UML™ FOR THE IT BUSINESS ANALYST,
SECOND EDITION:

A PRACTICAL GUIDE TO REQUIREMENTS GATHERING
USING THE UNIFIED MODELING LANGUAGE

Howard Podeswa

Course Technology PTR

A part of Cengage Learning

COURSE TECHNOLOGY
CENGAGE Learning™

Australia, Brazil, Japan, Korea, Mexico, Singapore, Spain, United Kingdom, United States

COURSE TECHNOLOGY
CENGAGE Learning™

UML for the IT Business Analyst, Second Edition: A Practical Guide to Requirements Gathering Using the Unified Modeling Language
Howard Podeswa

Publisher and General Manager, Course Technology PTR:
Stacy L. Hiquet

Associate Director of Marketing:
Sarah Panella

Manager of Editorial Services:
Heather Talbot

Marketing Manager:
Mark Hughes

Acquisitions Editor:
Mitzi Koontz

Project Editor:
Kate Shoup

Editorial Services Coordinator:
Jen Blaney

Copy Editor:
Kate Shoup

Interior Layout:
Shawn Morningstar

Cover Designer:
Mike Tanamachi

Indexer:
Katherine Stimson

Proofreader:
Laura Gabler

Library of Congress Control Number: 2009924527

ISBN-13: 978-1-59863-868-4

ISBN-10: 1-59863-868-8

Course Technology, a part of Cengage Learning
20 Channel Center Street
Boston, MA 02210
USA

Cengage Learning is a leading provider of customized learning solutions with office locations around the globe, including Singapore, the United Kingdom, Australia, Mexico, Brazil, and Japan. Locate your local office at: **international.cengage.com/region**

Cengage Learning products are represented in Canada by Nelson Education, Ltd.

For your lifelong learning solutions, visit **courseptr.com**

Visit our corporate website at **cengage.com**

Printed in the United States of America
5 6 7 8 9 16 15 14 13 12

For my incredible kids, Yasha and Sam.
And for Joy Walker. You are the prototype.[1]

---

[1]From the song "Prototype" on the album *Speakerboxxx/The Love Below*, 2003, by Outkast.

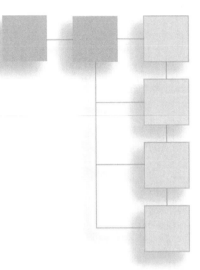

PREFACE

From 1998 to 2000, I spent part of my winters on the Cape Town peninsula in South Africa. It was one of those rare times when all aspects of life lined up. There were times when I prepared for an art exhibition, facilitated workshops in poor neighborhoods, and analyzed IT systems—all in the same day. This book is one of the products of that exciting and very productive time: Its case study is drawn from IT work my company did there for the Community Peace Program (CPP), an organization that aims to reduce violence in poverty-stricken neighborhoods through a process of dispute resolution called restorative justice.

One of the communities I visited often due to my work was the township of Zweletemba. There is a point in the trip to Zweletemba when you enter a tunnel that goes right through the mountains. Inevitably, it was at that point in the journey that I always fell asleep, awakening just as we exited the tunnel into what seemed like a magical world. Zweletemba, situated in the mountainous interior of the peninsula, is a place of contradictions. There is great poverty, with many people living in ramshackle homes built of materials salvaged from junk piles, but there is also great physical beauty, personal warmth, music, and humor.

It was in Zweletemba that the CPP was conducting a pilot project when I arrived in South Africa. The CPP was, at that time, interested in growing the organization using the lessons learned from Zweletemba—and, in the years that have followed, has in fact expanded to include numerous communities in the country. It was in advance of this expansion that the organization had asked my company to prepare requirements for an IT solution that would assist them in case management.

The CPP's restorative justice system came to mind when I began work on the first edition of this book. I was looking for a case study that would be complex enough to include the intricacies of typical systems. I chose the CPP's system because it has stakeholders who play multiple roles (in the same manner as customers of an insurance firm who appear as beneficiaries, policy holders, etc.); a key business object to which events, action, and information items are tied (similar to a customer call in a CRM system), as well as other complex characteristics that show up time and again in business systems. And, as an unfamiliar system, it puts the reader in the position of extreme business analysis—really not knowing anything about the system at the start of the project.

Projects like the CPP case study exemplify what I love most about business analysis—that it has introduced me to a variety of systems and, through them, to the people behind those systems. Through business analysis, I have met and worked with people from all walks of life—defense contractors, social workers, investment bankers, funeral directors—and they have, in turn, satisfied my inquisitiveness about people and how they do things. This quality of endless curiosity is a trait I've seen in many of the business analysts I've met. If it describes you, you've found a great profession. I hope that this book will help you excel at it so that it gives you the enjoyment it has given to me over the years.

—Howard Podeswa

ACKNOWLEDGMENTS

Special thanks go out to Charlie Orosz, Scott Williams, Tim Lloyd, Gerry de Koning, Fern Lawrence, Clifford Shearing, Ideaswork (formerly Community Peace Program), and the Zweletemba Peace Committee. Many thanks, also, to Adrian Marchis and the business analyst community at modernanalyst.com for the extensive input they have provided with respect to planning and tailoring business activities for specific projects. Thanks also to Adam Kahn, David Barrett, and Amy Ruddell of Diversified Business Communications for promoting the business-analysis profession and the ideas in this book through the BA World conferences they have organized, the Noble workshops my company has delivered there over the years, as well as their publication, *Business Analyst Times*.

And a personal thank you to the technical editor of the book's first edition, Brian Lyons, for an incredibly knowledgeable and thorough review. In the time that has passed between the two editions, Brian was tragically killed in a road accident. I am honored to have been able to benefit from his advice while he was alive. The experience of being put under the Lyons microscope was a challenging one—but one I wouldn't have missed for the world.

ABOUT THE AUTHOR

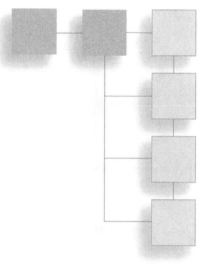

Howard Podeswa is the co-founder of Noble, Inc. (www.nobleinc.com), a business-analysis (BA) consulting and training company. Podeswa has contributed to the formalization of the business-analysis profession as a subject-matter expert for NITAS—a BA apprenticeship program (a CompTIA and U.S. federal government initiative)—and as a member of the review team for the *Business Analysis Body of Knowledge (BABOK)*.

Podeswa has 30 years' experience in many aspects of the software industry, beginning as a developer for Atomic Energy of Canada, Ltd. and continuing as systems analyst, business analyst, consultant, lead designer of business-analysis programs, and author of *The Business Analyst's Handbook*, a BA reference manual incorporating ITIL, the *BABOK*, BPMN, UML, agile, and other best practices and standards of importance to the BA. He has provided consulting and training services to a diverse client base, including the Mayo Clinic, Thomson Healthcare, Canadian Air Force (MASIS), the South African Community Peace Program, and major financial institutions (Deloitte, CIBC bank, CGU, etc.). Podeswa is also a sought-after speaker at international BA conferences. In addition, Podeswa has collaborated with CDI Education on object-oriented projects and training and has designed BA training programs for numerous institutions, including Boston University Continuing Education Center and New Horizons.

Podeswa is also a recognized visual artist whose artwork has been exhibited and reviewed internationally and supported by the Canada Council for the Arts. His exhibition, Object Oriented Painting Show (OOPS)—from which the images on the cover were taken—was the first to combine his two passions: OO technology and painting. His artwork is represented by the Peak Gallery (www.peakgallery.com).

Contact Info

The author may be contacted at howardpodeswa@nobleinc.ca. For questions and support material related to this book, please visit the Noble Inc. Web site at www.nobleinc.ca. For a full suite of business-analysis courses based on this and other writings by the author, please visit the Noble Inc. Web site at www.nobleinc.ca or contact the company at info@nobleinc.ca. To download electronic versions of business-analysis templates, please visit http://nobleinc.ca/downloads.html.

Nobleinc

TABLE OF CONTENTS

Introduction xix

Chapter 1   **Who Are IT Business Analysts?** 1
Chapter Objectives 1
The IT and Non-IT BA 1
Perspective on the IT BA Role 2
Why Modeling Is a Good Thing 3
The Behavioral (Dynamic) Model 3
The Structural (Static) Model 4
For Those Trained in Structured Analysis 5
Mapping the BABOK 2 to This Book 6
Chapter Summary 13
Endnotes 14

Chapter 2   **The BA's Perspective on Object Orientation** 17
Chapter Objectives 17
What Is OO? 18
The UML Standard 18
Cognitive Psychology and OO 18
Objects 19
    The BA Perspective 19
Attributes and Operations 19
    The BA Perspective 19
Operations and Methods 20
    The BA Perspective 20
Encapsulation 20
    The BA Perspective 20

OO Concept: Classes 21
  The BA Perspective 22
OO Concept: Relationships 22
  OO Concept: Generalization 22
  OO Concept: Association 24
  OO Concept: Aggregation 25
  OO Concept: Composite Aggregation (Composition) 26
OO Concept: Polymorphism 27
  Polymorphic Objects 27
  Polymorphic Operations 27
  The BA Perspective 28
Use Cases and Scenarios 28
  The BA Perspective 29
Business and System Use Cases 29
  The BA Perspective 30
Chapter Summary 30
Endnotes 31

Chapter 3   Steps of B.O.O.M. . . . . **.33**
Chapter Objectives 33
B.O.O.M. and SDLCs 33
The B.O.O.M. Steps 34
  Step 1: Initiation 34
  Step 2: Discovery 35
  Step 3: Construction 37
  Step 4: Final Verification and Validation (V&V) 37
  Step 5: Closeout 37
What Do You Define First—Attributes or Operations? 37
Developing the Structural Model Alongside the Behavioral Model 38
Tailoring B.O.O.M. for Your Project 38
What Do You Show Stakeholders? 41
Chapter Summary 42
Endnotes 42

Chapter 4   Analyzing End-to-End Business Processes . . . . **.43**
Chapter Objectives 43
Interviews During the Phases 43
B.O.O.M. Steps 45
Step 1: The Initiation Phase 45
  What Happens During the Initiation Phase? 45
  How Long Does the Initiation Phase Take? 45
  Deliverables of the Initiation Step: BRD (Initiation Version) 45
Step 1a: Model Business Use Cases .46

How Do You Document Business Use Cases? .47

Step 1ai: Identify Business Use Cases (Business Use-Case Diagram) 47

Other Model Elements 48

Putting Theory into Practice 48

Case Study D1: Business Use-Case Diagrams .49

Step 1aii: Scope Business Use Cases (Activity Diagram) 63

Activity Diagrams for Describing Business Use Cases 65

Case Study D2: Business Use-Case Activity Diagram
with Partitions (Swimlanes) 73

Chapter Summary 78

Endnotes 78

Chapter 5   **Scoping the IT Project with System Use Cases** 79

Chapter Objectives 79

Step 1b: Model System Use Cases 79

Step 1bi: Identify Actors (Role Map) 80

Finding Actors 80

Stereotypes and Actors 81

The Role Map 82

Modeling Actors with Overlapping Roles 82

What's the Point of Defining Generalized Actors? 84

Case Study E1: Role Map 84

Step 1bii: Identify System Use-Case Packages
(System Use-Case Diagram) 86

What Criteria Are Used to Group System
Use Cases into Packages? 86

Naming Use-Case Packages 86

Diagramming System Use-Case Packages .87

What If a Use-Case Package Is Connected to
All of the Specialized Actors of a Generalized Actor? 88

Case Study E2: System Use-Case Packages 89

Step 1biii: Identify System Use Cases (System Use-Case Diagram) 91

Features of System Use Cases 91

What Is the Purpose of Segmenting
the User Requirements into System Use Cases? 92

Modeling System Use Cases 92

Is There a Rule of Thumb for How
Many System Use Cases a Project Would Have? 95

Case Study E3: System Use-Case Diagrams 95

Step 1c: Begin Structural Model
(Class Diagrams for Key Business Classes) 101

Step 1d: Set Baseline for Discovery (BRD/Initiation) 101

Chapter Summary 102

Endnotes 102

Chapter 6   **Storyboarding the User's Experience** **103**

Chapter Objectives 103

Step 2: Discovery 104

    Lifecycle Considerations 104

    Step 2ai: Describe System Use Cases .104

The Use-Case Description Template 105

    The Fundamental Approach Behind the Template 106

Documenting the Basic Flow 109

    Use-Case Writing Guidelines 109

    Basic Flow Example: CPP System/Review Case Report 110

Documenting Alternate Flows 111

    Typical Alternate Flows 111

    Alternate Flow Documentation 112

    Example of Use Case with Alternate Flows:
    CPP System/Review Case Report 113

    Documenting an Alternate of an Alternate 114

Documenting Exception Flows 114

Guidelines for Conducting System Use-Case Interviews 115

Activity Diagrams for System Use Cases 115

Related Artifacts 115

    Decision Tables 116

Case Study F1: Decision Table 119

    Decision Trees 122

Case Study F2: Decision Tree 123

    Condition/Response Table 124

    Business Rules 124

Advanced Use-Case Features 125

    Include 126

    Extend 129

    Generalized Use Case 133

Case Study F3: Advanced Use-Case Features .136

Chapter Summary 138

Endnotes 138

Chapter 7   **Lifecycle Requirements for Key Business Objects** **141**

Chapter Objectives 141

What Is a State-Machine Diagram? 142

Step 2aii: 1. Identify States of Critical Objects 144

    Types of States 144

Case Study G1: States 145

Step 2aii: 2. Identify State Transitions 147

    Depicting State Transitions in UML 147

    Mapping State-Machine Diagrams to System Use Cases 149

Case Study G2: Transitions 150

Step 2aii: 3. Identify State Activities 153

Case Study G3: State Activities 155

Step 2aii: 4. Identify Composite States 157

Case Study G4: Composite States 158

Step 2aii: 5. Identify Concurrent States 160

    Concurrent State Example 160

Chapter Summary 161

Endnotes 162

Chapter 8
Gathering Across-the-Board Business Rules with Class Diagrams **163**

Chapter Objectives 163

Step 2b: Structural Analysis 164

    FAQs about Structural Analysis 165

Step 2bi: Identify Entity Classes 166

    FAQs about Entity Classes 167

    Indicating a Class in UML 167

    Naming Conventions 167

    Grouping Classes into Packages 168

    The Package Diagram 169

    Why It's Worth Pausing to Do Some Structural
    Modeling When Stakeholders Introduce New Terms 169

    Interview Questions for Finding Classes 170

    Challenge Questions 170

    Supporting Class Documentation 171

Case Study H1: Entity Classes 172

Step 2bii: Model Generalizations 175

    Subtyping 175

    Generalization 175

Case Study H2: Generalizations 179

Step 2biii: Model Transient Roles 180

    Example of Transient Role 181

    How Does a Transient Role Differ from a Specialization? 181

    Some Terminology 182

    Why Indicate Transient Roles? 182

    Rules about Transient Roles 182

    Indicating Transient Roles 182

    Sources of Information for Finding Transient Roles 182

    Interview Questions for Determining Transient Roles 183

    What If a Group of Specialized Classes Can All Play the Same Role? . .183

Case Study H3: Transient Roles 184

Step 2biv: Model Whole/Part Relationships 186
The "Whole" Truth 186
Examples of Whole/Part Relationships 186
Why Indicate Whole/Part Relationships? 186
How Far Should You Decompose a Whole into Its Parts? 187
Sources of Information for Finding Aggregation
and Composite Aggregation 187
Rules Regarding Aggregation and Composite Aggregation 187
Indicating Aggregation and Composite
Aggregation in the UML 187
The Composite Structure Diagram 188
Interview Questions for Determining Aggregation
and Composite Aggregation 189
Challenge Question 190
Case Study H4: Whole/Part Relationships 190
Step 2bv: Analyze Associations 192
Examples of Association 192
Why Indicate Association? 192
Why Isn't It the Developers' Job to Find Associations? 193
Discovering Associations 193
Rules Regarding Associations 193
The Association Must Reflect the Business Reality 195
Redundant Association Rule of Thumb 196
Exception to the Rule of Thumb 196
Case Study H5: Associations 199
Step 2bvi: Analyze Multiplicity 202
Example of Multiplicity 202
Why Indicate Multiplicity? 202
Indicating Multiplicity in the UML 202
Rules Regarding Multiplicity 203
Sources of Information for Finding Multiplicity 204
The Four Interview Questions for Determining Multiplicity 204
Case Study H6: Multiplicity 205
Chapter Summary 208
Endnotes 209

Chapter 9   Optimizing Consistency and
               Reuse in the Requirements Documentation 213
Chapter Objectives 213
Where Do You Go from Here? 214
Does the Business Analyst Need to Put Every
Attribute and Operation in the Structural Model? 214

Step 2bvii: Link System Use Cases to the Structural Model 215

How Do You Find the Modeling Elements Involved
in a System Use Case? 215

How Do You Document the Links Between System
Use Cases and the Structural Model? 215

Case Study I1: Link System Use Cases to the Structural Model 216

Step 2bviii: Add Attributes 221

Example 221

Why Indicate Attributes? 221

Don't Verification Rules about Attributes
Belong with the System Use-Case Documentation? 221

Sources of Information for Finding Attributes 222

Rules for Assigning Attributes 222

Derived Attributes 223

Indicating Attributes in the UML 223

Meta-Attributes 225

Case Study I2: Add Attributes 226

Step 2bix: Add Lookup Tables 231

Why Analyze Lookup Tables? 231

Example 231

Rules for Analyzing Lookup Tables 231

Challenge Question 232

Indicating Lookup Tables in the UML 232

Case Study I3: Analyze Lookup Tables 233

Step 2bx: Add Operations 236

An Example from the Case Study 236

How to Distribute Operations 237

Case Study I4: Distribute Operations 238

Step 2bxi: Revise Class Structure 241

Rules for Reviewing Structure 242

Challenge Question 242

Case Study I5: Revise Structure 242

Chapter Summary 244

Endnotes 244

Chapter 10   Designing Test Cases and Completing the Project 245

Chapter Objectives 245

Step 2c: Specify Testing 246

Who Does These Tests and How Does the BA Fit In? 246

What Is Testing? 247

General Guidelines 247

Structured Testing 248

When Is Testing Performed? 248

        Principles of Structured Testing (Adapted for OO) 248

        Structured Walkthroughs 250

        Requirements-Based (Black-Box) Testing 252

        Test Template 253

    Decision Tables for Testing 254

    Case Study J1: Deriving Test Cases from Decision Tables 255

    Boundary-Value Analysis 256

    Case Study J2: Select Test Data Using Boundary-Value Analysis 258

    White-Box Testing 260

        Who Does White-Box Testing? 260

        Limitations of White-Box Testing 260

        White-Box Coverage Quality Levels 260

        Sequencing of White-Box Tests 261

    System Tests 263

    Beyond the System Tests 266

    Step 2d: Specify Implementation Plan 267

        Post-Implementation Follow-Up 268

    Step 2e: Set Baseline for Development 268

    Chapter Summary 268

    Endnotes 270

Chapter 11   What Developers Do with Your Requirements **271**

    Chapter Objectives 271

    OO Patterns 272

        Examples 272

    Visibility 272

        Example 273

        Visibility Options 273

    Control Classes 274

    Boundary Classes 274

    Sequence Diagrams 274

        Example: A Sequence Diagram 275

    Communication Diagrams 277

    Other Diagrams 277

        Timing Diagrams 278

        Deployment Diagrams 278

    Layered Architecture 278

        Monolithic, Two-Tier, Three-Tier, and N-Tier Architecture 279

    Interfaces 279

    Mix-Ins 280

    Implementing OO Using an OO Language 280

    Implementing OO Using Procedural Languages 281

Implementing a Database from a Structural OO
Model Using an RDBMS 281
Chapter Summary 281
Endnotes 282

Appendix A   The B.O.O.M. Process 283
1: Initiation 284
2: Discovery 284

Appendix B   Business Requirements Document (BRD) Template 287
Business Requirements Document (BRD) 288
Table of Contents 289
Version Control 291
Executive Summary 292
Scope 294
Risk Analysis 295
Business Case 296
Timetable 296
Business Use Cases 296
Actors 296
User Requirements 298
State-Machine Diagrams 301
Nonfunctional Requirements 301
Business Rules 302
State Requirements 302
Structural Model 303
Test Plan 304
Implementation Plan 305
End-User Procedures 306
Post Implementation Follow-Up 306
Other Issues 306
Sign-Off 306
Endnote 306

**Appendix C   Business Requirements Document Example:
CPP Case Study 307**
Business Requirements Document (BRD) 308
Table of Contents 309
Version Control 312
Executive Summary 313
Scope 314
Risk Analysis 316

Business Case 318

Timetable 318

Business Use Cases 319

Actors 323

User Requirements 324

State-Machine Diagrams 332

Nonfunctional Requirements 333

Business Rules 334

State Requirements 334

Structural Model 334

Test Plan 341

Implementation Plan 341

End-User Procedures 342

Post Implementation Follow-Up 342

Other Issues 342

Sign-Off 342

Appendix D   Decision Table Template **343**

Appendix E   Test Script Template **345**

Test Template 345

Appendix F   Glossary of Symbols **347**

Appendix G   Glossary of Terms and Further Reading **353**

Index **359**

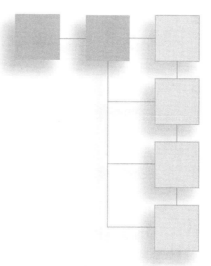

INTRODUCTION

I began working on the first edition of this book in the year 2000. As a former developer and current IT business analyst, I could see an approaching technological wave affecting my colleagues. Thanks in large part to client-server applications and the Internet, object-oriented (OO) languages like C++ and Java were taking over the development world. This had already changed the way the technical members of an IT team (systems analysts, coders, and so on) were working, but business analysts—the people who communicated requirements to the developers—were still working by and large as though OO didn't exist. The result was BA documentation that had to first be translated into OO terms and standards by the developers—an inefficient and error-prone step. I knew it was only a matter of time before companies began to expect their BAs to work with OO conventions, so I put together Business Object-Oriented Modeling (B.O.O.M.), a step-by-step program to mentor and train BAs to work efficiently on projects using the Unified Modeling Language (UML), the prevailing standard for modeling business and IT systems on OO projects (though not confined to OO projects, since the standard has non-OO modeling elements as well).

Since developing B.O.O.M., I have used it to mentor BAs working on UML projects in wealth management, insurance, accounting, defense, government, credit-card systems, telecommunications, hospitality, and other business areas. They have, in turn, helped me improve the process by sharing with me their best practices, templates, and other tools they use on the job. This knowledge has made its way back into B.O.O.M.

Thanks to contacts made through a colleague in corporate training, Charlie Orosz, I had an opportunity to publish B.O.O.M. as a book. I believe it fills a real need. Today, BAs often find themselves working on UML projects; yet they still have a long way to go to exploit the technology beyond the adoption of use cases (just one part of the UML). When BAs look for guidance in the UML, however, they find a dearth of UML literature written for the BA. There are some BA books on narrow aspects of the UML (such as use cases) and UML books with a technical perspective, but there is little that explains how a BA can pull together all the UML tools and fully exploit them during an IT project. I wrote this book to fill that gap.

This is not a "theory" book. I believe that people learn best by doing. In keeping with that, you and I will, together, develop and validate the requirements for an IT system as we move through the steps. By the time you have completed the book—and the case study in it— you will have hands-on experience in using OO standards (UML 2) and techniques and in integrating these with other, non-OO techniques over the course of an OO IT project.

Who This Book Is For

This book is intended for anyone performing the role of the information-technology business analyst (IT BA)—an integral part of a software-development team responsible for documenting and verifying the business and user requirements for a software system. If you are a new IT BA, or if you are an experienced BA who is new to the UML standard, this book is for you. This does not mean, however, that the intended reader necessarily has "IT business analyst" as a job title. Other titles that may overlap with the IT BA role include[2] business analyst, business process analyst, requirements engineer, business systems analyst, systems analyst, data analyst, functional architect, usability/UX analyst, product manager, and user experience analyst. If you're doing any of these jobs and your responsibilities include the gathering of requirements or the modeling of the business domain on a project for an IT solution, this book is for you. For example, this book will be of benefit to the developer who is interested in expanding his or her role to encompass IT BA activities. In this case, you may be wondering how you can exploit the UML tools and techniques you already know to include the gathering and documentation of business requirements. This book will guide you through that process.

What Types of IT Projects Will Benefit from This Book?

As noted by some readers of the first edition, this book is more about a requirements-gathering approach that happens to use the Unified Modeling Language (UML) standard than it is about the UML per se. As such, it has applicability to both UML and non-UML projects. That said, to use this book most directly, your project should be using the UML standard.

---

[2]Thanks to Adrian Marchis for pointing out the need to expound on alternate job titles.
For a discussion on BA roles, please see the *Modern Analyst* article "The Roles of the Business Analyst" at http://www.modernanalyst.com/TheProfession/Roles/tabid/73/Default.aspx.

Often, this means the contemplated solution is one that will be built using an object-oriented (OO) language, but this is not necessarily the case because the UML contains many diagrams that have little to do with OO—and those that do may be easily converted.[3] If your project is not using the UML, you will not be able to use this book directly, but you should be able to use the overall approach it describes in moving from the business problem to the IT requirements. You will need, however, to replace the UML terms and diagrams in this book with non-UML equivalents—for example, using the term business services and processes instead of the UML term business use cases; level 1 data flow diagrams instead of UML use-case diagrams; non-UML swimlane workflow diagrams instead of UML activity diagrams with partitions; etc.

You may be wondering about the relevance of this book to your project based on the life-cycle approach being used to define its phases, tasks, and roles. This book is applicable to all lifecycle approaches. How the techniques are applied, however, must be tailored for each lifecycle approach and, indeed, for each project. The section "Tailoring B.O.O.M. for Your Project" in Chapter 3, "Steps of B.O.O.M.," provides guidance in this area. In short, with respect to lifecycle, the artifacts described in this book are produced in greater depth on definitive (well-defined) lifecycles than on empirical (less defined, more adaptable) ones. For example, while a large project using Rational Unified Process (RUP)—an iterative, but definitive, lifecycle—might require textual system use-case descriptions (specifications) and class diagrams to a level of detail comparable to that shown in the book, a small project using an empirical lifecycle might only require higher-level documentation: system use-case diagrams, system use-case briefs (short descriptions of user tasks), and—only where necessary—business class diagrams. Why go even that far on an empirical project? You need that level of detail to estimate the cost, time, and resources for the project and to uncover sometimes subtle and elusive business rules. However, you are unlikely to create complete use-case textual descriptions or complete structural models (class diagrams, etc.) on empirical projects (such as those that use an agile approach), where the guiding principle is to do just enough documentation and to do it as late in the process as possible.

This last point brings us to the impact of the project lifecycle approach on the sequence in which the business analysis steps described in this book are carried out. On an iterative project, where there are numerous cycles of analysis, design, coding, and testing throughout the project, all the analysis is not done up front but is instead done incrementally as the project progresses (typically, during the iteration in which they will be implemented, just before they are to be designed and coded). On the other hand, on traditional, waterfall projects, where all the analysis is performed before design begins, all the documentation described in this book is created up front.

---

[3]For example UML class diagrams of the business domain may be readily converted into entity relationship diagrams (ERDs) for use in data design. The procedure for doing the conversion is described in Chapter 11, "What Developers Do with Your Requirements," in the section "Implementing a Database from a Structural OO Model Using an RDBMS."

As to which approach is best: When it is appropriate, an iterative, agile lifecycle is preferred because business stakeholders are more likely to get what they really want when the solution comes through a process of trial-and-error rather than from an abstract preconception of what the requirements might be. However, I do not advocate any one particular approach for all projects; I have been in this business long enough to know that one size will never fit all. On one project, you might be working for a client with a low tolerance for uncertainty (perhaps because of the cost or regulatory requirements) and, consequently, be using a waterfall approach, where there are few unknowns. On another project, you might be working with clients who are unsure of what they want (perhaps because of a rapidly changing business environment or because the service is so new) and, therefore, be using an agile lifecycle, where the expectation of change is built into the lifecycle approach. Over your career as a business analyst (or as anyone whose role includes business-analysis responsibilities), you need to be prepared to work under all these lifecycle approaches. This book will provide you with a full spectrum of techniques available to the BA, but you shouldn't expect to be doing everything on every project.

How You and Your Organization Can Benefit from B.O.O.M.

Many organizations are excellent at developing good software products. Where they are often weak is in developing the *right* software product. The mismatch between what the user wants and what the developers deliver can often be traced to poor practices in business analysis and quality control. B.O.O.M. provides a step-by-step procedure that helps ensure the completeness, correctness, and clarity of the requirements documentation.

In addition, many IT projects experience time and cost overruns due to the difficulty in responding to a rapidly changing business environment. A major contributing factor to this problem is the "ripple effect"—one change in the business that leads to many changes in project deliverables. B.O.O.M. helps by using UML techniques to minimize redundancies in the requirements. With "one fact in one place,"[4] the requirements are easier to revise.

Finally, many project failures are due to faulty communication between those who know the business and those who write the software. With B.O.O.M., the BA documents business rules and requirements using the same types of diagrams, concepts, and terminology used by OO developers, thus reducing the risk of miscommunication. Improvements in communication are even more dramatic if the organization uses a software-development tool like IBM Telelogic DOORS, Blueprint Requirements Center, or the RUP suite of products. In those environments, you'll use software tools right from the start to model business requirements. You can then pass the model (one or more digital files) to the developers,

---

[4]Thanks to Tony Alderson for this description of non-redundancy.

who can use it as the starting point for their design. It doesn't get much more efficient or direct than that. (Keep in mind, however, that you don't need to use business modeling software to benefit from OO BA practices or from this book.)

Once You've Read This Book, You'll Be Able to...

- Create a business requirements document (BRD) that conforms to the UML 2.2 standard and that incorporates use cases, class diagrams, and other object-oriented analysis (OOA) techniques.
- Follow a step-by-step UML-compliant process for interviewing, researching, and documenting requirements.
- Incorporate still-useful pre-OO techniques within OOA.
- Actively use the accompanying job aids while working on the job.
- Use the following artifacts:
  - Business use-case diagrams
  - System use-case diagrams and use-case templates
  - Package diagrams
  - Class diagrams
  - Composite structure diagrams
  - Object diagrams
  - Activity diagrams with and without partitions
  - State-machine diagrams
  - Decision tables

The CPP Case Study

One case study runs throughout the book. It is based on a business-analysis project my company performed for the Community Peace Program (CPP) in Cape Town, South Africa (with adjustments made for learning purposes). I encourage you to work through the case study yourself. Only by trying out the ideas as you learn them will you really be able to practically apply the techniques presented in this book.

The Appendices

This book includes a set of job aids in Appendices A through G. These appendices contain the condensed methodology, including examples of every diagram covered in the book, templates, and a glossary of UML symbols and terms.

Remember: It's All Just a Game!

As you read this book, you will spend a lot of time analyzing complex relationships in a system. It's easy to get uptight about whether you've got the right solution. Well, here's the good news: There is no "right" solution because there is more than one way to model the real world. So the best approach is to just play with an idea and see where it leads you.

How to Decide If You've Made a Good Modeling Decision

You'll know you've gone in a good direction if your model has these qualities:

- **Elegance:** A simple solution to a complex problem

- **Adaptability:** Can easily be changed to reflect a change in the requirements

- **Non-redundancy:** Does not repeat itself—each fact is "in one place"

What's Changed in This Edition

This edition of this book—the second edition—includes updates to best practices and standards that have emerged since the book was first published. It includes a new section on the *Business Analysis Body of Knowledge* (*BABOK*), whose most recent release, *BABOK 2*, was published in March of 2009. The *BABOK*, a publication of the International Institute for Business Analysis (IIBA), defines the BA profession and is the basis for a BA certification process and exam administered by the IIBA. The new section of the book describes the *BABOK 2* knowledge areas (areas of expertise) and describes how they and their component tasks map to this book. I hope this information will be of help to those who wish to prepare for certification.

Also included are changes to the UML. The current version, UML 2.2, was published in February of 2009. Changes from UML 2.0 reflected in the book include new definitions and changes in the terminology. The terminology changes reflected in this edition are as follows:

- Static modeling and static diagrams are now referred to as structural modeling and structure diagrams, respectively.

- Dynamic modeling is now referred to as behavioral modeling.

- The term inclusion use case has been replaced by the term included use case.

- The term extension use case has been replaced by the term extending use case.

- The term composition has been replaced by the term composite aggregation.

This book also takes into account differences in lifecycle approaches. I had intended to steer clear of these issues in the first edition because to properly cover the topic seemed beyond the scope of this book. It has since occurred to me, however, that the unintended side effect of this decision was to leave the impression in the minds of some readers that a waterfall lifecycle approach is being advocated—contrary to my intention. (In a waterfall approach, project activities in one phase, such as requirements analysis, must be completed before the next phase begins; in iterative approaches, all activities may occur in any phase, albeit to varying degrees.) In the current edition, I've introduced the issue of different lifecycle approaches and their impact on the business analyst. Also, the phase names used in the original edition as well as their descriptions have been changed to be generic enough to encompass all approaches, including agile lifecycles. This has the added advantage of keeping the phase names in line with those in the *Business Analyst's Handbook*. The changes to phase names are as follows:

- The second phase, previously referred to as Analysis, is now referred to as Discovery to reflect the fact that, on iterative projects, requirements analysis is not the only activity going on in this phase and that analysis is not exclusive to this phase.
- The Test phase is now referred to as Final Verification and Validation (V&V) to better reflect the fact that other (non-final) testing activities occur elsewhere in the lifecycle.

Finally, the instructions for using IBM Rational Rose have been removed from this edition of the book. Since the first edition of the book was written, IBM has shifted its marketing focus to other modeling products. There are so many modeling tools in use today and marketplace preferences are changing so rapidly that removing tool-specific instructions seemed the best approach.

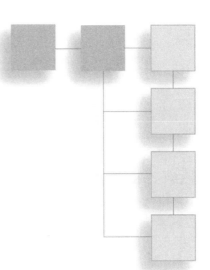

CHAPTER 1

WHO ARE IT BUSINESS ANALYSTS?

Chapter Objectives

At the end of this chapter, you will understand the following:

- The role of the IT business analyst throughout a project's lifecycle
- What is meant by the terms business model, behavioral model and structural model
- How the BABOK maps to this book

The IT and Non-IT BA

There are two types of business analysts. Just to clear up any possible confusion:

- A *non-IT business analyst* is someone who works within the context of the business. This person is involved in process improvement, cost-cutting, and so on.
- An *information technology business analyst* (IT BA) works within the context of IT projects—projects to buy, purchase, or modify some software. This person liaises with business and technical stakeholders and is responsible for gathering the requirements that originate from the business.

This book is directed at anyone acting as an IT BA on a project. As noted in the introduction, people with IT BA responsibilities do not necessarily have a BA or IT BA job title. For example, they may be developers who do double duty as requirements elicitors (a common practice, for example, on agile projects), or systems analysts whose responsibilities include modeling the business domain (as is the case on RUP projects). For a list of job titles that may include IT BA responsibilities, please see the section "Who This Book Is For" in the introduction. If your responsibilities include liaising with stakeholders, or eliciting, analyzing, or documenting requirements on an IT project, you are, in effect—if not in title—an IT BA, and the intended reader of this book. If you are a non-IT BA, you may find some of the techniques in this book useful, as there is some overlap between the non-IT and IT roles; other techniques in the book, however, are specific to the IT BA role. (For example, workflow diagrams are used by both while system use cases are specific to the IT BA.)

Perspective on the IT BA Role

The discipline of business analysis has evolved over the past few years into a mature profession with well-defined responsibilities and areas of expertise. The National IT Apprenticeship System (NITAS)—a BA program sponsored by the U.S. Dept. of Labor in conjunction with the Computing Technology Industry Association (CompTIA)—began working on a definition of the knowledge areas and activities of a BA a number of years ago. Since then, the International Institute of Business Analysis (IIBA) has taken the lead internationally in defining the knowledge areas required for the practice of business analysis and creating a certification process for the professional BA.[1] The IIBA's *Business Analysis Body of Knowledge Version 2.0* (*BABOK 2*) defines business analysis and the business analyst as follows:

> "Business analysis is the set of tasks and techniques used to work as a liaison among stakeholders in order to understand the structure, policies, and operations of an organization, and to recommend solutions that enable the organization to achieve its goals."[2]

> "A business analyst is any person who performs business analysis activities, no matter what their job title or organizational role may be."[3]

Note that the IIBA definition, referring as it does to business analysis (rather than IT business analysis), makes no restriction that the recommended solution involve an IT component. Despite the potential confusion, in practice, most organizations have a pretty similar idea of what the IT BA does: An IT BA is a liaison between the stakeholders of a software system and the developers who create or modify it. A *stakeholder* is a person or an organization affected by a project: a user, a customer who does not directly use the system, a sponsor, and so on. The IT BA's primary function is to represent stakeholders' interests to designers, programmers, and other team members.

The IT BA is expected to discover, analyze, negotiate, represent, and validate the requirements of a new or modified software system. Basically, this means capturing the requirements and supporting the testing of the software solution to ascertain whether it meets those requirements.

Why Modeling Is a Good Thing

> ### Business Model
>
> A *business model* is an abstract representation of a clearly delimited area of a business. It may take many forms—for example, pictures with supporting text or the underlying format used by a tool such as IBM Rational Software Modeler (RSM), Rational Rose, or Blueprint's Requirements Center to produce diagrams and generate code.

In this book, you'll be asked to draw a lot of diagrams. You may be wondering, "What's the point?" After all, most users can't read them, and they are reluctant to sign off on anything but text. The fast answer is that the diagrams are for the developers. That is, the diagrams are important because they get across the requirements in an unambiguous, standardized[4] way. The slow answer is that the diagrams are more than that. Here's how to get the most out of them:

- **Use diagrams to drive the interviews.** There is a logical, step-by-step process to drawing a diagram. At each step, you have to ask the user certain questions to discover what to draw next. The act of drawing the diagram tells you what questions to ask and when, and even when the interview is complete (which is when all the diagram elements have been resolved).
- **Use diagrams whenever you need to reconcile differing viewpoints.** For example, on a consulting job for an accountancy firm, I was asked to help the team make changes to its customer-relations management (CRM) processes. The current system involved too much double entry. Here, a workflow diagram[5] was useful to pool together the group's views on what was and what should be happening during these processes.

In this book, you'll learn how to create two different types of diagrams, or models:

- Behavioral model (also known as the dynamic model)
- Structural model (also known as the static model)

The Behavioral (Dynamic) Model

Behavioral modeling asks—and tries to answer—the question, "What does the system *do*?" It's very verb-oriented: The behavioral model judges (analyzes) the system by its *actions*.

> ### Behavioral Model
>
> A *behavioral model* is an abstract representation of what the system *does*. It is a collection of all useful stimulus and response patterns that together define the behavior of the system.[6]

In this book, the artifacts that fall into this category are as follows:

- Activity (workflow) diagrams
- State-machine diagrams
- Timing diagrams
- System use-case diagrams
- Business use-case diagrams
- Sequence diagrams (described briefly)
- Communication diagrams
- Use-case descriptions (referred to in RUP as use-case specifications)
- Decision tables
- Decision trees

The Structural (Static) Model

The motto of structural modeling would be, "Ask not what you do, ask what you *are*." The structural model answers the question, "What *is* this system?" As a structural modeler, you want to know what every noun used within the business really means. For example, while working with a telecommunications team, I asked the members to define exactly what they meant by a "product group." I used structural modeling diagrams to help me pin down its meaning and its relationship to other nouns, such as "line" and "feature." This process brought out the fact that there were two different definitions floating around among the team members. Using structural modeling, I was able to discover these two definitions and help the team develop a common language.

In this book, the artifacts that fall into this category are as follows:

- Class diagrams (the main diagrams used by the BA for structural modeling)
- Package diagrams
- Composite structure diagrams
- Static object diagrams

Structure Diagram

"Structure diagrams show the static structure of the objects in a system. That is, they depict those elements in a specification that are irrespective of time. The elements in a structure diagram represent the meaningful concepts of an application, and may include abstract, real-world and implementation concepts. For example, a structure diagram for an airline reservation system might include classifiers that represent seat assignment algorithms, tickets, and a credit authorization service."[7] (UML)

Not all of the diagrams and other artifacts described in this book will be created for every project, nor will they always be created with the same level of detail. See the section "Tailoring B.O.O.M. for Your Project" in Chapter 3, "Steps of B.O.O.M.," for guidelines on determining how much analysis and modeling to do on a project.

For Those Trained in Structured Analysis

The diagrams I've have been discussing focus on an object-oriented (OO) view of a business or system. OO is an approach to viewing and creating a complex system as an assembly of smaller components. (We'll look more deeply into OO in the next chapter.) The OO approach is often at odds with an older and still-used approach called structured analysis. This being the case, those with prior experience with structured analysis may be wondering at this point whether they have to throw away everything they already know because of OO. The good news is that despite the theoretical differences between the approaches, many of the OO diagrams are quite similar to the structured analysis ones—at least as they are used in a BA context. (Things are much more serious for programmers switching to OO.)

Table 1.1 lists diagrams used within structured analysis and matches them with their approximate counterparts in the Unified Modeling Language (UML)—a widely used standard that incorporates OO concepts.

TABLE 1.1   Structured Analysis Diagrams and Their UML Counterparts

Structured Analysis Diagram	UML Counterpart
Data flow diagram (DFD)	There is no exact counterpart because OO views a system as objects that pass messages to each other, while a DFD views it as processes that move data. However, some UML diagrams have similarities to the DFD: ■ A use-case diagram is similar to a level 1 DFD. ■ An activity diagram (with object flows) can be used similarly to a level 2 or lower-level (levels 3, 4, etc.) DFD.

TABLE 1.1 Structured Analysis Diagrams and Their UML Counterparts *(continued)*

Structured Analysis Diagram	UML Counterpart
System flowchart	Activity diagram
Workflow diagram	Activity diagram with partitions
Entity relationship diagram (ERD)	Class diagram

Table 1.2 matches terms used within structured analysis with their approximate counterparts in the UML.

TABLE 1.2 Structured Analysis Terms and Their UML Counterparts

Structured Analysis Term	UML Counterpart
Entity	Class, entity class
Occurrence	Instance, object
Attribute	Attribute
Process	Use case, operation, method
Relationship	Association

Mapping the *BABOK 2* to This Book

The *Business Analysis Body of Knowledge Version 2.0* (*BABOK 2*) describes business analysis through a set of areas of expertise, referred to as knowledge areas (KAs). "Knowledge areas define what a practitioner of business analysis needs to understand and the tasks a practitioner must be able to perform."[8] Table 1.3 summarizes the KAs of *BABOK 2*, lists the KA tasks that are addressed in this book, and describes where the reader may find guidance on the performance of each of those tasks.

TABLE 1.3   Mapping of *BABOK 2* Knowledge Areas to This Book

KA	Definition	KA Task (*BABOK* 2)	Coverage in This Text
Business Analysis Planning and Monitoring	"covers how business analysts determine which activities are necessary in order to complete a business analysis effort. It covers identification of stakeholders, selection of business analysis techniques, the process that will be used to manage requirements, and how to assess the progress of the work."[9]	2.1 Plan Business Analysis Approach	For guidance on process models (which may be used to define and document the business analysis approach), see Chapter 4, "Analyzing End-to-End Business Processes."
			For guidance on structured walkthroughs (which may be used as a means of validating a business analysis approach[10]), see the section "Structured Walkthroughs" in Chapter 10, "Designing Test Cases and Completing the Project."
		2.2 Conduct Stakeholder Analysis	On modeling business stakeholders and their relationships to business processes (business use cases), see Chapter 4, section "Step 1ai: Identify Business Use Cases (Business Use-Case Diagram)."
			For guidance on modeling stakeholders who interact directly with an IT solution, see the section "Step 1bi: Identify Actors (Role Map)" in Chapter 5, "Scoping the IT Project with System Use Cases."[11]
		2.3 Plan Business Analysis Activities	For planning BA activities over the project lifecycle, see Chapter 3.

TABLE 1.3 Mapping of *BABOK 2* Knowledge Areas to This Book *(continued)*

KA	Definition	KA Task (*BABOK 2*)	Coverage in This Text
		2.4 Plan Business Analysis Communication	On options for planning communication events, see the section "Interviews During the Phases" in Chapter 4.
Elicitation	"describes how business analysts work with stakeholders to identify and understand their needs and concerns, and understand the environment in which they work. The purpose of elicitation is to ensure that a stakeholder's actual underlying needs are understood, rather than their stated or superficial desires."[12]	3.2 Conduct Elicitation Activity	Guidance on structuring the interview and lists of questions for elicitation events over the lifecycle are provided throughout the book. For example, see Chapter 6, "Storyboarding the User's Experience"—specifically, the sections "Guidelines for Conducting System Use-Case Interviews" and "A Step-by-Step Procedure for Using a Decision Table During an Interview to Analyze System Behavior." See also Chapter 8, "Gathering Across-the-Board Business Rules with Class Diagrams"—specifically, the sections "Interview Questions for Finding Classes" and "Interview Questions for Determining Aggregation and Composite Aggregation."

TABLE 1.3   Mapping of *BABOK 2* Knowledge Areas to This Book *(continued)*

KA	Definition	KA Task (*BABOK 2*)	Coverage in This Text
Requirements Management and Communication	"describes how business analysts manage conflicts, issues, and changes in order to ensure that stakeholders and the project team remain in agreement on the solution scope, how requirements are communicated to stakeholders, and how knowledge gained by the business analyst is maintained for future use." [13]	4.3 Maintain Requirements for Reuse	On managing requirements for maximum reuse, see Chapter 9, "Optimizing Consistency and Reuse in Requirements Documentation."
		4.4 Prepare Requirements Package	In this book, the requirements package is referred to as a business requirements document (BRD). For a sample template, see Appendix B, "Business Requirements Document (BRD) Template." For an example of a completed BRD, see Appendix C, "Business Requirements Document Example: CPP Case Study."
		4.5 Communicate Requirements	On options for communicating requirements, see the section "Interviews During the Phases" in Chapter 4. On reviewing requirements with stakeholders, see the section "Structured Walkthroughs" in Chapter 10.

TABLE 1.3   Mapping of *BABOK 2* Knowledge Areas to This Book *(continued)*

KA	Definition	KA Task (*BABOK 2*)	Coverage in This Text
Enterprise Analysis	"describes how business analysts identify a business need, refine and clarify the definition of that need, and define a solution scope that can feasibly be implemented by the business. This knowledge area describes problem definition and analysis, business case development, feasibility studies, and the definition of solution scope." [14]	5.2 Assess Capability Gaps	On modeling as-is and to-be (solution) business processes in order to identify gaps, see Chapter 4. On models used in the context of the enterprise architecture[15]— a key input to this task—see Chapter 4 (for business process descriptions), Chapter 6 (specifically, the sections "Decision Tables" and "Decision Trees" [for business rules]), and Chapter 8 (for the definition of business concepts and relationships).
		5.4 Define Solution Scope	On the definition of the solution scope (for an IT solution), see Chapter 5.
Requirements Analysis	"describes how business analysts prioritize and progressively elaborate stakeholder and solution requirements.... It involves analyzing stakeholder needs to define solutions that meet those needs, assessing the current state of the business to identify and recommend improvements, and the verification and validation of the resulting requirements." [16]	6.2 Organize Requirements	For guidance on managing a large number of system use cases, see the section "Step 1bii: Identify System Use-Case Packages" in Chapter 5. On mapping the behavioral and structural models to each other, see the section "Step 2bvii: Link System Use Cases to the Structural Model" in Chapter 9.

TABLE 1.3   Mapping of *BABOK 2* Knowledge Areas to This Book   (continued)

KA	Definition	KA Task (*BABOK 2*)	Coverage in This Text
		6.3 Specify and Model Requirements	On the definition of user classes, see the section "Step 1bi: Identify Actors (Role Map)" in Chapter 5.
			On the definition of concepts and relationships, see Chapter 8.
			Techniques listed in the *BABOK* for this task are covered in this text as follows:
			■ Business rules analysis: On documenting business rules, see the section "Business Rules" in Chapter 6. On operative business rules, see the section "Decision Tables" in Chapter 6. On structural business rules, see Chapter 8.
			■ Data modeling: See Chapter 8 for the UML approach (class diagrams).
			■ Functional decomposition: On the include relationship (which allows hierarchical composition)[17], see the section "Advanced Use-Case Features" in Chapter 6.
			■ Process modeling: See Chapter 4.
			■ Scenarios and use cases: See Chapter 6.
			■ Sequence diagram: See Chapter 11, "What Developers Do with Your Requirements."
			■ State diagrams: See Chapter 7, "Lifecycle Requirements for Key Business Objects."

TABLE 1.3 Mapping of *BABOK 2* Knowledge Areas to This Book *(continued)*

KA	Definition	KA Task (*BABOK 2*)	Coverage in This Text
		6.5 Verify Requirements	Structured walkthroughs, a technique used in this task[18], are discussed in the section "Structured Walkthroughs" in Chapter 10.
		6.6. Validate Requirements	Structured walkthroughs, a technique used in this task[19], are discussed in Chapter 10 in the section "Structured Walkthroughs."
Solution Assessment and Validation	"describes how business analysts assess proposed solutions to determine which solution best fits the business need, identify gaps and shortcomings in solutions, and determine necessary workarounds or changes to the solution. It also describes how business analysts assess deployed solutions to see how well they meet the original need so that the sponsoring organization can assess the performance and effectiveness of the solution." [20]	7.2 Allocate Requirements	The following techniques listed in the *BABOK* for this task[21] are addressed in the text: ■ Business rules analysis: On operational rules that may be managed through the software, see the section "Decision Tables" in Chapter 6. On structural business rules, see Chapter 8. ■ Process modeling: See Chapter 4. ■ Scenarios and use cases: On removal of alternate flows so they can be later implemented as an extending use case, see the section "Advanced Use-Case Features" in Chapter 6.

TABLE 1.3 Mapping of *BABOK 2* Knowledge Areas to This Book *(continued)*

KA	Definition	KA Task (*BABOK 2*)	Coverage in This Text
		7.3 Assess Organizational Readiness	On process models, used to identify activities and stakeholders likely to be affected by the implementation of the solution[22], see Chapter 4.
		7.5 Validate Solution	For designing tests used as acceptance criteria for validating solutions, see Chapter 10. In particular, see the following sections of Chapter 10: ■ "Decision Tables for Testing" ■ "System Tests" (on testing of non-functional [service-level] requirements)

Chapter Summary

In this chapter, you learned the following:

■ The role of the IT BA is to represent the business stakeholders to the development community.

■ The main duties of the IT BA are to discover and communicate requirements to the developers and to support testing.

■ A business model is a collection of diagrams and supporting text that describes business rules and requirements.

■ A behavioral model describes what a system does.

■ A structural model describes what a system is.

■ The International Institute for Business Analysis (IIBA) is a professional body that offers a professional BA certification and whose publication, the *Business Analysis Body of Knowledge* (*BABOK*), defines knowledge areas (KAs) relevant to the practice of business analysis.

Endnotes

[1]I was involved with both these initiatives, as subject-matter expert on NITAS and as an editor of the *BABOK*.

[2]*A Guide to the Business Analysis Body of Knowledge (BABOK Guide) Version 2.0*, International Institute of Business Analysis, page 3, 2009.

[3]*A Guide to the Business Analysis Body of Knowledge (BABOK Guide) Version 2.0*, International Institute of Business Analysis, page 4, 2009.

[4]The standard used in this book is UML 2.2.

[5]The diagram was an activity diagram with partitions (swimlanes). It describes the sequence of activities and who (or what) is responsible for each activity.

[6]The diagrams covered under the "Behavioral Model" heading are sometimes referred to as *process models* (showing activities but not necessarily sequencing) and *workflow models* (which do show sequencing).

[7]UML Superstructure Specification, v2.2, OMG, 2009, page 686. The UML (Unified Modeling Language) is a standard used in object-oriented development.

[8]*A Guide to the Business Analysis Body of Knowledge (BABOK Guide) Version 2.0*, International Institute of Business Analysis, page 6, 2009.

[9]*A Guide to the Business Analysis Body of Knowledge (BABOK Guide) Version 2.0*, International Institute of Business Analysis, page 6, 2009.

[10]See *A Guide to the Business Analysis Body of Knowledge (BABOK Guide) Version 2.0*, International Institute of Business Analysis, Section 2.1.5 Techniques, page 23, 2009.

[11]For a discussion of process modeling and use cases in the context of this task, see *A Guide to the Business Analysis Body of Knowledge (BABOK Guide) Version 2.0*, International Institute of Business Analysis, Section 2.2.5 Techniques, page 28, 2009.

[12]*A Guide to the Business Analysis Body of Knowledge (BABOK Guide) Version 2.0*, International Institute of Business Analysis, page 7, 2009.

[13]*A Guide to the Business Analysis Body of Knowledge (BABOK Guide) Version 2.0*, International Institute of Business Analysis, page 7, 2009.

[14]*A Guide to the Business Analysis Body of Knowledge (BABOK Guide) Version 2.0*, International Institute of Business Analysis, page 7, 2009.

[15]The enterprise architecture is "a description of an organization's business processes, IT software and hardware, people, operations and projects, and the relationships between them." (*A Guide to the Business Analysis Body of Knowledge (BABOK Guide) Version 2.0*, International Institute of Business Analysis, page 226, 2009.)

[16]*A Guide to the Business Analysis Body of Knowledge (BABOK Guide) Version 2.0*, International Institute of Business Analysis, page 7, 2009.

[17]"The include relationship allows hierarchical composition of use cases as well as reuse of use cases." OMG Unified Modeling Language (OMG UML), Superstructure, V2.2, page 596, February 2009.

[18]*A Guide to the Business Analysis Body of Knowledge (BABOK Guide) Version 2.0*, International Institute of Business Analysis, page 117, 2009.

[19]*A Guide to the Business Analysis Body of Knowledge (BABOK Guide) Version 2.0*, International Institute of Business Analysis, page 120, 2009.

[20]*A Guide to the Business Analysis Body of Knowledge (BABOK Guide) Version 2.0*, International Institute of Business Analysis, page 8, 2009.

[21]*A Guide to the Business Analysis Body of Knowledge (BABOK Guide) Version 2.0*, International Institute of Business Analysis, Section 7.2.5 "Techniques", page 126, 2009.

[22]*A Guide to the Business Analysis Body of Knowledge (BABOK Guide) Version 2.0*, International Institute of Business Analysis, Section 7.3.5 "Techniques", page 129, 2009.

CHAPTER 2

THE BA'S PERSPECTIVE ON OBJECT ORIENTATION

Chapter Objectives

At the end of this chapter, you will

- Understand how OO affects the BA role on IT projects.
- Understand key OO concepts:
  - Objects
  - Operations and attributes
  - Encapsulation
  - Classes
  - Entity classes
  - Relationships
  - Generalization
  - Association
  - Aggregation
  - Composite aggregation
  - Polymorphism
  - System use cases
  - Business use cases
  - Unified Modeling Language (UML)

What Is OO?

OO

OO is an acronym for "object-oriented." The OO analyst sees a system as a set of objects that collaborate by sending requests to each other.[1]

OO is a complete conceptual framework that covers the entire lifecycle of an IT project.

- OO affects the way the BA analyzes and models the requirements.
- OO affects the way the software engineer (technical systems analyst) designs the system specifications.
- OO affects the way the code itself is structured. Object-oriented programming languages such as C++ and the .NET languages support OO concepts and structures.

All of these are based on the same theoretical framework—one that we'll explore in this chapter.

The UML Standard

UML is an acronym for Unified Modeling Language, a widely accepted standard incorporating OO concepts first developed by the "Three Amigos"—Grady Booch, Jim Rumbaugh, and Ivar Jacobson—and now owned by the Object Management Group (OMG). The UML standards cover terminology and diagramming conventions. This book uses the latest version of that standard, UML 2.2.

I've seen many projects get bogged down over arguments about whether it's "legal" to do this or that according to the UML. If this happens with your team, ask what difference the outcome of the argument will have on the quality of the resulting software. In many cases, particularly during business analysis, there *are* no ramifications. In such cases, discuss it, make a decision, and move on.

Cognitive Psychology and OO

As a business analyst, your job is to get inside the heads of your stakeholders so that you can extract what they know about a piece of the real world—a *business system*—and pass it on to the developers, who will simulate that system on a computer. If you were choosing an approach for doing all this, you'd want something that goes as directly as possible from the stakeholders' heads to the IT solution. This approach would have to begin with an understanding of how people actually think about the world, and would have to be broad enough to take the project from requirements gathering right through to construction of the software. Object orientation is one such approach. It begins by proposing that the object is the basic unit by which we organize knowledge. In the following discussion, we'll see how OO takes this simple idea and builds an entire edifice of powerful concepts that can be used to understand and build complex systems.

Objects

OO begins with the observation that when you perceive the world, you don't just take it in as a blur of sensations. Rather, you distinguish individual objects, and you have internal images of them that you can see in your mind's eye. Taken together, these internal objects model a segment of the real world.

The BA Perspective

You begin to analyze a business area by asking stakeholders to describe the business objects it encompasses. A business object is something the business (and the IT system that automates it) must keep track of or that participates in business processes. Examples of such an object might include an invoice, a customer-service representative, or a call.

Attributes and Operations

OO theory continues by examining the kind of knowledge that is attached to each internal object. Because we can recognize an object again after having seen it once, our internal representation of an object must include a record of its properties. For example, we remember that a shirt object's color is blue and its size is large. In OO, *color* and *size* are referred to as attributes; *blue* and *large* are attribute values. Every object has its own set of attribute values.

Something else we remember about an object is its function. For example, the first time you saw a crayon, it took you some time to learn that it could be used to scribble on the walls. Unfortunately for your parents, the next time you saw that crayon, you knew exactly what to do with it. Why? Because you remembered that scribble was something you could do with that object. In OO, *scribble* is referred to as an operation.

To sum up what we've established so far: Two things we remember about objects are

- The *values of their attributes*
- The *operations* that we can do with them

The BA Perspective

The next step in analyzing a business system is to find out what attributes and business operations apply to each object. For example, two attributes that apply to an account object are *balance* and *date last accessed*; two operations that relate to the object are *deposit* and *withdraw*.

An object's operations usually change or query the values of its attributes. For example, the *withdraw* operation changes the value of the object's *balance* attribute. But this is not always the case. For example, *view transaction history*—another operation that applies to the account object—displays information about all the transaction objects tied to the account; however, it might not refer to any of the account's attributes.

Operations and Methods

Going one step further, you don't just remember what you can do with an object, you also remember how you do it. For example, you know that you can place a call with a particular mobile phone—but you also remember that to do so, you must follow a particular procedure: First you enter the phone number and then you press the Send key. In OO terms, *place a call* is an operation; the procedure used to carry it out is called a method.

The BA Perspective

Next, you take each operation and ask stakeholders what procedure they use to carry it out. You document the procedure as a method. For example, you ask stakeholders what procedure they follow when withdrawing funds from an account. They tell you that they first check to see if there is a hold on the account and whether there are sufficient funds available for withdrawal. If everything is in order, they reduce the balance and create an audit trail of the transaction. You document this procedure as the method used to carry out the *withdraw* operation.

Encapsulation

Every day you use objects without knowing how they work or what their internal structure is. This is a useful aspect of the way we human objects interact with other objects. It keeps us from having to know too much. It also means that we can easily switch to another object with a different internal structure as long as it behaves the same way externally.

This is the OO principle of *encapsulation*: Only an object's *operations* are visible to other objects. Attributes and methods remain hidden from view.

The BA Perspective

When you describe the method of an object, don't mention the attributes of another object or presume to know how another object performs its operations. The benefit to this approach is that if the methods or attributes related to a business object ever change, you'll have to make corrections to only one part of the model.

OO Concept: Classes

You have seen that our ability to internally model an object allows us to use it the next time we encounter it without relearning it. This does not automatically mean, however, that we can apply what we've learned to other objects of the same type. Yet we do this all the time. For example, once we've learned how use one iPhone 3G, we know how to use all iPhone 3G objects. We can do this because we recognize that all these objects belong to the same type: iPhone 3G. In OO, the category that an object belongs to is called its class.

What If We Couldn't Classify Objects?

If you weren't able to group objects into classes, you wouldn't realize that a blue metallic pot and a green ceramic pot belong to the same group but that a blue metallic pot and a blue metallic car do not. (Oliver Sacks has an interesting book on the subject, called *The Man Who Mistook His Wife for a Hat*. He speaks of one of his patients who, unable to classify objects, wrongly concluded that his wife was a hat and tried to put her on his head as he was leaving the office.)

The minute you know that two objects belong to the class, *iPhone 3G*, you know a number of things about them:

- The same attributes apply to both objects. For example, you know that both objects will have a serial number, a phone number, and various camera settings.
- Each object will have its own values for these attributes.
- The same operations apply to both objects. For example, you can place a call and take a picture with each of these objects.
- The same methods apply. For example, the procedure for placing a call is the same for both phones.

See the following sidebar to find out how the Unified Modeling Language (the UML)—the predominant standard for Object-Orientation—defines a class.

What They Say:

"*Class*: A class describes a set of objects that share the same specifications of features, constraints, and semantics." [2] (UML)

What They Mean:

A class is a *category*. All objects that belong to the same category have the same attributes and operations (but the values of the attributes may change from object to object).

Let's summarize what we've learned so far:

- Attributes and operations are defined at the class level and apply to all objects within that class.
- All objects in a class have the same attributes. This means that the same properties are significant for all objects in a class. That said, the value of the attributes may change from object to object within a class—e.g., the color of one pen may be blue while the color of another is green.
- All objects in a class have the same operations and methods. In other words, all objects in a class can do the same things—and they do them the same way.
- You'll learn later that relationships (such as the relationship between a customer and an invoice) can also be stated at the class level.

The BA Perspective

Despite the name *object*-oriented analysis, you'll be spending most of your time defining classes, not objects. The classes you'll be interested in are those that relate to the business. These are termed entity classes. For example, in a banking system, you'd define the characteristics of an Account entity class and a Customer entity class.

OO Concept: Relationships

We often define one class in terms of another class. For example, a Car is a kind of a Vehicle. Both Car and Vehicle are classes. The phrase "a kind of" describes a *relationship* between the two classes.

The UML defines a number of types of relationships that are useful to the BA: generalization, association, aggregation, and composite aggregation.

OO Concept: Generalization

The concept of a class allows us to make statements about a set of objects that we treat exactly the same way. But sometimes we run into objects that are only partially alike. For example, we may own a store that has a number of iPhone 3G objects and a number of Motorola Razr phone objects. The iPhone 3Gs are not exactly like the Motorola Razr phones, but they do share some characteristics—for example, the ability to place a mobile call. We treat this situation by thinking of these objects not only as iPhone 3G or Motorola Razr phones but also as mobile phones. A particular phone object, for example, might be able to run a particular iPhone application by virtue of being an iPhone 3G—but it can also place a mobile call by virtue of being a mobile phone. In OO, Mobile Phone is referred to as the generalized class; iPhone 3G and Motorola Razr are referred to as its specialized classes. The relationship between the Mobile Phone class and either of its subtypes (iPhone 3G or Motorola Razr) is called generalization.

Why do we generalize? It allows us to make statements that cover a broad range of objects. For example, when we say that a mobile phone can receive a text message, we are stating a rule that applies to all of its specializations.

What They Say:

"A generalization is a taxonomic relationship between a more general classifier and a more specific classifier. Each instance of the specific classifier is also an indirect instance of the general classifier. Thus, the specific classifier inherits the features of the more general classifier." [3] (UML)

What They Mean:

When an object belongs to a specialized class (for example, iPhone 3G), this automatically implies that it belongs to a generalization of that class (for example, Mobile Phone). Any attribute or operation that applies to the generalized class also applies to the specialized class. Furthermore, any relationships specified for the generalized class also apply to the specialized class. (For example, the relationship "Customer OWNS [one or more] Accounts," though specified for the Account class, applies also to Checking Account, Savings Account, and all other Account types [specialized classes of Account].)

Other terms in use include the following:

Generalized Class	Specialized Class
Superclass	Subclass
Base class	Derived class
Parent	Child

The idea that a specialized class automatically adopts the attributes, operations, and relationships of its generalized class is given a special name in OO: *inheritance*.

What They Say:

"*Inheritance*: The mechanism by which more specific elements incorporate structure and behavior of more general elements." [4] (UML 2)

What They Mean:

Inheritance refers to the mechanism by which a specialized class adopts—that is, *inherits*—all the attributes, operations, and relationships[5] of a generalized class.[6]

The BA Perspective

You look for classes of business objects that are subtypes of a more general type. For example, Checking Account and Savings Account are two kinds (specialized classes) of Accounts. Then you document which attributes and operations apply to all Accounts, which apply only to Checking Accounts, and which to Savings Accounts. By structuring your requirements this way, you only have to document rules common to all account types once. This makes it easier to revise the documentation if these business rules ever change. It also gives you the opportunity to state rules about Accounts that must apply to all future account types—even ones you don't know about yet.

OO Concept: Association

Another way that classes may be related to each other is through association. When you connect a mouse to a PC, you are associating *mouse* with *PC*.

What They Say:

"An *association* specifies a semantic relationship that can occur between typed instances. An instance of an association is called a *link*." [7] (UML 2)

What They Mean:

An association between two classes indicates that objects (instances) of one class may be related (linked) to objects of the other class. You specify an *association* at the class level; you specify a *link* at the object level.

The BA Perspective

You analyze how the business links objects of one class with those of another (or, sometimes, with other objects of the same class). For example, the military needs to track which mechanics serviced each piece of equipment, what the maintenance schedule is for each one, and so on. As a BA, you document these types of rules as associations. This is a critical part of your job. Miss an association—or document it incorrectly—and you may end up with software that does not support an important business rule.

Why It's Important to Analyze Associations

I once worked with a municipality that had just purchased a human-resources (HR) system. Since they only intended to purchase ready-made software, they didn't think it necessary to do much analysis and, therefore, did not analyze associations. Had they done so, they would have included in their requirements the fact that the business needed to be able to associate each employee with one or more unions.[8] (The business context for this was that some employees held a number of positions, each covered by a different union.) As a result of the omission, not only did the municipality end up purchasing HR software that did not support this requirement, they also had to absorb the cost of customization. Had they included the requirement, they would have been unlikely to purchase this software in the first place—and even if they had, they would have been able to pass the modification cost on to the vendor.

OO Concept: Aggregation

Aggregation is the relationship between a whole and its parts. For example, the trade organization CompTIA is an aggregation of member organizations; an insurance policy is an aggregation of a basic policy and amendments to the policy, and a stamp collection is an aggregation of stamps.

What They Say:

"*Aggregation*: A special form of association that specifies a whole-part relationship between the aggregate (whole) and a component part. [9] (UML)

What They Mean:

Formally, in the UML, aggregation is considered to be a specific type of association, where the class on one end of the association represents a whole and the class at the other end represents a part. Aggregation may be used by the BA as an alternative to modeling an association with the name "is a part of".

With aggregation, a part may belong to more than one whole. For example, a *catalogue* object is a collection (aggregation) that consists of many product objects. However, any particular product object may appear in more than one *catalogue* object.

The BA Perspective

You look for business objects that are made of other business objects. You model these relationships as aggregations. Then you focus on which rules (attributes, operations, and relationships) apply to the whole and which apply to the parts. One thing this process enables you to do is reuse the requirements of a part object in a new context. For example, you model an ATM card as an aggregate, one of whose parts is a PIN. You define the attributes and operations of a PIN. Later you reuse the PIN requirements for a credit-card system that also uses PINs.

OO Concept: Composite Aggregation (Composition)

Composite aggregation, also known as *composition*, is a special form of aggregation wherein each part may belong to only one whole at a time.

What They Say:

" *Composite aggregation* is a strong form of aggregation that requires a part instance be included in at most one composite at a time. If a composite is deleted, all of its parts are normally deleted with it."[10] (UML)

What They Mean:

Formally, composition is a specific kind of aggregation. In aggregation, a part may belong to more than one whole at the same time; in composite aggregation, however, the object may belong to only one whole at a time. The parts are destroyed whenever the whole is destroyed—except for those parts that have been removed prior to the deletion of the whole.

Let's recap what OO says about association, aggregation, and composite aggregation:

The most general relationship is association, followed by aggregation, and, finally, composite aggregation.

What If You're Not Sure What Type of Whole-Part Relationship to Use?

Don't get too distraught if you are unable to decide whether a particular whole-part relationship is best described as an *aggregation* or *composite aggregation*. While the distinction (from a BA perspective) is helpful, it is not critical. If you have any problem deciding, specify the whole-part relationship as *aggregation*. If you're not even sure whether the relationship is best described as a whole-part relationship, then model it as an association. In fact, there is nothing wrong with the BA modeling all whole-part relationships as simple associations. You lose a little bit of nuance in the model – but it will make no difference to the resulting IT solution.

The BA Perspective

You model strong whole-part relationships between classes of business objects as composite aggregation. For example, in analyzing a CRO (clinical research organization) system, I modeled a *Case Report Form* as a composite aggregation of *Modules*. The *Case Report Form* was a record of everything that was recorded about a patient with respect to the drug being researched; each *Module* was a record of one visit to the clinic by the patient. The developers understood from this model that each *Module* could only belong to one *Case Report Form* at a time and that when a *Case Report Form* was removed from the system, all of its *Modules* needed to be removed as well.

OO Concept: Polymorphism

Polymorphism means the ability to take on many forms. The term is applied both to objects and to operations.

Polymorphic Objects

Suppose a financial company handles different subtypes of *Funds*, such as an *Asia Fund*, *Domestic Fund,* and so on, each with its own idiosyncrasies. The BA models this situation using a generalized class, *Fund*, and a specialized class for each subtype of *Fund*. Next, the BA moves on to capture investment rules in an *Investment* class. Checking with the stakeholders, the BA finds that one of its operations, *invest capital*, deals with all *Funds* the same way, regardless of subtype. The BA handles this by ensuring that the documentation for the *invest capital* operation refers exclusively to the generalized class *Fund*—not to any of its specializations. When the operation is actually executed, though, the *Fund* object will take on one of many forms—for example, an *Asia Fund* or a *Domestic Fund*. In other words, the *Fund* object is polymorphic.

Polymorphic Operations

Continuing with the same example, since all the *Fund* subtypes have to be able to accept deposits, the BA defines a *Fund* operation called *accept deposit*. This operation is inherited by all the specializations. The BA can also specify a method for this *Fund* operation that will be inherited by the specializations. But what if one or more of the specializations— for example, the *Asia Fund*—uses a different procedure for accepting deposits? In this case, the BA can add documentation to the *Asia Fund* class that describes a method that overrides the one inherited from the generalized class. For example, the method described might involve supplementary charges. In practice, when capital investment causes a *Fund* to perform an *accept deposit* operation, the method that is used to carry out the operation will take on one of many forms. This is what is meant by a polymorphic operation. With polymorphic operations, the selection of the method depends on which particular class (*Asia Fund*, *Domestic Fund,* and so on) is carrying it out.

One Operation, Many Methods

A *polymorphic operation* is one whose method may take on many forms based on the class of the object carrying it out.

The BA Perspective

When you define operations for a generalized class, you look for those that all specializations must be able to support. If you can, you define a method that describes how the operation is typically carried out. If any specialized classes have different ways of doing the operation, you define a new method for it at the specialized class level. This simplifies the documentation. You don't need to write, "If the type is *X*, then do one method; if it is *Y*, do another one." Instead, you get this across by *where* you document the method in the model.

One Interface, Many Implementations

Polymorphism means "one interface, many possible implementations." Cars, for example, are designed with polymorphism in mind. They all use the same interface—an accelerator pedal—to change speed, even though the internal method may differ from model to model. The auto industry designs cars this way so that the drivers do not have to learn a new interface for each new model of car.

Use Cases and Scenarios

A *use case* is a use to which the system will be put that produces an observable result and usually provides value to one or more entities that interact with the system. It's an external perspective on the system from the point of view of the user. For example, some of the use cases that customers need in a Web-based banking system are *Make bill payment*, *Stop payment*, and *Order checks*.

What They Say:

"*Use case*: A use case is the specification of a set of actions performed by a system, which yields an observable result that is, typically, of value for one or more actors or other stakeholders of the system."[11] (UML 2)

What They Mean:

A use case is a usage of the system that provides an observable and (usually) meaningful result. The use-case documentation (diagrams and/or text) should delineate the series of steps that take place during the interaction and include different ways that this interaction could play out.

What They Say:

"Scenario: A specific sequence of actions that illustrates behaviors. A scenario may be used to illustrate an interaction or the execution of a use-case instance."[12] (UML 2)

What They Mean:

A *scenario* is one path through a use case—one way that it might play out.

For example, the *Make bill payment* use case may play out in one of the following ways:

- Scenario 1: Attempt to make a payment from an account and succeed in doing so.
- Scenario 2: Attempt to make a payment from an account and fail because there is a hold on the account.

The BA Perspective

During behavioral analysis, you identify and document the use cases of the system—what the users want to do with it. You do this by identifying and describing its scenarios— all the ways the interaction could play out. These use cases and scenarios are your user requirements.

Business and System Use Cases

Over time, practitioners began to distinguish between two kinds of use cases: business use cases and system use cases. This distinction is not part of the core UML but it is a valid and widely accepted UML extension.[13]

- A *use case* (unqualified) refers to an interaction with any type of system. The question is, what type of system is being referring to?
- A *business use case* is an interaction with a business system. For example, *Process Claim* is a business use case describing an interaction with an insurance company.

- A *system use case*[14] is an interaction with an IT system. For example, system use cases that support the aforementioned business use case are *Record Claim*, *Validate Coverage*, *Assign Adjuster*, and so on. Each of these describes an interaction between a user and the computer system. A system use case typically involves one active (primary) user and takes place over a single session on the computer. At the end of the system use case, the user should feel that he or she has achieved a useful goal.

The BA Perspective

Early in a project, you identify and describe the business use cases that the IT project will affect. At this point, you focus on the business aspect of proposed changes—how they will affect workflow and the human roles within the business. Next, you analyze each business use case, looking for activities that the IT project will cover. You group these activities into system use cases, taking care to ensure that each system use case gives the user something of real benefit. These system use cases then drive the whole development process. For example, in each release, a planned set of system use cases is analyzed (unless this was done up front), designed, coded, and implemented. With this use case–centered approach, users get features that add real value to their jobs with each software release.

Chapter Summary

In this chapter, you learned the following concepts:

- *OO* is an acronym for object-oriented, an approach to analysis, design, and programming that is based on dividing a system up into collaborating objects.
- An *object* is a particular "thing" that plays a role in the system and/or that the system tracks—for example, the customer *Jane Dell Ray*. An object has *attributes* and *operations* associated with it. The object is the basic unit of an OO system.
- An *attribute* is a data element of an object.
- An *operation* is a service that a class of objects can carry out.
- A *method* is the process used to carry out an operation.
- *Encapsulation* is an OO principle stating that everything about an object—its operations and properties—is contained within the object. No other object may refer directly to another's attributes or rely on a knowledge of how its operations are carried out.
- A *class* is a category of object. Objects of the same class share the same attributes and methods.
- An *entity class* is something the business keeps information about—for example, *Customer.*

- A *relationship* is a connection between classes. A number of different types of relationships were discussed in this chapter: generalization, association, aggregation, and composite aggregation.

- *Generalization* is an OO property that models partial similarities among objects. A *generalized class* describes the commonalities. Each variation is called a *specialized class*. A specialized class *inherits* all the operations, attributes, and relationships of the generalized class.

- An *association* between classes indicates a link between its objects—for example, between an *Account* object and its *Customer* owner.

- *Aggregation* is a relationship between a whole and its parts.

- *Composite aggregation* is a specific form of aggregation wherein the parts have no existence independent of the whole.

- *Polymorphism* is an OO concept allowing one operation name to stand for different procedures that achieve the same end. The class of the acting object determines which action is selected.

- A *use case* is a typical interaction between the user and system that achieves a useful result for the user.

- A *business use case* is a business process.

- A *system use case* is a typical interaction with an IT system.

- The *unified modeling language* (*UML*) is a widely accepted standard for modeling business and IT systems that incorporates OO concepts.

Endnotes

[1] Another way of phrasing this is that the objects pass messages to each other.

[2] *UML Superstructure Specification*, v2.2, OMG, page 49, 2009.

[3] *UML Superstructure Specification*, v2.2, OMG, page 63, 2009.

[4] *UML 2.0: Infrastructure—Final Adopted Specification*, OMG, page 10, 2003. (No definition for inheritance appears in the latest version, UML 2.2.)

[5] An example of an inherited relationship is the relationship "accessed by" between a generalized class, Account, and a Customer class. All specializations (subtypes) of Account inherit this relationship—i.e., a Checking Account is accessed by a Customer, a Savings Account is accessed by a Customer, and so on. In this example, "accessed by" is an association relationship.

[6] A specialized class inherits not only the operations of the generalized class but also the methods for carrying out those operations. However, an inherited method may be overridden by a method specified for the specialized class. This last property is referred to as polymorphism.

[7] *UML Superstructure Specification*, v2.2, OMG, page 39, 2009.

[8]The "one or more" aspect of the association is known as *multiplicity*.

[9]*UML 2.0: Infrastructure—Final Adopted Specification*, OMG, page 4, 2003. (No definition for aggregation appears in the latest version, UML 2.2.)

[10]*UML Superstructure Specification*, v2.2, OMG, page 41, 2009. The term composition was defined in the UML 2 infrastructure. The UML 2.2 contains references to the term composition in this context but formally names the relationship composite aggregation.

[11]*UML Superstructure Specification*, v2.2, OMG, page 596, 2009.

[12]*UML 2.0: Infrastructure—Final Adopted Specification*, OMG, page 15, 2003. (No definition for scenario appears in the latest version, UML 2.2.)

[13]The extensions are realized through the invention of new stereotypes for existing UML model elements. A stereotype extends the meaning of a model element. For example, in business modeling, a *business actor* is a stereotype of the UML actor. For a more complete discussion of business modeling, see Pan-Wei Ng, "Effective Business Modeling with UML: Describing Business Use Cases and Realizations," *Rational Edge*. UML business modeling extensions are described in the jointly authored paper, "UML Extension for Business Modeling, Version 1.1," by Rational Software, Microsoft, Hewlett-Packard, Oracle, Sterling Software, MCI Systemhouse, Unisys, ICON Computing, IntelliCorp, i-Logix, IBM, ObjecTime, Platinum Technology, Ptech, Taskon, Reich Technologies, and Softeam, 1 September 1997.

[14]In some circles, the term *business use case* refers to an interaction with a business (conforming to the usage in this book); *use case* (without a qualifier) refers to an interaction with an IT system and is equivalent to the term *system use case* in this book. I prefer the term *system use case* as it avoids confusion regarding the type of system involved in the interaction.

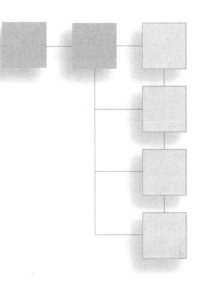

CHAPTER 3

STEPS OF B.O.O.M.

Chapter Objectives

At the end of this chapter, you will know the steps of Business Object Oriented Modeling (B.O.O.M.), a procedure for eliciting, analyzing, documenting, and testing requirements using object-oriented and complementary techniques.

B.O.O.M. and SDLCs

Many large companies adopt a systems development lifecycle (SDLC) for managing their IT projects. The SDLC defines the specific phases and activities of a project. The names of the phases differ from SDLC to SDLC, but most SDLCs have something close to the following phases[1]:

- **Initiation:** Make the business case for the project. Work also begins on the user experience and on drafts of architectural proof of concepts. The prototyping effort during the Initiation phase should be risk-driven and limited to gaining confidence that a solution is possible.

- **Discovery:** Conduct investigation leading to an understanding of the solution's desired behavior. (On iterative projects, requirements analysis peaks during this phase but never disappears entirely.) During this phase, architectural proofs of concept are also constructed.

- **Construction:** Complete the analysis and design, code, integrate, and test the software. (On iterative projects, these activities are performed for each iteration within the phase. Design and coding appear in all phases, but peak during this phase.)

- **Final Verification and Validation (V&V):** Perform final testing before the product or service is transitioned into production. (While final testing occurs in this phase, testing activities may occur throughout the SDLC—for example, before design or as a replacement for it.)

- **Closeout:** Manage and coordinate deployment into production and close the IT project.[2]

The B.O.O.M. Steps

A deeper assessment of these phases and their relationship to the B.O.O.M. steps follows.

Step 1: Initiation

The objectives of the Initiation phase are to develop the business case for the project, establish project and product scope, and explore solutions, including the preliminary architecture. The BA assists the project manager by identifying stakeholders, business services and processes, and IT services affected by the project. By the end of this phase, key functionality is identified, such as key system use cases (user tasks) and IT services. When a non-agile process is used, these requirements are baselined and subsequent changes to scope are managed in a controlled manner using a change-management process.

The Initiation phase poses a conundrum for the BA. The purpose of this phase is to get a rough cut at the business case for a proposed IT project. The trouble is that without knowing the requirements, it's impossible to estimate the cost of the project; at the same time, without a business justification for the project, it is difficult to justify much requirement analysis. The answer is to do *just enough* research to be able to create a ballpark estimate. In this book, you'll do this using a number of UML techniques that keep you focused on high-level needs. These techniques are as follows:

- **Business use cases:** A tool for identifying and describing end-to-end business processes affected by the project.
- **Activity diagrams:** Used to help you and stakeholders form a consensus regarding the workflow of each business use case.
- **Actors:** These describe the users and external systems that will interact with the proposed IT system.
- **System use cases:** Used to help stakeholders break out the end-to-end business processes into meaningful interactions with the IT system.

By the end of this phase, you will have a rough idea about the project as well as a fairly comprehensive list of system use cases, and you will know which users will be involved with each system use case. You won't know the *details* of each system use case yet, but you will know enough to be able to ballpark the project—for example, to say whether it will take days, weeks, or months.

The main deliverable of this phase is an early draft of a business requirements document (BRD). This book takes a "living document" approach to the BRD. You'll create it in this phase, and revise it as the project progresses. To help manage scope, you'll save a copy of the document at the end of each phase. This is what I mean by "set baseline" in the following list. *Baselining* allows you to see what the requirements looked like at various checkpoints in order to see, for example, whether a feature requested later by a stakeholder was within the scope as defined at that time.

Following is a list of the steps you'll carry out during this phase.

1a) Model business use cases

    i)   Identify business use cases (business use-case diagram)

    ii) Scope business use cases (activity diagram)

1b) Model system use cases

    i)   Identify actors (role map)

    ii) Identify system use-case packages (system use-case diagram)

    iii) Identify system use cases (system use-case diagram)

1c) Begin structural model (class diagrams for key business classes)

1d) Set baseline (BRD/Initiation)

Step 2: Discovery

The main objective of the Discovery phase is to understand the solution's desired behavior and baseline the architecture. This and the previous phase are the key phases for the BA. Requirements analysis peaks during this phase. (In iterative processes, analysis continues throughout the lifecycle; in waterfall processes, it is completed in this phase.) Some system use cases are selected for development during this phase in order to demonstrate architectural proofs of concept.

BA responsibilities during this phase focus on eliciting *detailed* requirements from stakeholders, analyzing and documenting them for verification by stakeholders and for use by solution providers. You will exploit a number of UML and complementary techniques to assist in requirements elicitation, analysis, and documentation during this phase. Some of the main techniques you'll use include the following:

- System use-case descriptions (specifications), storyboarding the interaction between users and the proposed IT system as each system use case is played out
- State-machine diagrams describing the lifecycle of key business objects
- Class diagrams describing key business concepts and business rules that apply to business objects such as accounts, investments, complaints, claims, and so on

Testing, in the sense used in this book, is not just the running of programs to uncover errors; it includes other validation and verification activities as well as test planning and preparation. Following accepted quality assurance practices, I introduce testing long before the code is written. Hence, you'll find some testing activities also included in this phase. You'll learn to specify the *degree* of technical testing (white-box and system testing) required from the developers as well as how to design *effective* requirements-based test cases (black-box tests). By doing this during the Discovery phase, not only do you allow for enough lead time to set up these tests, but you also declare measurable criteria for the project's success: If the tests you've described don't "work as advertised," the product will not be accepted.

Following are the steps you'll carry out during this phase

2a) Behavioral analysis
　　　i) Describe system use cases (use-case description)
　　　ii) Describe state behavior (state-machine diagram)
　　　　　1. Identify states of critical objects
　　　　　2. Identify state transitions
　　　　　3. Identify state activities
　　　　　4. Identify superstates
　　　　　5. Identify concurrent states

2b) Structural analysis (object/data model) (class diagram)
　　　i) Identify entity classes
　　　ii) Model generalizations
　　　iii) Model transient roles
　　　iv) Model whole-part relationships
　　　v) Analyze associations
　　　vi) Analyze multiplicity
　　　vii) Link system use cases to the structural model
　　　viii) Add attributes
　　　ix) Add lookup tables
　　　x) Distribute operations
　　　xi) Revise class structure

2c) Specify testing (test plan/decision tables)
　　　i) Specify white-box testing quality level
　　　ii) Specify black-box test cases
　　　iii) Specify system tests

2d) Specify implementation plan (implementation plan)

2e) Set baseline for development (BRD/Discovery)

Please note than on an iterative project this phase may include a number of cycles, or iterations, in which case the above steps are repeated for each iteration (cycle) within the phase. (See the section "Tailoring B.O.O.M. for Your Project" later in this chapter for a more complete discussion of lifecycles and their impact on analysis steps.)

Step 3: Construction

Business-analysis activity during this phase depends on the lifecycle approach being used. On waterfall projects, where all the analysis is done up front, there is no requirements gathering or analysis during this phase; however, the BA is involved in supporting quality assurance and validating that the technical design meets the requirements (for example, by reviewing test plans and design specifications). On iterative projects, where requirements analysis and solution development take place over a number of iterations, the steps described for the Discovery phase (steps 2a through 2e) are carried out during each iteration of the Construction phase. (See the section "Tailoring B.O.O.M. for Your Project" later in this chapter for a more complete discussion of lifecycles and their impact on analysis.)

Step 4: Final Verification and Validation (V&V)

The business analyst supports final testing before the completed solution is deployed, reviewing test plans and results and ensuring that all requirements are tested.

Step 5: Closeout

The business analyst supports the deployment process, reviewing transition plans and participating in a post-implementation review (PIR) to evaluate the success of the change.

What Do You Define First—Attributes or Operations?

The OO principle of encapsulation suggests that in understanding how each object is used in a system, it's more important to know its operations than its attributes; operations are all that objects see of each other. However, within the context of business analysis, it's usually easy to identify the attributes of a class: The attributes show up as fields on screens and reports, and it's often fairly obvious what class of objects they describe. Ascribing operations to classes is not quite as easy—and I like to do the easy things first. (However, when I'm doing OOD, I start with the operations.)

Feel free to make changes to the order described for analyzing operations, attributes, or any other step. Consider B.O.O.M. your starting point. By following it, you *will* get to the end result—comprehensive requirements—relatively effortlessly. But you should, over time, customize the process as you see fit. The section "Tailoring B.O.O.M. for Your Project" in this chapter provides some guidelines for doing this.

Developing the Structural Model Alongside the Behavioral Model

B.O.O.M. steps 2a (behavioral analysis) and 2b (structural analysis) should be performed in parallel. In working through the case study in this book, I've separated these activities for pedagogical purposes; it's difficult, when learning this for the first time, to jump back and forth continually between the two types of modeling. Here's how you should intersperse these steps once you have some experience behind you:

1. During the Initiation phase, you identify system use cases in the behavioral model. Nouns discovered during this process are added to the structural model if they relate to new business concepts or objects. For example, the system use case Adjudicate Loan Application introduces the term Loan Application, which you define in the structural model. You continue working on the structural model during the Initiation phase, describing key business classes and their relationships to each other.

2. Following the Initiation phase, as you describe each system use case (step 2ai), you verify it against the existing structural model. Does the system use case comply with rules expressed in the structural model? Has the system use case introduced new classes? You resolve any differences between the system use case and the structural model and update the structural model if necessary.

3. By the time you have described the last system use case, the structural model should be complete and fully verified.[3]

Tailoring B.O.O.M. for Your Project

The B.O.O.M. steps are meant to be used as a checklist of items for the BA to consider when planning BA activities for a project—but not every step is required on every project. As a BA, your guiding principle in this regard should be, "If it isn't going to make a difference to the outcome, don't do it." Yet I see a lot of confusion amongst BAs about how much analysis to do on a given project. Are structural models (class diagrams and ERDs) always worth doing, or are they a waste of time? How much detail should you put into the user requirements? Obviously, blindly creating documentation without understanding its value—or if it even has any value—is not useful. The problem is when to do what. Following are some general guidelines.

The degree of documentation and analysis required for a project and the order in which analysis activities are carried out depends on a number of factors:[4]

- **The degree of formality versus adaptiveness of the lifecycle:** The degree of a lifecycle's formality versus its adaptiveness (capacity to adjust to environmental conditions) is indicated by whether it is classified as a definitive or an empirical lifecycle. At one end of the continuum are definitive lifecycles, which follow a formal, well-defined process. Projects using this style of lifecycle will produce much of the documentation described in this book and to a comparable level of detail. At the other end of the continuum are empirical processes—less formal, adaptive processes, such as those that use an agile approach. Empirical processes require less analysis and documentation than definitive ones. Detailed user requirements are not documented on such projects because the requirements are in a constant state of flux and because the process relies on a heavily collaborative process of trial and error in order to determine what stakeholders want. On these projects, you might analyze the impact of the proposed change on business use cases and on their internal workflow, and identify and briefly describe system use cases and their main alternate flows (optional and error pathways), but not create detailed system use-case descriptions. Brief descriptions of system use cases are sufficient for project estimation and for planning iterations, but anything more than that is generally not necessary with this approach. Structural analysis still has a place in empirical lifecycles, especially when it relates to the business architecture, because of its value in defining business concepts and in discovering across-the-board business rules that are easy to miss. However, you are unlikely to produce a complete structural model on such projects. For empirical lifecycles, these are the rules to follow:

  - Do as little documentation as you can get away with.

  - Do it as late in the process as possible.

  - Don't baseline the requirements unless they are in the process of being implemented.

- **Whether an iterative approach is being used:** How analysis activities are sequenced within the development process is determined by whether the project is using a waterfall or an iterative lifecycle. With a waterfall lifecycle, all the analysis must be done up front before implementation begins. Hence, all the B.O.O.M. analysis steps must be completed by the end of the Discovery phase, before the Construction phase. On an iterative project (also referred to as iterative-incremental), the solution is developed in cycles, called iterations. Each iteration is like a mini-project, involving some degree of analysis, design, and coding, and should result in an increment of functionality; in other words, the user must be able to do something he or she could not do before. On such projects, the analysis is not all performed up front but continues through the Construction phase. For example, you might identify and briefly describe system use cases during the Initiation phase (as shown in the B.O.O.M. steps), fully describe those system use cases that exercise key architectural features during the Discovery phase, and complete the description of each system use case during the Construction iteration in which it will be implemented.

- **The degree of uncertainty tolerated by the sponsor and the size of the budget:** The type of lifecycle that is most appropriate for a project—and hence the timing and amount of analysis and documentation it entails—depends on many factors. One is the degree of uncertainty that the project sponsor and stakeholders are willing to accept. If the budget is large, clients are less likely to be willing to sign off on high-level documentation that leaves many of the details unknown. They often want to know exactly what they are paying for up front, before any development or procurement begins. In this case, the situation may dictate that a definitive, waterfall process be used. On the other hand, where a small budget is involved, clients may be willing to live with more uncertainty and, hence, be comfortable with an empirical approach.

- **Regulatory requirements:** Regulatory requirements have an impact on how much of the requirements must be pinned down in writing. If they require an extensive paper trail, the use of a definitive lifecycle is indicated.

- **The size of the team and the physical distance between analyst, the solution team, and business stakeholders:** Close proximity of solution providers and business stakeholders and small team sizes both argue for an empirical approach. Verbal communication works fine in these settings; indeed, formal, written documentation only slows down the process. On the other hand, when large teams or distances are involved, a definitive, well-defined process with formal documentation may be needed to facilitate coordination and communication.

- **The capabilities of developers:** The greater the expertise of the developers, the less documentation may be required. For example, if the team has deep experience handling software internationalization, then the requirements related to this issue need not be spelled out in detail.

- **The type of solution being contemplated (in-house or vendor solution):** In-house and custom solutions favor more documentation; vendor-supplied off-the-shelf solutions favor less documentation. Some of the business rules and requirements for the project are likely to be standard across the industry and are, therefore, likely to be supported in an off-the-shelf solution. These requirements entail less risk—and hence, less need for documentation—than those that are peculiar to the client organization.

- **The maturity of the organization:** In mature organizations, many processes and systems may already be documented, so the extent of new analysis and documentation required on a new project is less than on a less mature organization, where existing documentation is sparse.

What Do You Show Stakeholders?

Not every document you produce is aimed at the same audience. You need to tailor what you show to the audience that will see it. All the artifacts described in this book are appropriate for developers and other analysts on your team, but not all are appropriate for business stakeholders—at least not without some translation. The following is a summary of the artifacts described in this book and how they are presented to business stakeholders. You may want to re-read this section once you've learned more about these artifacts.

- **Activity (workflow) diagrams:** Show these to stakeholders, but only use the basic modeling elements described in this book. (Examples of other elements excluded from this book and inappropriate for stakeholders include signals and expansion regions.) Activity diagrams with partitions (swimlanes) help business stakeholders visualize the internal workflow of a business use case (business process); simple activity diagrams attached to system use cases help them visualize user-IT interactions when the flows though a system use case connect in complex ways.

- **State-machine diagrams:** Show business stakeholders simple diagrams only, indicating states and transitions but excluding advanced features (such as internal actions within a state and send events).

- **Use-case diagrams:** Show these to stakeholders, but only include actors and their relationships to use cases. Business use-case diagrams provide stakeholders with an overview of who participates in which processes; system use-case diagrams provide a useful overview of who does what with the IT solution. However, hide other modeling elements such as include, extend, and generalization relationships; these are useful internally for the team in reducing redundancies but they are apt to confuse stakeholders. (An exception may be made with respect to the include relationship if stakeholders are comfortable with it.)

- **Use-case descriptions (referred to in RUP as use-case specifications), decision tables, and decision trees:** Show these to stakeholders.

- **Class diagrams:** Do not show these to stakeholders. Note, however, that they do contain important business rules; convert these to text and obtain sign-off on them. See the section "Step 2bvi: Analyze Multiplicity" in Chapter 8, "Gathering Across-the-Board Business Rules with Class Diagrams," for guidance in expressing associations and multiplicities as sentences (as in, "Each case generates zero or more payments").

Chapter Summary

In this chapter, you learned the following concepts:

- The phases during which the B.O.O.M. steps apply are as follows
  - *Initiation*, during which a business case is made for the project.
  - *Discovery*, during which the eliciting, analysis, and documentation of detailed requirements peaks. Testing activities also occur during this phase.
  - *Construction*, during which the solution is built and—if an iterative lifecyle approach is being used on the project—requirements, elicitation, analysis, and documentation continue.

Endnotes

[1]For example, RUP has Inception, Elaboration, Construction, and Transition phases. The SDLC described in these pages uses the generic phase names introduced in my book, *The Business Analyst's Handbook*. The B.O.O.M. steps are derived from *The Noble Path*, also described in that book. For a broader discussion of lifecycle approaches and their impact on the BA and for more on the Noble Path, see *The Business Analyst's Handbook*, Chapter 1, "Overview of BA Activities Throughout the Life Cycle."

[2]For more on the impact of project attributes and lifecycles on business analysis, see *The Business Analyst's Handbook*, 1st edition, Chapter 1, "Overview of BA Activities Throughout the Life Cycle," pages 3–4.

[3]Both the behavioral and structural models are completed during the Discovery phase when a waterfall lifecycle is used. When an iterative process is used, they continue to be developed during the Construction phase.

[4]Thanks to Adrian Marchis and the many members of the BA online community at modernanalyst.com for their contributions to this discussion. For more on this topic, see my blog post "How Much Analysis Do You Really Need to Do?" and readers' comments at http://www.modernanalyst.com/Community/ModernAnalystBlog/tabid/181/articleType/ArticleView/articleId/921/How-much-analysis-do-you-really-need-to-do.aspx#Comments.

CHAPTER 4

ANALYZING END-TO-END BUSINESS PROCESSES

Chapter Objectives

By the end of this chapter, you will

- Be able to gather requirements about end-to-end business processes using business use cases.
- Know the layout of a business requirement document (BRD).
- Know how to fill the role of the IT business analyst during the Initiation phase of a project.
- Identify business use cases.
- Use business use-case diagrams effectively to gain consensus about which stakeholders interact with the business as each business use case is carried out.
- Use activity diagrams to gain consensus about workflow.

Interviews During the Phases

As a BA, you'll carry out interviews with users at various phases of a project. During the Initiation phase, you'll interview stakeholders in order to establish the business rationale and scope for the project and to collect initial requirements. During the Discovery phase (and, on iterative projects, during the Construction phase), you'll meet with users to discover and document the business requirements for the new (or revised) software system. As you gather the requirements in these phases, you'll hold review sessions with stakeholders to verify the correctness and completeness of the requirements documentation. During the Final V&V phase, you'll meet with stakeholders to validate that the software meets their requirements.

As you go through this book, you'll learn what questions to ask during these interviews. This section looks at the structure of those interviews. Table 4.1 describes different interview formats and when each type is used during the project lifecycle. Please note that on an iterative project, any interview type associated in the table with the Discovery phase is also used during the Construction phase, since requirements analysis continues as the solution is developed.

TABLE 4.1   Interview Formats

Format	What	When	Benefits	Disadvantages
One-on-one interviews		During the Initiation and Discovery phases	Is easy to organize	Reconciling discrepancies is time consuming
Brainstorming	Group interview for enlisting new ideas	During Initiation phase and whenever the project is "stuck"	Breaks old ways of thinking	Does not yield detailed requirements
Joint application development (JAD)	Group interview to gather requirements	During Discovery phase	Simplifies reconciling of discrepancies, decreasing analysis time; can be used to create various deliverables, including the following: ▪BRD ▪Proof of concept ▪Strategy ▪Screens ▪Decision tables	Difficult to get all the interviewees in one room at same time Group-think
Structured walkthrough	Group interview to verify requirements	During Discovery phase, after early draft of requirements is available. During Construction phase, to review technical specifications and, on iterative projects, to verify remaining requirements.	Moves testing forward, reducing the impact of mistakes	Difficult to get interviewees in one room at same time Group-think

B.O.O.M. Steps

In this chapter, we'll be walking through the following B.O.O.M. steps in the Initiation phase:

1a) Model business use cases.
  i) Identify business use cases (business use-case diagram).
  ii) Scope business use cases (activity diagram).

Step 1: The Initiation Phase

The first phase in a project is the Initiation phase. Different approaches to IT project management each have their own terms for this phase and the precise activities that go on within it. Approximate counterparts for this phase include the following:

- Envisioning (Microsoft Solutions Framework—MSF): This chapter addresses the following MSF objectives regarding the Envisioning phase: "High-level view of project goals," "Business requirements must be identified and analyzed."[1]
- Inception (RUP)
- Initiate (PMI)

What Happens During the Initiation Phase?

During the Initiation phase, the project grows from an idea in someone's mind into a barebones proposal that outlines the main aspects of the project and describes the main reasons for pursuing it. During this phase, your job as a business analyst is to identify and analyze the business requirements for the project. You'll identify high-level business goals as business use cases. You'll be working with stakeholders to analyze stakeholder participation using business use-case diagrams. And you'll communicate to stakeholders an emerging consensus regarding workflow using activity diagrams.

How Long Does the Initiation Phase Take?

Basically, it "should be a few days' work to consider if it is worth doing a few months' work of deeper investigation."[2] For larger projects, it may take months.

Deliverables of the Initiation Step: BRD (Initiation Version)

As you work through the B.O.O.M. steps, you'll use a single document, the business requirements document, or BRD, to describe business requirements throughout the project lifecycle. You begin working on the BRD during the Initiation phase. Different organizations handle this documentation in different ways. The BRD may be a single living document or a requirements package that resides as separate components that are assembled in different ways for different audiences.

)r the documentation produced during the Initiation phase include

valuation: Documents the proposed benefits of the project

and scope: Describes what the project hopes to achieve

1 and scope: Describes the objectives for the software product

Key components of the BRD produced during the Initiation phase are as follows:

- Business use-case descriptions (referred to in RUP as specifications), including business use-case diagrams
- Role map
- System use-case diagram
- Initial class diagram, describing key business classes

Please see Appendix B, "Business Requirements Document (BRD) Template," to see where these components fit into the overall requirements documentation.

Step 1a: Model Business Use Cases

In your first meetings with stakeholders, you want to identify the end-to-end business processes that the IT project will affect. These processes are *business use cases*. A business use case is a business process representing a specific workflow in the business—an interaction that a stakeholder has with the business that achieves a business goal. It may involve both manual and automated processes and may take place over an extended period of time.

Business Use Case

"A business use case defines what should happen in the business when it is performed; it describes the performance of a sequence of actions that produces a valuable result to a particular business actor [someone external to the business]." (*Source: Rational Rose*)

Any IT project has the potential to change the business environment—how steps (both manual and automated) within a business are performed and the roles and responsibilities of employees. By focusing on business use cases at the outset of the project, you ensure that this business perspective is not forgotten.

How Do You Document Business Use Cases?

Use business use-case diagrams to describe the players who take part in each business use case. Use text or a workflow diagram (such as an activity diagram) to describe the interaction between the players and the business as the use case is played out. Let's start with the business use-case diagram.

Step 1ai: Identify Business Use Cases (Business Use-Case Diagram)

A business use-case diagram is a use-case diagram where the system that it models is the real-world business area. It provides an overview of business processes and services (business use cases) and the entities that use those services or participate in their implementation.

Business Use-Case Diagrams

"The business use-case model is a diagram illustrating the scope of the business being modeled. The diagram contains business actors [roles played by organizations, people, or systems external to the business] and the services or functions they request from the business." (*Source: IconProcess*)

Recall that the business use-case diagram is not a part of the core UML standard, but rather an extension of it. Because of this, the terms and symbols related to business use cases are not as standardized as those that are part of the UML proper. Figure 4.1 shows some of the symbols used in business use-case diagrams.

Figure 4.1 illustrates the following modeling elements:

- **Business actor:** Someone external to the business, such as a customer or supplier.
- **Worker:** Someone who works within the business, such as an employee or a customer-service representative.
- **Association:** An association between an actor and a business use case indicates that the actor interacts with the business over the course of the business use case—for example, by initiating the use case or by carrying it out.

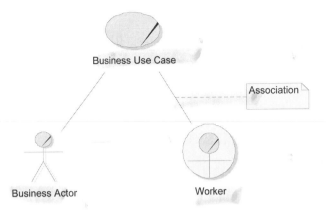

Figure 4.1
Business use-case diagram symbols. Note that the "stroke" in each of these symbols differentiates them from symbols used in system use-case diagrams.

Other Model Elements

Other types of actors are also sometimes used in business modeling. *The UML Extension for Business Modeling*, version 1.1, for example, allows for the subdivision of workers into *case workers* and *internal workers*.

- **Case worker:** A worker who interacts directly with actors outside the system.
- **Internal worker:** A worker who interacts with other workers and entities inside the system.

In this book, we will confine ourselves to the more generic term "worker."

Putting Theory into Practice

When the BA walks onto a project, some preliminary work has often already been done: Someone has had an idea for the project and developed a preliminary business case for it. Based on the business case, a decision has been made to assemble a project team. One of the first steps for the BA is to review this preliminary documentation, often in a kick-off meeting with stakeholders. The purpose of the meeting is to review stakeholder interests in the project and to identify the business use cases that the project could affect.

Here is also where our case study begins. Together, we'll walk through the B.O.O.M. steps for analyzing and documenting the requirements of this system and, in doing so, gain hands-on experience in being a UML business analyst. I urge you to work through each of the steps yourself before viewing the resulting documentation. Then compare your work to the documentation I've provided in this book. It's perfectly okay for you to come up with a different result; after all, there is more than one way to analyze a system. But you should be able to justify any decision you've made.

Case Study D1: Business Use-Case Diagrams

In Case Study D1, you'll be introduced to the Community Peace Program (CPP) project, a project you'll follow throughout this book as you learn to apply B.O.O.M. steps in practice. In this case study, you'll see an example of BRD documentation based on the template described in Appendix B. As the BRD is a living document, it will change as the project progresses. Case Study D1's version is a draft produced during the Initiation phase of the project.

Problem Statement

As a business analyst assigned to a new project, you've convened a kickoff meeting with stakeholders to discuss their interests in the project and to identify the business processes potentially affected by it. Based on what you learn at the kickoff meeting, you have put together the following first draft of a business requirements document (BRD). Your next step is to summarize stakeholder interests, by creating a business use-case diagram, showing business use cases and the business actors and workers involved in each use case.

Suggestions

Read through the following BRD. Then identify the stakeholders as workers or business actors and document their involvement with each business use case in a business use-case diagram. Do not include systems in your model at this stage; your focus should be on the activities that need to occur and the humans involved.

CPP Business Requirements Document (BRD)/Initiation

Project No.: <u>1000</u>

Production Priority: <u>High</u>
Target Date: _____

Approved by:

_____   _____

Name of user, department   Date

_____   _____

Name of user, department   Date

Prepared by:

_____   _____

Name of user, department   Date

Filename: _____

Version No.: <u>0.1 (1st draft)</u>

Table of Contents

- Version Control
  - Revision History
  - RACI Chart for This Document
- Executive Summary
  - Overview
  - Background
  - Objectives
  - Requirements
  - Proposed Strategy
  - Next Steps
- Scope
  - Included in Scope
  - Excluded from Scope
  - Constraints
  - Impact of Proposed Changes
- Risk Analysis
  - Technological Risks
  - Skills Risks
  - Political Risks
  - Business Risks
  - Requirements Risks
  - Other Risks
- Business Case
- Timetable
- Business Use Cases
  - Business Use-Case Diagrams
  - Business Use-Case Descriptions

- Actors
  - Workers
  - Business Actors
  - Other Systems
  - Role Map
- User Requirements
  - System Use-Case Diagrams
  - System Use-Case Descriptions
- State-Machine Diagrams
- Nonfunctional Requirements
- Business Rules
- State Requirements
  - Testing State
  - Disabled State
- Structural Model

Version Control

Revision History

Version #	Date	Authorization	Responsibility (Author)	Description
0.1	06/05		Mbuyi Pensacola	Initial Draft

RACI Chart for This Document

RACI Chart

Each person's connection to the BRD is documented in the following chart as *, R, A, S, C, I. The following chart explains the meaning of each of these codes.

Codes Used in RACI Chart

*	Authorize	This individual has ultimate signing authority for any changes to the document.
R	Responsible	Responsible for creating this document.
A	Accountable	Accountable for accuracy of this document (for example, the project manager).
S	Supports	Provides supporting services in the production of this document.
C	Consulted	Provides input (interviewee, etc.).
I	Informed	Must be informed of any changes.

Name	Position	*	R	A	S	C	I
C. Ringshee	Director, CPP	X					
J. Carter	Manager, Operations			X			
Mbuyi Pensacola			X				

Executive Summary

Overview

This project is for a software system to govern the tracking and reporting of cases by the Community Peace Program (CPP).

Background

The project is being developed for the Community Peace Program (CPP), a South African non-profit organization that provides infrastructure for community-based justice systems based on the model of restorative justice.[3] The main objective of the CPP is to provide an effective alternative to the court system. Its advantages are improved cost-effectiveness and a decreased recurrence rate, since problems are treated at their source. All parties to a dispute must consent to having the case diverted to the CPP. The advantage to the *perpetrator* is the avoidance of incarceration and other severe punishment; for the *complainant*, the advantages lie in the possibility for a true resolution to the problem and a decreased likelihood that the problem will recur. The advantages to the *justice system* are as follows:

- A reduction in case volume due to the offloading of cases to the CPP and a decrease in recurrence rates
- A decrease in the cost of processing a case

The system is being deployed in the townships of South Africa under the auspices of the CPP and with the support of the Justice Department. Similar approaches are being used throughout the world—for example, the "Forum," in use by Canada's Royal Canadian Mounted Police (RCMP).

The CPP operates by working with local communities to set up Peace Committees. Most of these are currently in townships on the Cape Town peninsula. Each Peace Committee is composed of peacemakers—members of the community who are trained in conflict-resolution procedures based on principles of restorative justice. The complainants and accused must all agree to adhere to the procedure or the case is passed on to the state justice system.

Due to increasing demand for its services in conflict resolution, the CPP is undergoing a rapid expansion. Current manual practices will not be able to keep up with the expected rise in case volume.

Objectives

The most urgent need is for timely statistics regarding cases handled by the CPP. Because of the anticipated increase in caseload, these statistics will be difficult to derive using the current, manual systems. Timely statistics will be essential in justifying the project to its funders. Also, the tracking of funds disbursement and monitoring of cases will become increasingly difficult as the program expands.

Requirements

The project will leave current manual systems in place for the initial recording of case information up to and including the convening of a Peace Gathering and the completion of subsequent monitoring. Workflow after that point will be within the scope of the project—that is, recording of case data, validation of CPP procedures, disbursement of payments, and the generation of statistical reports.

Proposed Strategy

An iterative SDLC will be employed as follows: The business analyst(s) will analyze all use cases at the start for the project (the Discovery phase); the design and coding will proceed iteratively during the Construction phase. In the first Construction iteration, general administration and case tracking will be developed. In the second iteration, payments will be disbursed and reports generated.

Next Steps

- **Action:** Select software developer
- **Responsibility:** J. Carter
- **Expected Date:** One month after acceptance of this document

Scope

Included in Scope

The system will provide statistical reports for use by funders. Also, it will provide limited tracking of individual cases to the degree required for statistics and, wherever possible, in a manner that will facilitate expansion of the system to include complete case monitoring. The project includes manual and automated processes. The system will encompass those activities that occur after a case has been resolved. These are primarily as follows: the recording of case data, the disbursement of payments, and the generation of reports. CPP members will be the only direct users of this system.

Excluded from Scope

The system becomes aware of a case only when it has been resolved. All activities prior to this point are not included in this project—i.e., it excludes the tracking of cases from the time of reporting, convening of Peace Gathering, and monitoring of cases before resolution. These activities will continue to be performed manually, although the manual forms will be changed to comply with new system requirements.

Constraints

- Eighty-percent match (minimum) between CPP's needs and commercial-off-the-shelf (COTS) product(s).
- One integrated solution is preferred. No more than two COTS products should be needed.
- Mbuyisela Williams will be main liaison for the project.
- Final approval for a system is estimated to take six weeks to two months.

Impact of Proposed Changes

The following table lists the end-to-end business processes that stand to be affected by the project. Each process is identified as a business use case. The table documents whether the process is new (as opposed to an update to an existing process), what the stakeholder would like the process to do, and what the process currently does. The difference between the desired and current functionality defines the project's scope. Each business use case is linked to stakeholders and prioritized. Prioritization helps the project manager plan the project and, when competing software vendors are being considered, to short-list viable solutions.

Business Use Case	New?	Desired Functionality	Current Functionality (If a Change)	Stakeholders/ Systems	Priority
Manage administration	Yes	General administrative functions, e.g., creation/updating of Peace Committees, members, etc.	Manual systems only in place	CPP general administration	High
Manage case		Manage a case: identify new cases, update case information, etc.	Manual systems only in place		High
Administer payments	Yes	Make payments to individuals who assisted in a case and to various funds.	Manual systems only in place	Convener, Peace Committee member, AP system	Medium
Gererate reports	Yes	Report on cases by region and by period: compile stats on caseload, # cases per type of conflict, etc.	Manual systems only in place	Any worker (members of the CPP), government body (any governmental organization receiving reports), funder	High

Risk Analysis

Technological Risks

To Be Determined (TBD).

Skills Risks

TBD.

Political Risks

Political forces that could derail or affect the project include the following:

- Cancellation of funding: Funding for this project is provided by a foreign government and is granted only on an annual basis after yearly inspections of the organization and based on the government's policy toward foreign aid.
  - Likelihood: Medium.
  - Cost: Cancellation of the project.
  - Strategy:
    - Avoid: Through regular project reports to funders and lobbying of government ministers
    - Mitigate: Search out "plan B" funders: University of Cape Town School of Governance

Business Risks

TBD.

Requirements Risks

TBD.

Other Risks

TBD.

Business Case

This section of the BRD describes the business rationale for the project. The estimates at this stage are ballpark only and will be revised as the project progresses.

- Initial investment: Two person-years @ US$50,000/yr = $100,000.
  Hardware: Use existing PCs at office location.
- Annual cost: One new half-time position, IT maintenance staff = US$25,000/yr.
- Annual benefits: Reduce administration staff by two due to automatic generation of reports to funders and increased efficiency of case tracking = US$60,000/yr.
- ROI: ([annual benefit] – [annual cost]) / [initial investment] = (60,000 – 25,000) / 100,000 = 35%.
- Payback period: [initial investment] / ([annual benefit] – [annual cost]) = 100,000 / (60,000 – 25,000) = 2.9, or approximately three years.

These numbers are expected to improve over the years as the project expands, since the efficiencies of the IT system relative to a manual system are more pronounced the greater the volume of the cases.

Timetable

Only a ballpark timetable can be provided at this stage:

- **Discovery:** To begin one month after the project is approved to go beyond the Initiation phase.
- **Construction:** To begin three months after the project is approved. Verification of requirements and planning of requirements-based testing to begin during the Discovery and Construction phases. Actual tests of software to be run as modules become available.

- **Final V&V:** Final testing, including system testing of nonfunctional requirements, to occur during Final V&V phase, which is to begin 9–11 months after project approval.
- **Closeout:** To begin one year after project is approved. Closeout to take one month.

Business Use Cases

This section of the BRD describes changes to the workflow of end-to-end business processes affected by the project.

Business Use-Case Diagrams

TBD: This subsection of "Business Use Cases" identifies stakeholder involvement in each business process.

Business Use-Case Descriptions

TBD: This subsection of "Business Use Cases" describes the interaction between actors and the business for each business use case.

Actors

Workers

This subsection of "Actors" describes stakeholders who act within the business in carrying out business use cases.

Department/ Position	General Impact of Project
Convener	(Member of the CPP.) Will use IT system to update cases and administer payments.
CPP general admin	(Member of the CPP.) Will use IT system to perform administrative functions, such as updating Peace Committees and members in the system.

Business Actors

This subsection of "Actors" describes external parties, such as customers and partners, who interact with the business.

Other Systems

System	General Impact of Project
AP system	Existing system for tracking accounts payable. This system must remain in place.

Role Map

The subsection of "Actors" models users and external systems that interact with the IT system.

TBD: This section will be completed later during the Initiation phase.

User Requirements

TBD: Portions of this section will be completed later in the Initiation phase; other portions will be added during the Discovery phase.

System Use-Case Diagrams

TBD: This section will be completed later during the Initiation phase.

System Use-Case Descriptions

TBD: Later in the Initiation phase, short descriptions of the system use cases will be provided as well as detailed descriptions of selected high-risk system use cases—for example, those that are to be developed early because they involve new and poorly understood technology.

State-Machine Diagrams

TBD: This section will be completed during the Discovery phase.

Nonfunctional Requirements

TBD.

Business Rules

TBD.

State Requirements

TBD: This section of the BRD describes which features shall be available and which shall be disabled when the IT system is in various states.

Testing State

TBD: This subsection of "State Requirements" describes what the user may and may not do while the system is in the test state.

Disabled State

TBD: This subsection of "State Requirements" describes what is to happen as the system goes down.

Structural Model

TBD: During the Initiation phase, only strategic classes are to be modeled. Other classes are to be added during the Discovery phase.

Case Study D1 Solution: Resulting Documentation

The following business use-case diagram was created by the BA to summarize the business use cases potentially affected by the project and the stakeholders involved with each one (see Figure D1.1).

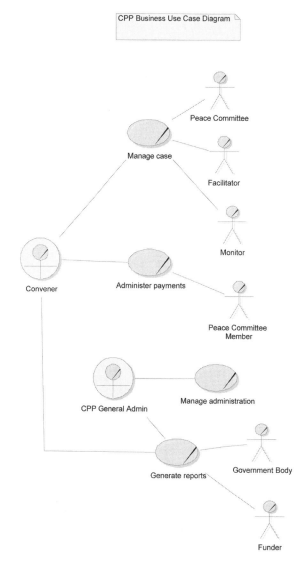

Figure D1.1
Business use-case diagram.

Step 1aii: Scope Business Use Cases (Activity Diagram)

Now that you have a business use-case diagram that matches up stakeholders with business processes, you can begin to plan the next stage of the interviews. Each interview should focus on a subset of the business use cases. Be sure to invite all stakeholders associated with the use case (as shown on the diagram) as well as off-stage stakeholders—those who do not directly interact with the process but still have a stake in it, such as regulators and high-level management.

The purpose of these interviews is to analyze the workflow of each business use case. *Workflow* means the sequencing of activities and (optionally) a clear designation of who carries out each activity. Workflow can be documented in text and/or through the use of a workflow diagram. The business façade—the interaction between the business area and entities outside of it—is best described in text. If you are analyzing business use cases for the broad purpose of improving the business process, you may want to use a formal template for documenting the interaction. In this case, use the use-case template provided within the BRD template in Appendix B. If you are analyzing business use cases only as a means to an end—the end being the system use cases—then an informal text description will probably suffice. This is the situation we are presuming for the case study. In either case, if the workflow for the interaction is too complex to describe clearly in text, append the text with an activity diagram. To document the internal process used to carry out the business use case (referred to in RUP as a business use-case realization), use an activity diagram with partitions (swimlanes). Activity diagrams are UML-compliant examples of workflow diagrams.

Table 4.2 summarizes some of the commonly used workflow diagrams.

TABLE 4.2 Diagrams for Depicting Workflow

Diagram	Description	Advantages	Disadvantages
System flowchart	Earliest form for depicting sequencing of activities.	■ Intuitive. Each type of input and output is clearly marked with its own symbol. ■ Includes logic symbols.	■ Not compliant with UML. ■ Can be hard to learn (many symbols).

TABLE 4.2   Diagrams for Depicting Workflow *(continued)*

Diagram	Description	Advantages	Disadvantages
Swimlane workflow diagram	Tool used for describing process logic. UML equivalent is an activity diagram with partitions (swimlanes).	▪ Intuitive. ▪ Can handle many situations in one diagram ▪ Shows who is responsible for which action (using swimlanes).	▪ Not compliant with UML.
Sequence diagram	UML tool used to describe one path (*scenario*) through a use case.	▪ Part of UML standard. ▪ Encourages thinking in objects. Clearly specifies who does what. ▪ Simplifies logic: Only one situation dealt with in each diagram. ▪ Sometimes recommended for business modeling.	▪ Diagramming style is often non-intuitive for business analysts and users. ▪ Requires analyst to determine not only who carries out each activity, but who requests it.
Activity diagram	UML tool for describing logic. Used to describe entire system, a use case, or an activity within a use case. Has two versions: ▪ Activity diagram without partitions (swimlanes): Does not show who does what. ▪ Activity diagram with partitions: shows who does what.	▪ Part of UML standard. ▪ Can handle many situations in one diagram. ▪ Simple diagramming conventions. ▪ Encourages thinking about opportunities for parallel activities (more than one activity going on at the same time).	▪ Ability to handle many situations can lead to a diagram that is too complex to follow.
Business process diagram (BPD)	Business process modeling notation (BPMN) tool for describing workflow	▪ Part of BMN standard, managed by the OMG ▪ Rich symbol set can model complex and subtle workflow requirements better than activity diagrams.	▪ Not UML-compliant ▪ Difficult to understand without prior training

Activity Diagrams for Describing Business Use Cases

The activity diagram is the one most useful to the IT BA for depicting workflow. It is simple to understand—both for BAs and end-users.

Although some practitioners advocate sequence diagrams for this purpose, you should not use sequence diagrams as a BA tool. Compared to activity diagrams, they are not as readily understood by non-technical people. The best time to use sequence diagrams is during the technical design of the system, an activity that is beyond the scope of the BA.

Activity Diagram (Without Partitions)

The following diagram describes the Initiate Peace Gathering process, a sub-goal of the business use case Manage Case. Initiate Peace Gathering is the process of setting up a Peace Gathering to deal with a case (dispute). The diagram illustrates most of the major features of an activity diagram without partitions (swimlanes) that are useful to the IT BA. I have added other diagrams to illustrate the remaining features.

Activity Diagram Elements

Activity diagrams may include the following elements (see Figure 4.2):

- **Initial node:** Indicates where the workflow begins.
- **Control flow:** An arrow showing the direction of the workflow.
- **Activity:** Indicates a step in the process.
- **Decision:** A diamond symbol, indicating a choice. Workflow will proceed along one of a number of possible paths, according to the guard conditions.
- **Merge:** Use this symbol if you wish to adhere to strictly to the UML standard when modeling a number of alternative flows that lead to the same activity. Rather than terminating them at the same activity, terminate them at a merge, and draw a flow from the merge to the activity.[4] For business-analysis purposes, however, you might want to consider relaxing the standard by dispensing with the merge as it does hinder readability.
- **Guard condition:** A condition attached to a control flow. When the guard condition is true, workflow may flow along the control flow. Guard conditions are usually attached to control flows that come out of a decision symbol. (However, they can also be used without the decision symbol.) A guard is shown within square brackets.
- **Event:** A trigger attached to a control flow. The event must occur for the flow to move along the control flow. Declaring something as an event has a stronger implication than calling it a guard. An event actually triggers the control flow by forcing the previous activity to end, whereas a guard only governs whether a flow that was triggered for another reason (such as the completion of the previous activity) is allowed to flow along the control flow. An event is indicated without the use of square brackets.

- **Fork and join:** Bars used to document parallel activities. In the UML, parallel activities are those that may begin in any sequence—either at the same time or one before the other. A fork indicates the point after which a number of activities may begin in any order. A join indicates that workflow may commence only once the parallel activities that flow into it have all been completed.

- **Final node:** Indicates the end of the process.

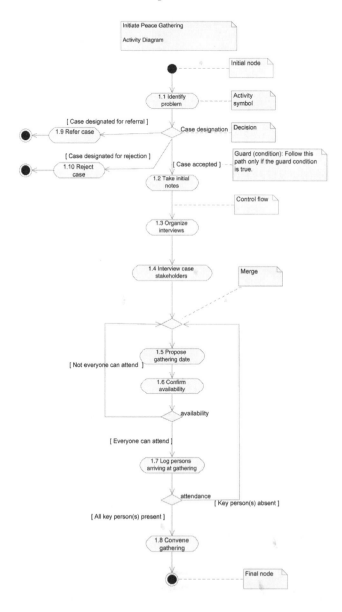

Figure 4.2
Activity diagram describing workflow for the Initiate Peace Gathering business use case.

Note

The symbol that looks like a piece of paper with an end folded over is the UML Note icon. You can use notes freely to add your own annotations to diagrams and you can tie your notes to diagramming elements as I've done in Figure 4.2.

Figure 4.3 shows the use of fork and join.

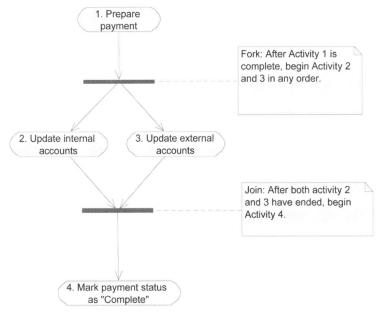

Figure 4.3
A diagram using fork and join.

Figure 4.4 shows a control flow labeled with an event.

Nested Activities

The UML enables you to put an entire mini–activity diagram inside an activity symbol (see Figure 4.5). The inner activities are *nested* inside the larger one.

In Figure 4.5, the initial node indicates the beginning of the activity, Organize Interviews, and the final node indicates its end.

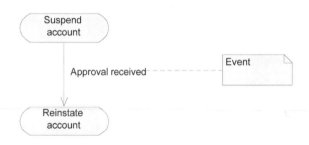

Figure 4.4
A control flow labeled with an event.

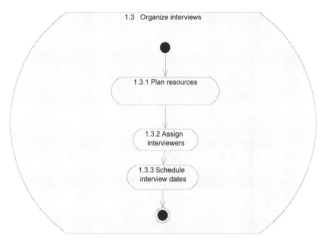

Figure 4.5
Activities nested within an activity symbol.

Object Flows

If you find the preceding notation communicates enough about a workflow to stakeholders, you won't need the extra notations described next. But the UML does give you the option of indicating the inputs and outputs of any activity on the diagram by adding *object flows*. (If you are a reader versed in structured analysis, it may help to think of object flows as the UML equivalent of the data flows in a data-flow diagram.)

Add object flows to your activity diagrams if you wish to show the point at which business objects are created, changed, or required by activities. Examples of business objects that you might think of including in this way are claims, complaints, reports, invoices, and paychecks. On the activity diagram, you will not only be able to identify the object, but you can also indicate what state it'll be in at that point.

What Is a State?

Objects may be considered to be in various states during their lifetimes. For example, invoices pass through some of the following states: Created, Due, Paid, Past 30 Days, Written Off. To find out what these states are, simply ask the stakeholders to tell you what statuses they consider a business object to be in. Anything they refer to as a *status* can generally be treated as a UML state.

What makes some changes to a business object important enough to be considered changes of state? The business treats the object differently because of the change: For example, there are rules for the sequence in which the object may move in and out of the state, or the objects' response to external events differs. You'll learn more about states in Chapter 7, "Life Cycle Requirements for Key Business Objects."

Figure 4.6 shows how object flows are depicted in the UML.

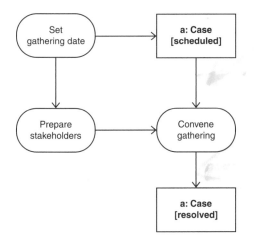

Figure 4.6
Indicating object flows on activity diagrams.

Figure 4.6 indicates that the Set Gathering Date activity causes a case to move into the Scheduled state. After this, a Prepare Stakeholders activity is performed. This is followed by the Convene Gathering activity, which takes as input a case in the Scheduled state. Once the activity has been completed, the case will be in the Resolved state. The previous example illustrates some of the main features of object flows:

- **Object flow:** A solid line with an open arrowhead. An object flow connects an object to an activity. When the arrow points away from an activity, the object flow indicates that the object (or object state) at the tip of the flow is a result (output) of the activity. When the arrow points to an activity, it indicates that the object at the source of the flow is required by (input to) an activity.

- **Object:** The object that is required, created, or altered by an activity. Name the object according to the format ⟨objectName⟩: ⟨ClassName⟩ ⟨[statename]⟩—for example, a:Case [resolved]. You may omit objectName—for example, :Case[resolved]. As well, you may omit the statename—for example, a:Case.

An object may be a source or destination of an object flow, or both. One activity diagram may include objects of many classes and different objects of the same class. As well, the same object may appear more than once on an activity diagram, as in Figure 4.6.

If an activity produces an object as output, and this same object is the input for the next activity, you may omit the control flows between the two activities. In Figure 4.7, a control flow between the Set Up Interviews and Interview Stakeholders activities is not required.

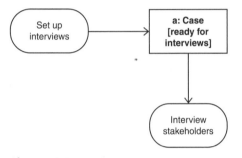

Figure 4.7
No object flow required.

Figure 4.8 shows a draft of an activity diagram segment for the Initiate Peace Gathering process, with object flows added to indicate how a case changes its state during the process.

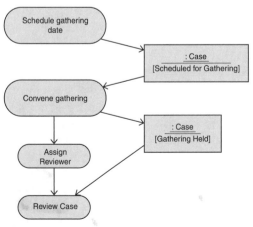

Figure 4.8
Activity diagram with object flows: draft of Initiate Peace Gathering.

The activity diagram shown in Figure 4.8 is interpreted as follows:

- The activity, Schedule Gathering Date, results in a case's state being set to Scheduled for Gathering.
- Next, the activity, Convene Gathering, takes a case that has been Scheduled for Gathering and results in it being set to the Gathering Held state.
- The next activity is Assign a Reviewer.
- The next activity, Review Case, requires as its input a case that is in the Gathering Held state.

Activity Diagram with Partitions (Swimlanes)

To indicate who performs each activity, you add partitions (commonly referred to as swimlanes) to the activity diagram. A *partition* is depicted as a column (or row) on an activity diagram. Allocate one partition for each object that takes an active part in the process flow. Each partition represents a stakeholder (business actor or worker) who carries out some activity. Although you shouldn't spend too much time focusing on technology at this time, you may also show a computer system as a partition.

Position every activity in the partition of the object that performs it. Name each partition at the top of the column, according to the participating object, as shown in Figure 4.9.

You may use an informal, simple name for the partition, identifying the actor who carries out the task—for example, Problem Identifier. A better approach is to use the more formal form `<objectName>` : `<className>`. `className` is the name of the role—that is, the worker, business actor, or external system that participates in the activities. `objectName` identifies a specific instance (or example) of the role—for example, Mr. Dudu: Problem Identifier. This format is recommended because it allows you to show the participation of more than one instance of the same actor—for example, two different Problem Identifiers involved in the same business case. The `objectName` in this format is optional. If you wish to omit it, don't forget to leave in the colon—for example, :Peace Committee Operations. When using a modeling tool, the formal format has the added advantage of allowing you to conveniently name the partition by dragging actors from the browser to the partition in the diagram window.

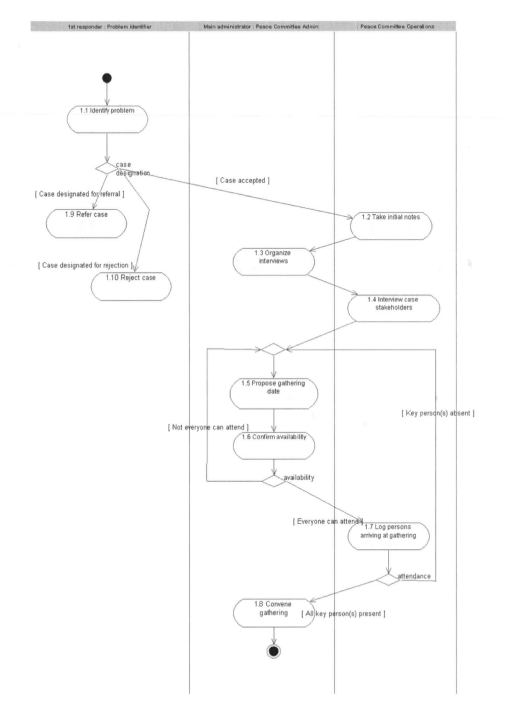

Figure 4.9
Activity diagram with partitions (swimlanes).

Case Study D2: Business Use-Case Activity Diagram with Partitions (Swimlanes)

The following case study walks you through the next evolution of the CPP project. During this case study, you meet with stakeholders to discuss the workflow for two business use cases. During the meeting, you draw and revise activity diagrams in order to help stakeholders work toward a consensus regarding workflow.

Problem Statement

You've met individually with stakeholders involved in the Manage Case and Administer Payments business use cases in order to discuss workflow for these processes. Not too surprisingly, everyone has a slightly different view of how best to sequence activities, so you decide to convene a meeting to reach a consensus. In preparation for the meeting, you plan to create activity diagrams with partitions to summarize your best understanding of the workflow for these business processes. You won't be including object flows, as you wish to focus on the sequencing of the activities. You'll distribute these to interviewees before the meeting to give them a chance to preview it. During the meeting, you'll post the diagrams and make changes to them based on feedback from stakeholders.

Suggestions

Don't get uptight about creating perfect activity diagrams right off the bat. All you need is a reasonable first guess. The main value of the diagrams at this point is that they give stakeholders something concrete to bounce ideas off of. During the meeting itself, you'll come up with a consensus regarding the workflow. Following is an informal textual description of the business use cases, based on your preliminary interviews. Your immediate goal is to convert these into activity diagrams with partitions—one for each business use case.

Business Use Case: Manage Case (Dispute)

The following business use case has been written fairly informally because it is being used as a means to an end. A more formal style uses the same format as the system use-case template. For more on the formal style, see the sections "Documenting the Basic Flow" and "Documenting Alternate Flows" in Chapter 6, "Storyboarding the User's Experience."

Despite the informal style, this example does use two sections found in the formal template, "Pre-Conditions" and "Post-Conditions."

- A *pre-condition* is something that must be true before the use case begins. In the following example, a Peace Committee must already have been set up before the CPP can manage a case.
- A *post-condition* is something that will be true after the use case ends.
- A *post-condition on success* is something that will be true after the use case ends, but only if the goal (expressed in the name of the use case) is accomplished. In the example, the post-condition on success is that a case report has been prepared for the case being managed during the business use case.
- A *post-condition on failure* (not shown in the example) is a condition that will be true after the use case is over if it ends with abandonment of the goal.

Pre-Condition

A Peace Committee has been established in the township.

Post-Condition on Success

A case report has been prepared.

Flow

1. The Peace Committee in the area initiates a Peace Gathering.
2. The Peace Committee prepares an individual interview report for each party to the dispute.
3. Once all reports have been taken, the facilitator summarizes the reports to the Peace Gathering.
4. The facilitator verifies the facts in the reports with those present.
5. The facilitator solicits suggestions from the gathering.
6. The facilitator solicits a consensus for a plan of action.
7. If the gathering has decided to refer the case to the police, the facilitator escorts the parties to the police station, after which the convener prepares a case report as per step 10.[5]
8. If, on the other hand, a consensus has been reached, the facilitator appoints a monitor.

9. The monitor performs ongoing monitoring of the case to ensure its terms are being met.

10. When the deadline for monitoring has been reached, the ongoing monitoring immediately ends. At this time, if the conditions of the case have been met, the convener prepares a case report. If the conditions have not been met, then the process begins again (return to step 1).

Business Use Case: Administer Payments

Pre-Condition

A case report has been submitted.

Post-Condition on Success

Payments have been made to funds and to accounts of Peace Committee members involved in the case.

Flow

1. The convener reviews the case report to determine whether rules and procedures have been followed.

2. If rules and procedures have been followed:

   a. The convener marks the case as payable.

   b. The convener then disburses payments to the various funds and to the accounts of Peace Committee members who worked on the case.

   c. The existing Accounts Payable system actually applies the payments. (Constraint: The AP system must continue to be used for this purpose when the project is implemented.)

3. If the rules and procedures have not been followed, the convener marks the case as non-payable.

Case Study D2: Resulting Documentation

Following are the workflow diagrams you will have created based on the preceding notes. You will have included these in the preparation notes sent to each stakeholder who will be attending the interview session. During the meetings, you'll have displayed these diagrams on a flipchart, whiteboard, or projection screen, and revised them based on comments from the interviewees.

Figure D2.1 is an activity diagram with partitions that describes the workflow of the business use case Manage Case.

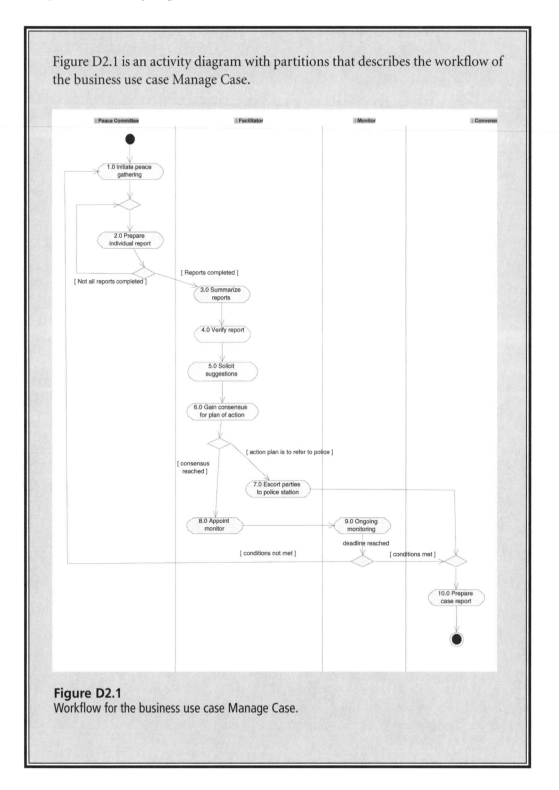

Figure D2.1
Workflow for the business use case Manage Case.

Figure D2.2, an activity diagram with partitions, describes workflow for the business use case Administer Payments.

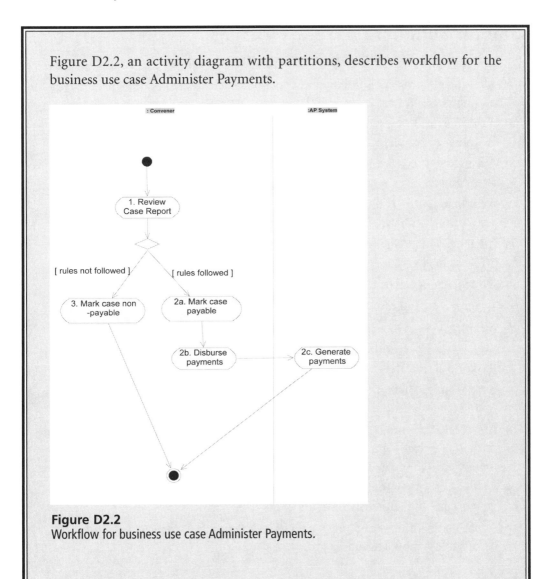

Figure D2.2
Workflow for business use case Administer Payments.

Next Steps

Review the diagrams with stakeholders and discuss ways that the process might be improved (if necessary) in the new system through the following:

- Changes to the sequencing of activities
- Changes to which actor is responsible for each activity
- Suggestions about which of these steps to include as part of the IT automation project

Chapter Summary

In this chapter, you learned the following concepts:

- A *business use case* is an interaction between a stakeholder and the business, yielding a valuable result for the stakeholder; a business process.

- A *business actor* is a stakeholder outside the business that interacts with it, such as a customer or supplier.

- A *worker* is a stakeholder who works within the business, such as a customer-service representative.

- A *business use-case diagram* is a diagram depicting business use cases and their associations with actors.

- An *activity diagram* is a diagram that depicts the sequencing of activities.

- An *activity diagram with partitions (swimlanes)* is a diagram that depicts the sequencing of activities and the object that performs each activity.

- A *guard* is a condition that restricts flow along a transition.

- A *control flow* shows the direction of the workflow.

- An *event* is a trigger that forces the end of an activity and flow to continue along the control flow that it labels.

- A *decision* is a diamond symbol that marks a point at which flows diverge based upon some condition.

- A *merge* is a diamond symbol that marks a point at which flows merge. If any of the activities leading into a merge have completed, flow will continue beyond the merge. Use the merge to avoid having more than one incoming flow for an activity.

- A *fork* marks a point after which parallel activities begin. Activities that are parallel may occur simultaneously or in any sequence.

- A *join* marks the end of parallel activities. All parallel activities must complete before a flow moves beyond a join.

Endnotes

[1] These are described in the MSF White Paper Process Model V3.1.

[2] M. Fowler, UML Distilled, 1997, page 16 (in his discussion of the Initiation phase of Objectory).

[3] The principles of restorative justice were developed by Terry O'Connel.

[4] The reason for this recommendation is that, in UML 2, two incoming flows on an activity are interpreted as an implicit join, meaning that both prior activities had to have been completed.

[5] The conditions described in step 10 do not apply to cases referred to police. That is, once the parties have been escorted to the police, a case report is always prepared.

CHAPTER 5

SCOPING THE IT PROJECT WITH SYSTEM USE CASES

Chapter Objectives

By the end of this chapter, you will be able to define the boundaries of the project during the Initiation phase by carrying out the following actions:

1. Initiation

   1b) Model system use cases

   i)   Identify actors (role map)

   ii) Identify system use-case packages (system use-case package diagram)

   iii) Identify system use cases (system use-case diagram)

   1c) Begin structural model (class diagrams for key business classes)

   1d) Set baseline for Discovery (BRD/Initiation)

New tools and diagrams you will learn to use in this chapter include the following:

- Role map
- System use-case diagram

Step 1b: Model System Use Cases

Now that you have an understanding of the end-to-end business processes, it's time to begin thinking about how the proposed IT system might help automate these processes. System use cases help you imagine the IT system from a user perspective, by focusing on the user's goals.

If the project is large, you will need to find a way to break up the work so that a number of analysts can work in parallel. First, you need to standardize common issues so that all team members handle them consistently. One of these issues is the way that users of the IT system will be documented. To address this issue, you create a diagram called a *role map*. Another issue is how to break up the user requirements into manageable pieces. You address this issue with *system use-case diagrams*.

Step 1bi: Identify Actors (Role Map)

In this step, you identify the IT system's users, or *actors*. Previously, when we spoke of actors, it was in relation to *business* use-case modeling. There we spoke of business actors and workers. From this point onward, however, we are doing *system* use-case modeling and will speak simply of actors. An actor, in this context, is a role played by a person or system that interacts with the IT system.

> **What They Say:**
>
> An actor specifies a role played by a user or any other system that interacts with the subject.[1] (UML)
>
> **What They Mean:**
>
> An actor is a type of user or an external system that interacts with the system under design.
>
> **Similar Terms:**
>
> ▪ **External agent/external entity:** Equivalent terms used in structured analysis.
>
> ▪ **Stakeholder:** A term more inclusive than *actor* as it includes anyone who the project will affect even if they do not have direct contact with it.

Finding Actors

To find actors, go through your list of business actors and workers, eliminating any who don't interact with the IT system. Then add any external systems and human users who are required because of the technology. (Remember that when you performed business use-case modeling, your focus was not on technology, so you may have missed some of these actors.)

FAQs about Actors

- **Why identify actors and why do it now?** By starting with the actors, you are working toward building a system that focuses on users' needs. This is a logical step to perform now, since at this point, you need to establish a list of interviewees for eliciting the next level of requirements. The actor list gives you this. This step also helps you estimate the length of the Discovery phase of the project. More *human actors* means more user groups to interview and a lengthier analysis. I use a ballpark figure of one day per interview—half a day to conduct the interview, the other half-day to cover preparation, analysis, and documentation. *System actors* also require increased analysis, because the interfaces to these systems need to be studied. External systems also increase the complexity of solution development because of the technical difficulty in getting systems to talk to each other. Later in the project, the actors you've identified will assist the network administrator in specifying user groups and access privileges.

- **If a user only receives reports from the system, is that user an actor?** Yes (although there is some controversy about this question).

- **How do you handle system use cases that aren't started by anybody, but just start up automatically at a given time? Where's the actor?** Define an actor called Time to act as the initiator of these use cases. (There is also controversy about this issue. Some practitioners, for example, prefer to see no actor and some prefer to indicate the actor who has asked that the use case be initiated at that time.)

- **If a customer calls in a request and a customer-service representative (CSR) keys it in, which one is the actor?** Only the actor who directly interacts with the computer system is considered an actor. In this case, it would be the CSR. Another option sometimes used is to name the actor CSR for Customer.

Stereotypes and Actors

A *stereotype* is an extension of a UML feature. Modelers can invent their own stereotypes to create extended meanings to UML model elements.

Stereotypes in the UML can be depicted either by using a special symbol, such as the stick figure, or by using the regular UML symbol and including the name of the stereotype inside guillemets, as in <<stereotype-name>>. In the case of actors, some people like to reserve the stick figure for human users and use the guillemet option for external systems. Figure 5.1 shows examples of both.

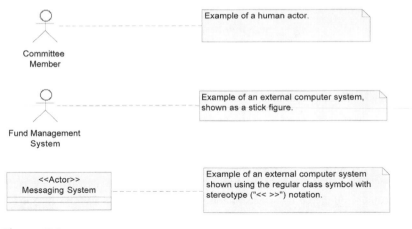

Figure 5.1
Depicting actors and stereotypes.

The Role Map

A *role map* is a diagram used to standardize the treatment of users and external systems throughout the project. A role map is a restricted form of a use-case diagram. Whereas the use-case diagram shows actors *and* their associations with use cases, the role map shows only actors.

Place icons for each of the actors you've identified in the role map. The role map then becomes the central diagram team members go back to whenever they want to know how to depict a user in the model. You can also use the role map to show the ways in which user roles overlap.

Modeling Actors with Overlapping Roles

You document actors with overlapping roles by drawing a *generalization relationship* between actors. Any time the phrase "a kind of" comes up in the discussion of actors, think about using the generalization relationship. For example, a Bookkeeper and an Accountant are two kinds of Accounting Staff. Exactly how you draw the generalization depends on how the roles overlap. We'll look at two types of situations:

▪ Actors whose roles partially overlap

▪ An actor whose role completely encompasses another's

Actors with Partially Overlapping Roles

When two actors have some overlap in their roles, but each actor can do things with the system that the other can't, model the actors as specialized actors and invent an *abstract generalized actor* to represent the overlap. The term *generalized* implies that the specialized actors inherit something from the generalized actor. In this case, the specialized actors inherit the ability to do all the things that the generalized actor can do. (Formally, the specialized actors inherit the *associations* that the generalized one has with system use cases.) The term *abstract* means that the invented actor is not real. (In OO-speak, the abstract actor is never *instantiated*.) The generalized actor is not a true role but an abstract concept meant to represent the shared aspects of other roles. Figure 5.2 shows how to depict actors with partially overlapping roles.

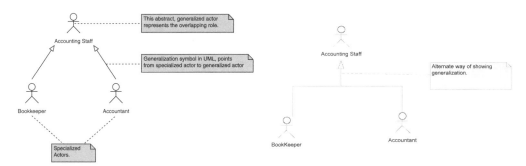

Figure 5.2
Depicting actors whose roles partially overlap.

Modeling an Actor Whose Role Totally Encompasses Another's

In other cases, an actor might be able to do everything that another actor can do and more. In this situation, model the actor with the restricted role as the generalized actor, and model the actor with the larger role as the specialized actor. This may look odd at first, since the diagram tends to make the lesser role "more important." This is due to the common practice of drawing the generalized actor above the specialized actor. The UML, however, does not dictate the placement of symbols on a diagram. If your users object, just draw the diagram "upside down." But make sure that the generalization symbol still points from the specialized actor to the generalized actor. Figure 5.3 shows how to depict such a relationship among actors.

A Generalized Actor May Represent a Real-World User Role

The generalized actor, in this case, is not an invention but a *real role*. It is therefore considered to be a *concrete* (as opposed to abstract) actor.

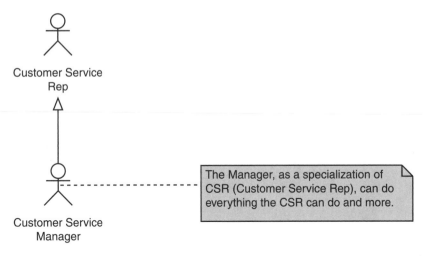

Figure 5.3
Depicting actors when one's role totally overlaps the other's.

What's the Point of Defining Generalized Actors?

They simplify the drawing of use-case diagrams. Soon, you'll be creating use-case diagrams that indicate which actors are associated with each use case. If all of the specialized actors of one generalized actor are associated with the same use case, you'll be able to draw a single association line between the generalized actor and the use case instead of lines from each of the specialized actors.

Case Study E1: Role Map

In this case study, we continue the analysis of the CPP system by focusing on the actors that interact with the IT system.

Problem Statement

You've again met with stakeholders to determine which of the business actors and workers involved in business use cases will interact with the proposed IT system —either directly, by using the software, or indirectly, by receiving reports, statements, and so on, from it. Also, you've investigated the computer systems with which the proposed system needs to communicate. The results of this investigation follow. Your next step is to document your findings in a role map.

Business Actor	Interaction with Proposed System?
Peace Committee	No. (Interaction is with individual members, not with the organization.)
Peace Committee member	Yes
Facilitator	No. (Automation begins after facilitator's role is complete.)
Monitor	No. (Automation begins after monitor's role is complete.)
Government body	Yes
Funder	Yes
Worker	**Interaction with Proposed System?**
CPP General admin	Yes. Role partly overlaps with convener. (Both can generate reports.)
Convener	Yes. See above.
External System	**Interaction with Proposed System?**
AP system	Yes

Case Study E1: Resulting Documentation

Figure E1.1. shows the role map diagram resulting from Case Study E1.

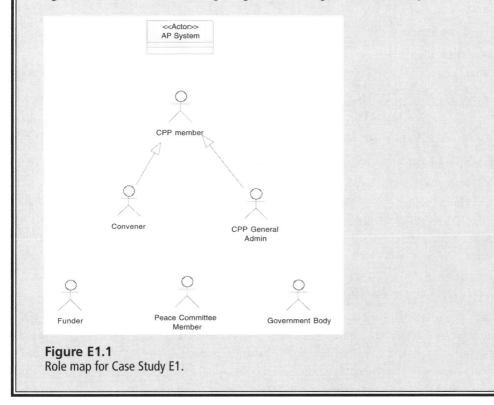

Figure E1.1
Role map for Case Study E1.

Step 1bii: Identify System Use-Case Packages (System Use-Case Diagram)

If your project supports only one business use case, you may proceed directly to the following step, identify system use cases. But if it supports a number of business use cases, consider creating system use-case packages. A *system use-case package* is a collection of system use cases and the diagrams that describe them. The UML package icon looks like (and acts similarly to) a Windows folder. By defining the packages now, you are, in effect, setting up a filing system that all members of the team will use once the analysis really gets under way.

What Criteria Are Used to Group System Use Cases into Packages?

The UML does not impose any criteria, but here are some common approaches:

- **Group system use cases by the main actor who uses them.** For example, group together into one package all the system use cases used by general administration.
- **Create a system use-case package for each business use case.** For example, in an insurance system, the customer sees the end-to-end process, Make a Claim. To the customer, this represents one business goal; however, to achieve it, the company's workers require a number of discrete interactions with the computer system:
  - Record claim
  - Validate policy
  - Adjust claim
  - Pay claim

  Each of these interactions qualifies as a system use case. Since they all contribute to the same high-level goal, a good way to group them is to bundle them all in the use-case package Make a Claim.

The second option has the advantage of placing logically related system use cases together. This is the approach you'll follow as you work through the case study. Look out for system use cases that can be reused in more than one business context. Place any of those system use cases, if you find them, in special packages reserved for system use cases that transcend any one business use case. Documenting commonly used system use cases in one central place promotes reuse and consistency of treatment.

Naming Use-Case Packages

Formally, because a package is a thing—specifically, a container—it should be named with a noun phrase. On the other hand, because of the way we are using the packages, it makes sense to name each package according to the business use case it supports. This makes tracing easier—from the business use-case model we worked on earlier to the system use-case model we are now developing. Either approach is acceptable.

Diagramming System Use-Case Packages

The diagram used to represent system use-case packages is, formally, a use-case diagram—though it looks a little odd in that it does not depict any actual use cases. Figure 5.4 shows some of the system use-case packages for a credit-card system and the actors who interact with them. Please note that the connecting of actors to packages, as shown in Figure 5.4, is a B.O.O.M. extension to the UML; it is not part of the standard but is a valid extension of it.

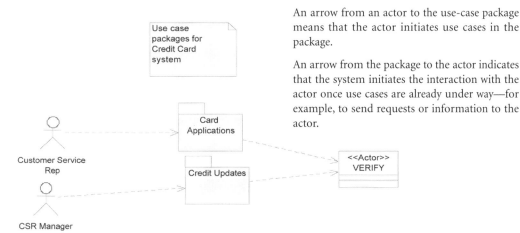

An arrow from an actor to the use-case package means that the actor initiates use cases in the package.

An arrow from the package to the actor indicates that the system initiates the interaction with the actor once use cases are already under way—for example, to send requests or information to the actor.

Figure 5.4
Use-case diagram showing system use-case packages and actors.

The direction of the arrow from the actor to the package indicates whether an actor initiates system use cases in the package (in which case the arrow points away from the actor) or whether the use cases initiate some action by the actor (the arrow points to the actor). Note that the arrow connecting the actors to the use-case packages is a dashed line with an open arrowhead. The dashed line indicates a *dependency*—a loose connection between modeling elements that means one element has some awareness of another one—and the arrowhead indicates the direction of the dependency. (Formally, the initiating actor is aware of system use cases in the package; in the case of non-initiating actors, it is the system that is aware of them.) You may avoid using the arrowheads but you must use the dashed line as opposed to a solid line; the UML does not allow a solid line (association) between actors and packages.

This diagram indicates that a customer-service representative can initiate use cases relating to card applications and that a CSR manager initiates updates to credit. In both cases, the system under design will need to be able to communicate with VERIFY (an external system that verifies the application against a person's credit record).

What If a Use-Case Package Is Connected to All of the Specialized Actors of a Generalized Actor?

Connect the package to the generalized actor. For example, suppose that VERIFY was only one of a number of systems able to verify a person's credit and that the system under design needed to be able to communicate with all of them. You'd indicate that as shown in Figure 5.5. (In the section "Interfaces" in Chapter 11, "What Developers Do with Your Requirements," you'll learn about another way to model this with interfaces.)

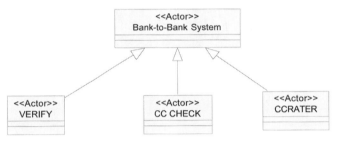

Figure 5.5
The role map updated for a system to communicate with several external systems.

The use-case package diagram would now look like Figure 5.6.

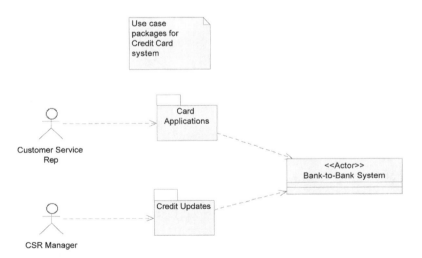

Figure 5.6
Use-case package diagram updated for a system to communicate with several external systems.

In the diagram in Figure 5.6, there is no need to show the specializations of the generalized Bank-to-Bank System, since they are described in the role map shown in Figure 5.5.

Case Study E2: System Use-Case Packages

In this case study, you organize the system use-case model into packages.

Problem Statement

Your project is large enough to justify system use-case packages. You begin by considering the business use-case model that you identified earlier. Also, you review the role map, which identifies users and external systems that interact with the IT system. (I've repeated both of these diagrams in the "Suggestions" section for convenience.) Based on these diagrams and the initial draft of the BRD, your next step is to define the system use-case packages for the project. You'll do this by creating a use-case diagram depicting actors and system use-case packages.

Suggestions

Create a system use-case package to correspond to each business use case. Figure E2.1 repeats the business use-case diagram and role map for the system.

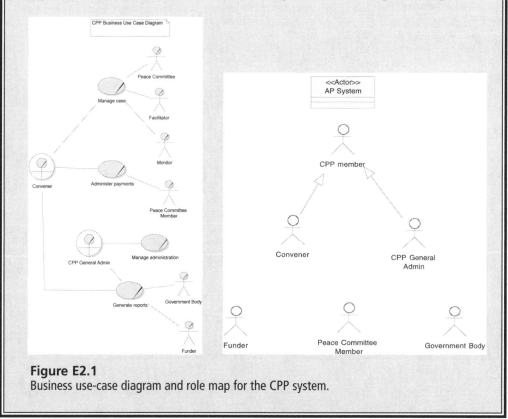

Figure E2.1
Business use-case diagram and role map for the CPP system.

Case Study E2: Resulting Documentation

Figure E2.2 shows the system use-case package diagram resulting from Case Study E2.

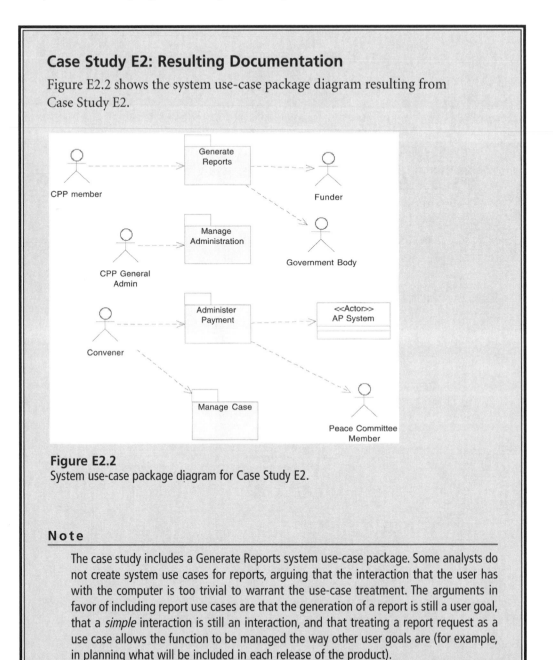

Figure E2.2
System use-case package diagram for Case Study E2.

Note

The case study includes a Generate Reports system use-case package. Some analysts do not create system use cases for reports, arguing that the interaction that the user has with the computer is too trivial to warrant the use-case treatment. The arguments in favor of including report use cases are that the generation of a report is still a user goal, that a *simple* interaction is still an interaction, and that treating a report request as a use case allows the function to be managed the way other user goals are (for example, in planning what will be included in each release of the product).

Step 1biii: Identify System Use Cases (System Use-Case Diagram)

The next step is to identify the system use cases that go into the packages. You do this by going back to the business use cases and reviewing the activities they describe. First try to determine, with stakeholders, which of these activities fall within the scope of the IT project. Where things are currently being done manually, you're looking for activities that could be either fully or partially automated by the IT project. Where things are being done using IT, you're looking for opportunities for improvement.

Once you've identified the activities, you'll need to group them into system use cases. Imagine the system.[2] How will someone sitting at a terminal actually use this system? What result is the user trying to achieve from the computer system with each interaction? Each of these results, expressed as a user goal, is a system use case. For example, for a Web banking system, some system use cases are View Transaction History, Transfer Funds, and Pay Bill.

Review

A *system use case* is an *interaction* between an actor and a computer system.

Features of System Use Cases

A system use case is an interaction that an entity (either a human user or an external computer system) has with the system under design. After executing a system use case, a user should be able to walk away from the terminal and feel that he or she has accomplished something of value. Purchasing stocks over the Web is a valid system use case; selecting a From Account is not. As a rule of thumb, use the "one user, one session" rule: Each execution of a system use case should involve only one initiating actor and should take place over a single session on the computer.

The system use-case approach involves diagrams and text. The UML provides strict rules for drawing use-case diagrams. It does not, however, standardize the writing of use-case text. Project-management methodologies, such as Rational Unified Process (RUP) and books on use cases,[3] have attempted to fill the gap. (I'll discuss this further in the section "The Use-Case Description Template" in Chapter 6, "Storyboarding the User's Experience.") While textual templates for use cases differ, they are always designed in keeping with the definition of a use case; they focus, therefore, on describing the *interaction* that the user has with the system, as opposed to the design. The text typically reads as a narrative: "The user does..."; "The system does...."

What Is the Purpose of Segmenting the User Requirements into System Use Cases?

System use cases become the central tool that governs the management of the project. With their user perspective, they keep the team focused on the user throughout the project. Here's how:

- **The requirements are written from the user's point of view.** Prior to use cases, requirements were often written as a list of capabilities, such as, "The system must be able to...." With system use cases, the documentation is instead written as a narrative describing the user's experience using the system.

- **System use cases help ensure that the user receives useful functionality with each release when a project is managed iteratively.** With iterative project management, the system is analyzed, designed, coded, and often released in several passes. At each pass, one or more system use cases (or selected use-case scenarios) are developed. Because each system use case achieves a meaningful goal for the user, the user is guaranteed useful functionality at the end of each iteration.

- **System use cases lead to user interfaces that are organized from a user perspective.** Most people have had experience with systems that require the user to bounce around screens or a site just to get one unit of work done. This happens because the developers have organized the user interface from their own point of view. When the interface is organized around system use cases, each option presented to the user represents a complete activity from the user's perspective.

- **System use cases yield a set of test cases that encompass the ways users use the system.** Because a system use case describes the way that an interaction plays out, it is very close to being a test script. And the way the text is typically organized, as separate "flows," makes it easy to identify test scenarios.

Modeling System Use Cases

Once you've decided what system use cases are required to support a business use case, you document your findings in a *system use-case diagram*. Create one (or more if necessary) system use-case diagram for each system use-case package.

The system use-case diagram shows which actors participate in each system use case. The diagram does *not* show sequencing; you can't tell from the diagram the order in which the system use cases should be used or the sequence of activities within each use case. (To show sequencing, use an activity diagram instead.) Figure 5.7 shows a system use-case diagram.

Figure 5.7 illustrates the following modeling elements:

- **Primary actor**: An actor who initiates a use-case interaction (indicated as an actor at the tail end of an arrow pointing to a use case).

- **Secondary actor**: An actor that the system initiates an interaction with after the use case has started (indicated as an actor at the tip of an arrow pointing from a use case).
- **System use case**: A user task (indicated as an oval).

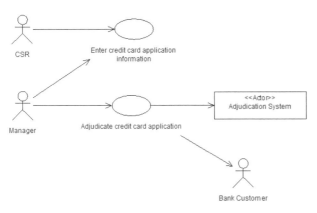

Figure 5.7
Example of a system use-case diagram.

Here's what the diagram says:

- A CSR (customer service representative) or a manager enters credit card–application information. (See the discussion in the following section for more on the subject of multiple primary actors.)
- A manager may adjudicate a credit-card application. The system use case, once under way, may involve an interaction with an external computer system, Adjudication System—for example, by requesting a maximum allowable credit limit for the customer based on application information and credit history. The system use case may also involve an interaction with a bank customer—for example, by e-mailing the customer a letter of acceptance or rejection.

How Many Primary Actors Can a Use Case Have?

In the situation modeled in Figure 5.7, either a CSR or a manager can initiate the system use case, Enter Credit Card Application Information. In this situation, the practice followed in this book (and in Figure 5.7) is to indicate both as primary actors—the implication being that either the CSR or manager may initiate the interaction. Others argue against this practice, however, because they would interpret this to mean that both actors are required to initiate the use case; those following this approach would indicate only one actor, a CSR, for this use case, since that is the role being played regardless of the user's job title. Be aware, in any case, that the issue of whether multiple primary actors indicates an *or* (either actor may initiate) or an *and* (both are required to initiate) is controversial.

What if the manager is acting in a truly *separate* role, however, as the authorizer of information previously entered during the use case by the CSR? In that case, all practitioners would model the manager as an additional actor for the use case. Whether the actor is primary or secondary depends on who *initiates* the interaction between the manager and the system. If the system does—for example, by sending a request for approval to the manager—then the manager is a secondary actor. If the manager does—for example, by signing in and selecting the case for review—then the manager is a primary actor.

To draw a system use-case diagram, follow these steps:

1. Copy all the actors connected to the package in the main use-case package diagram onto the new diagram. This will ensure that you don't forget any actors.

2. Draw a system use-case symbol (an oval) to represent each user goal within the package.

3. Connect the actors to the use cases using the UML *association* symbol: a solid line that may, if desired, be *adorned* (as UML puts it) with an open arrowhead. The following steps explain the rules for drawing the association.

4. Connect an actor to a system use case if the actor participates in any way while the use case plays out. If all you can say at this time is that the actor participates somehow, use a solid line.

5. If the actor *initiates* the system use case, draw an arrow that points from the actor to the use case. This designates the actor as a *primary actor* for the use case. Note that the direction of the arrow indicates who initiated the interaction (it always points away from the initiator). The arrow does not indicate the direction of the data. For example, a user initiates a query transaction. The arrow points away from the actor even though the data moves from the system to the actor.

6. If the actor gets involved only after the system use case has already begun, draw the arrow from the use case to the actor. In this case, it is the system (of which the use case is a part) that has initiated the interaction with the actor. This type of actor is termed a *secondary actor.*

7. If several possible actors may initiate the system use case, connect all of them to the use case as primary actors. This does not break the "one initiating actor" rule. In any particular execution of the system use case, only one of these primary actors is involved. (Keep in mind, however, that as previously discussed, there is controversy around this issue: Some interpret two primary actors to mean that *both* must be involved, as opposed to the interpretation of this book, that *either* may be involved.) You may also designate more than one secondary actor for the use case, if appropriate.

8. If all of the specialized actors of a generalized actor participate with the use case, draw an association between the generalized actor and the use case. It implies association with the specializations.

Is There a Rule of Thumb for How Many System Use Cases a Project Would Have?

No. Ivar Jacobson recommends about 20 use cases for a 10 person-year[4] project. Martin Fowler reports about 100 use cases for a project of the same size.[5]

Keep in mind that one reason for splitting requirements into system use cases is to assist *the planning of releases.* Try to size the system use cases so that you can roll out one or more complete system use cases (or use-case scenarios) in each release.[6]

Case Study E3: System Use-Case Diagrams

In this case study, you'll create system use-case diagrams that summarize who does what with the IT solution. Following are notes gathered from follow-up interviews regarding the business use cases for this project.

A) Manage Case

You have just conducted a meeting with stakeholders to discuss the Manage Case business use case. You've circulated the following business use-case description and activity diagram to attendees.

Business Use Case: Manage Case (Dispute)

Post-Condition on Success

A case report has been prepared.

Flow

1. The Peace Committee in the area initiates a Peace Gathering.
2. The Peace Committee prepares an individual interview report for each party to the dispute.
3. Once all reports have been taken, the facilitator summarizes the reports to the Peace Gathering.
4. The facilitator verifies the facts in the reports with those present.
5. The facilitator solicits suggestions from the gathering.
6. The facilitator solicits a consensus for a plan of action.
7. If the gathering has decided to refer the case to the police, the facilitator escorts the parties to the police station, after which the convener prepares a case report as per step 10.[7]

8. If, on the other hand, a consensus has been reached, the facilitator appoints a monitor.

9. The monitor performs ongoing monitoring of the case to ensure its terms are being met.

10. When the deadline for monitoring has been reached, the ongoing monitoring immediately ends. At this time, if the conditions of the case have been met, the convener prepares a case report. If the conditions have not been met, then the process begins again (return to step 1).

Figure E3.1 shows the diagram that results from this flow.

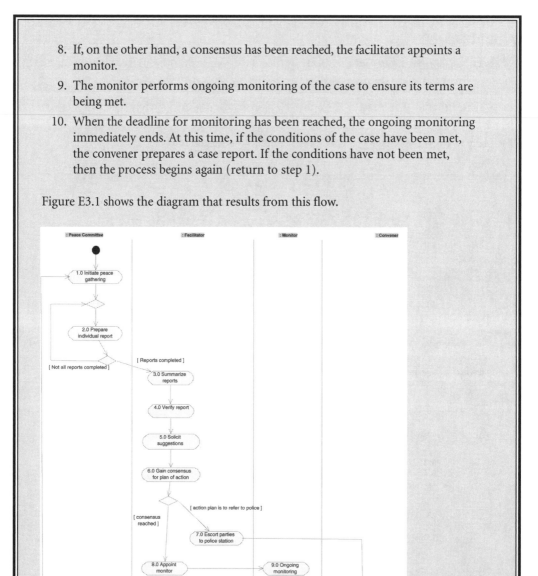

Figure E3.1
Activity diagram for business use case Manage Case.

Here's how the interview progresses from that point:

1. You ask stakeholders how much of this process can be automated. They tell you that there is no budget for automation in the communities themselves, but only at the head office. They clarify that a case moves out of the community to the head office when the convener performs the activity Prepare Case Report.

2. Next, you ask users to rephrase this activity as a goal they would be trying to achieve through their interaction with the IT system. They say that the goal would be to update case information; that is, to open up a new case and later to add information about the case if necessary. Accordingly, you name the system use case Update Case.

B) Administer Payments

Next, you discuss the Administer Payments business use case with the users. The following is the document, extracted from the business requirements document, that you've circulated, describing the process.

Business Use Case: Administer Payments

Pre-Condition

A case report has been submitted.

Post-Condition on Success

Payments have been made to funds and to accounts of Peace Committee members involved in the case.

Flow

1. The convener reviews the case report to determine whether rules and procedures have been followed.

2. If rules and procedures have been followed:

   a. The convener marks the case as payable.

   b. The convener then disburses payments to the various funds and to the accounts of Peace Committee members who worked on the case.

   c. The existing accounts payable (AP) system actually applies the payments. (Constraint: The AP system must continue to be used for this purpose when the project is implemented.)

3. If the rules and procedures have not been followed, the convener marks the case as non-payable.

Figure E3.2 shows the diagram that results from this flow.

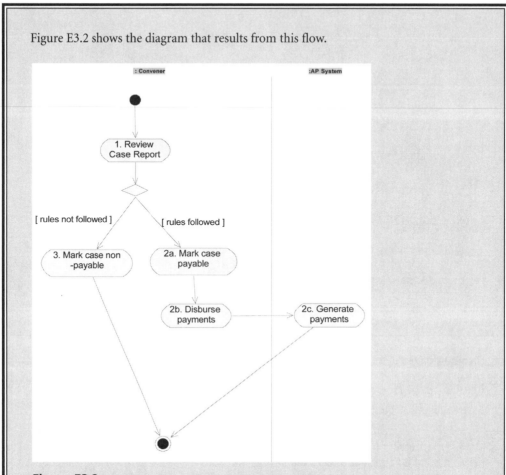

Figure E3.2
Activity diagram for business use case Administer Payments.

Once again, you have a discussion with the stakeholders about automation. You learn that, as originally scoped, the project will not incorporate the actual generation of payments; these will remain the responsibility of the existing AP system. However, the new system will need to interface with the AP system. Also, the new system should be able to assist the convener in performing all of the other steps in the process.

Next you ask stakeholders to group the activities, thinking of what they would expect to accomplish in each session with the computer. You learn that the process of reviewing a case and marking it as payable or non-payable is all part of the same user goal and would happen best as one session. Stakeholders imagine a convener reviewing a case and marking it, then moving on to the next case, and so on.

They envision a separate session for disbursing the payments for cases that have earlier been deemed payable. The transactions will be sent to the AP system at that time.

This yields the following use cases:

- Review Case
- Disburse Payments

Note how this meeting, focused on system use cases, really keeps you in tune with the users' experience; this is the main point of the use-case approach.

C) Other Business Use Cases

In similar meetings regarding the other business use cases, you've identified the following system use cases:

- Generate Reports Package:
  - Generate Funder Reports: Initiated by any CPP member. The reports are sent to the funders.
  - Generate Government Reports: Initiated by any CPP member. The reports are sent to a government body. (This is as specific as the stakeholders can be at this time.)
- Manage Administration Package:
  - Update Peace Committees: Initiated by the CPP general administrator to add or update information on the Peace Committees located in the communities.
  - Update CPP Member List: Initiated by the CPP general administrator to add or update information about members of the central CPP organization, working out of the head office.
  - Set System Parameters: Initiated by the CPP general administrator to "tweak" the system. Such parameters would include one-time setup operations as well as parameters affecting performance.

Your Next Step

Create system use-case diagrams that summarize what you learned in the meeting. You'll present these during the next meeting as a way of summarizing your conclusions. Later, these diagrams will serve to direct the next phase of the project, the Discovery phase.

Case Study E3: Resulting Documentation

Figure E3.3 shows the diagrams resulting from Case Study E3.

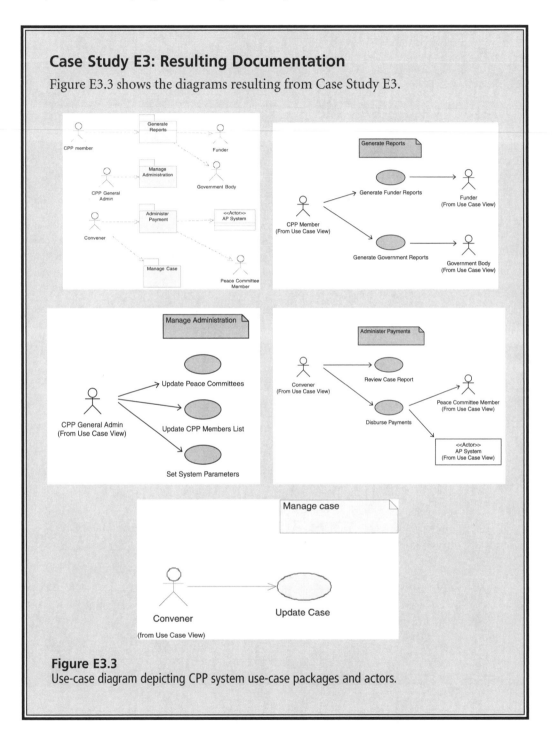

Figure E3.3
Use-case diagram depicting CPP system use-case packages and actors.

Step 1c: Begin Structural Model (Class Diagrams for Key Business Classes)

As you've worked through the Initiation phase of the project, business terms such as "case" and "Peace Gathering" have come up. Now is an appropriate time to begin formally defining these business concepts and their relationships to each other. You do this by beginning the structural model, drawing class diagrams for the main business classes. We'll explore structural analysis in Chapter 8, "Gathering Across-the-Board Business Rules with Class Diagrams," which is devoted to the topic. But just to give you an idea of what you might expect to see at this point in time, Figure 5.8 shows a class diagram describing some of the main business classes that have come up during the Initiation phase.

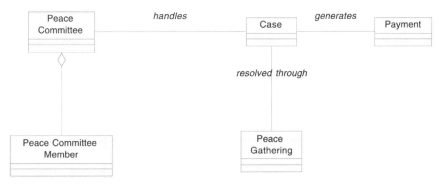

Figure 5.8
A class diagram describing several business classes discovered during the Initiation phase.

Don't be perturbed if you have trouble with this diagram right now; I've included it here only to provide context. Here's what it means:

- A Peace Committee handles a case.[8]
- A case is resolved through Peace Gatherings.
- A case generates payment(s).
- A Peace Committee consists of Peace Committee members.

Other information, such as the number of payments per case, can also be added to the structural model at this stage.[9] Since this is still early in the project, expect changes to be made to the structural model as the project progresses.

Step 1d: Set Baseline for Discovery (BRD/Initiation)

Once the Initiation phase of the project is over, you need to "baseline" your analysis. This simply means saving the state of the analysis at this point and putting it under change control. By baselining your documentation, you ensure that if changes are requested later, you'll be able to check whether they represent a change from the original scope of the project. (Keep in mind, however, the exception for agile projects, where the requirements are not baselined unless they are under development.) The analysis up to this point also becomes the starting point for the next phase of the project, the Discovery phase.

Chapter Summary

In this chapter, you completed the Initiation phase of the project by identifying and modeling the system use cases. These system use cases will now drive the rest of the analysis and development effort.

New tools and concepts introduced in this chapter include the following:

- *Actors* are roles, organizations, or systems that use or are contacted by the system.
- A *role map* is a diagram indicating actors and their relationships to each other.
- A *use-case package* is a container that holds use cases.
- A *system use-case diagram* is a diagram describing the system use cases (uses to which the IT system will be put) and the actors who interact with them.

Endnotes

[1] *UML Superstructure Specification*, v2.2, OMG, 2009, page 588.

[2] Thanks to Tim Lloyd for introducing me to this phrase.

[3] A key book in this area is Alistair Cockburn's *Writing Effective Use Cases*, 2001.

[4] 10 person-years means that the number of people multiplied by the number of years that each one works equals 10—for example, 1 person working 10 years or 10 people each working 1 year.

[5] Martin Fowler, *UML Distilled*, 1997, page 51.

[6] Releasing complete system use cases in each iteration helps simplify the management of the project, but is not a hard-and-fast rule. You may decide, for example, to release only select flows (pathways) of a use case in a particular iteration.

[7] The conditions described in step 10 do not apply to cases referred to police. That is, once the parties have been escorted to the police, a case report is always prepared.

[8] The diagram as shown has an ambiguity regarding the direction in which it should be read. For example, it either states that a Peace Committee *handles* a case or a case *handles* a Peace Committee. In practice, many BAs do not worry about this, since the statement usually only makes sense in one direction. However, the UML does allow for a solid triangular arrowhead to be placed next to the association name (*handles*) to indicate the direction it should be read. More on this in Chapter 8.

[9] This type of requirement is termed a *multiplicity* in the UML. You'll learn more about multiplicity in Chapter 8.

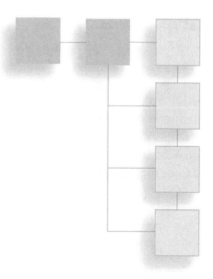

CHAPTER 6

STORYBOARDING THE USER'S EXPERIENCE

Chapter Objectives

Now that you've defined the scope of the project, you're ready to take your project "into analysis." There are various aspects to analysis. In this and the coming chapter, you'll learn how to analyze the dynamic aspects of the system in action.

You'll be able to carry out these B.O.O.M. steps:

2. Discovery

    2a) Behavioral analysis

        i) Describe system use cases (use-case description)

Tools and concepts you'll learn to use in this chapter include the following:

- Use-case description template
- Activity diagram
- Decision table
- Decision tree
- Condition/response table
- Advanced use-case features

Step 2: Discovery

The Discovery phase of the project is the one that takes up most of a business analyst's time. The objective of requirements analysis, which peaks during this phase, is to discover and document the requirements of the proposed system. The central product of analysis, the completed BRD, acts as a contract between the business and the developers. If a requirement is not in the BRD (or equivalent documentation), it's not part of the contract, so it's essential to ensure that you document all necessary requirements completely, correctly, and unambiguously. This and the following chapter will take you through a process to help you do just that.

The Discovery phase involves a number of steps:

2. Discovery
   2a) Perform behavioral analysis
      i) Describe system use cases (use-case description)
      ii) Describe state behavior (state-machine diagram)
   2b) Perform structural analysis (object/data model) (class diagram)
   2c) Specify testing (test plan/decision tables)
   2d) Specify implementation plan (implementation plan)
   2e) Set baseline for development (BRD/Discovery)

This chapter deals with step 2ai, "Describe system use cases."

Lifecycle Considerations

Please note that on waterfall projects, all requirements-analysis activities described above are performed during the Discovery phase since they must be complete before development may begin in the Construction phase. On iterative projects, analysis peaks during the Discovery phase but continues during the Construction phase, since not all requirements are gathered up front with this approach. As well, on such projects, a phase typically consists of a number of iterations—each incorporating a complete cycle of analysis, design, coding, and testing for the use-case scenarios selected for that iteration. Finally, for iterative projects that follow an agile approach, the requirements are not baselined unless they are being implemented.

Step 2ai: Describe System Use Cases

At the end of the Initiation phase, you identified system use cases in the BRD. This version was baselined for step 2 (the Discovery phase). By baselining the BRD, you ensured that you have a reference point to go back to. Updates to the BRD during the Discovery phase are made on a new working version.

For your first changes, review the list of system use cases. If needs have changed or you have obtained further information, update the system use-case diagrams and related text in the BRD. Once you've settled on a list of system use cases, your next step is to investigate and document each one thoroughly.

Deliverables of Step 2ai: Describe Use Cases

This step produces a number of deliverables, as described here:

- The BRD template contains a section for system use-case diagrams. These diagrams are updated.
- The BRD has a section called "System Use-Case Descriptions." For each system use case that appears in the system use-case diagrams, a use-case description is added that includes a completed use-case description template. The text documentation may be augmented with any of the following:
  - Activity diagrams
  - Decision tables
  - Decision trees
  - Other related artifacts containing supplementary documentation

The Use-Case Description Template

The UML, as we've learned, doesn't have a lot to say about text. The following template fills that gap by incorporating industry best practices. If you are working for an organization that doesn't have a template, use this as your starting point, but customize it as time goes on. If you already have a template, compare it to the following template. You may find features you'd like to add.

Keep one thing in mind when using this or any other template: Its main value is as a way to institutionalize best practices in your organization. You should customize it as time goes on, based on what works for you. As an example, this template requires the BA to keep detailed rules about field verification out of the use case proper; these rules are documented in class diagrams or in a data dictionary instead. But one organization I've worked with found that it couldn't get its developers to cross-reference; if a rule was not explicitly stated in the use case, the rule wasn't implemented in the software. Consequently, the organization decided to include such rules in its use cases. Remember that whatever choices you make, there is only one yardstick:

Does it work?

The Fundamental Approach Behind the Template

The underlying principle of this template is to describe workflow using a simple narrative style that avoids complex logic. The trick to keeping things simple is to handle variations in a separate area of the document rather than in one all-encompassing section. First, you document a normal, typical interaction in a section called "Basic Flow." Next, you describe alternative success scenarios in an "Alternate Flows" section. Finally, you describe error handling in an "Exceptional Flows" section.

Use-Case Description Template

1. **Use Case:** The use-case name as it appears on system use-case diagrams

   Perspective: Business use case/system use case

   Type: Base use case/extending/included/generalized/specialized

   1.1 **Brief Description:** Describe the use case in approximately one paragraph.

   1.2 **Business Goals and Benefits:** Briefly describe the business rationale for the use case.

   1.3 **Actors**

       1.3.1 **Primary Actors:** Identify the users or systems that initiate the use case.

       1.3.2 **Secondary Actors:** List the users or systems that receive messages from the use case. Include users who receive reports or online messages.

       1.3.3 **Off-Stage Stakeholders:** Identify non-participating stakeholders who have interests in this use case.

   1.4 **Rules of Precedence**

       1.4.1 **Triggers:** Describe the event or condition that "kick-starts" the use case, such as *Call received*; *inventory low*. If the trigger is time-driven, describe the temporal condition, such as *End-of-month*.

       1.4.2 **Pre-conditions:** List conditions that must be true before the use case begins. If a condition *forces* the use case to occur whenever it becomes true, do not list it here; list it as a trigger.

   1.5 **Post-conditions**

       1.5.1 **Post-conditions on Success:** Describe the status of the system after the use case ends successfully. Any condition listed here is guaranteed to be true on successful completion.

1.5.2   Post-conditions on Failure: Describe the status of the system after the use case ends in failure. Any condition listed here is guaranteed to be true when the use case fails as described in the exception flows.

1.6   Extension Points: Name and describe points at which extending use cases may extend this use case. Example of extension point declaration: "Preferred Customer: 2.5–2.9."

1.7   Priority

1.8   Status: Your status report might resemble the following:

Use-case brief complete: 2009/06/01

Basic flow + risky alternatives complete: 2009/06/15

All flows complete: 2009/07/15

Coded: 2009/07/20

Tested: 2009/08/10

Internally released: 2009/09/15

Deployed: 2009/09/30

1.9   Expected Implementation Date

1.10   Actual Implementation Date

1.11   Context Diagram: Provide a system use-case diagram showing this use case, all its relationships (include, extend, and generalization relationships) with other use cases, and its associations with actors.

2. Flow of Events

Basic Flow: Insert basic flow steps. Numbers begin with 2.1.

Alternate Flows

2.Xa   Insert the alternate flow name. The alternate flow name should describe the condition that triggers the alternate flow. "2.X" is the step number in the basic flow where the interruption occurs. Describe the steps in paragraph or point form.

Exception Flows

2.Xa   Insert the exception flow name. The exception flow name should describe the condition that triggers the exception flow. An exception flow is one that causes the use case to end in failure and for which "post-conditions on failure" apply. "2.X" is the step number in the basic flow where the interruption occurs. Describe the steps in paragraph or point form.

3. **Special Requirements:** List any special requirements or constraints that apply specifically to this use case.

   3.1 **Non-Functional Requirements:** List requirements not visible to the user during the use case—security, performance, reliability, and so on.

   3.2 **Constraints:** List technological, architectural, and other constraints on the use case.

4. **Activity Diagram:** If the flows connect in complex ways, include an activity diagram showing workflow for this system use case or for select parts of the use case.

5. **User Interface:** Initially, include description/storyboard/prototype only to help the reader visualize the interface, not to constrain the design. Later, provide links to screen design artifacts.

6. **Class Diagram:** Include a class diagram depicting business classes, relationships, and multiplicities of all objects participating in this use case.

7. **Assumptions:** List any assumptions you made when writing the use case. Verify all assumptions with stakeholders before sign-off.

8. **Information Items:** Include a link or reference to documentation describing rules for data items that relate to this use case. Documentation of this sort is often found in a data dictionary. The purpose of this section and the following sections is to keep the details out of the use case proper so that you do not need to amend it every time you change a rule.

9. **Prompts and Messages:** Any prompts and messages that appear in the use case proper should be identified by name only, as in Invalid Card Message. The "Prompts and Messages" section should contain the actual text of the messages or direct the reader to the documentation that contains the text.

10. **Business Rules:** The "Business Rules" section of the use-case documentation should provide links or references to the specific business rules that are active during the use case. An example of a business rule for an airline package is "Airplane weight must never exceed the maximum allowed for its aircraft type." Organizations often keep such rules in an automated business rules engine, other electronic files (such as spreadsheets and text files) or manually in a binder.

11. **External Interfaces:** List interfaces to external systems.

12. **Related Artifacts:** The purpose of this section is to provide a point of reference for other details that relate to this use case but would distract from the overall flow. Include references to artifacts such as decision tables, complex algorithms, and so on.

Documenting the Basic Flow

The basic flow describes the most common way that the use case plays out successfully. (Some people call it the "happy scenario.") It reads as a straightforward narrative: "The user does...; the system does...." As a rule of thumb, the basic flow should not list any conditions, since subsequent sections handle all errors and alternatives. To keep documentation consistent, employ a style guideline throughout your company for writing use-case requirements.

Use-Case Writing Guidelines

The following guidelines are industry best practices. The template and case study adopt the numbering scheme proposed by Alistair Cockburn.[1] Many other schemes are used in the industry for numbering requirements, including the practice of not numbering them at all.[2]

- Tell a story. Write sentences that describe the unfolding narrative of the user's interaction with the system.
- Use a simple subject-verb-object sentence structure.
- Use a consistent tense (present or future tense).
- Each step should contain one testable, traceable requirement.
- Keep the number of steps in a flow small (maximum 9 to 25 steps).
- Minimize the use of the word "if." Use alternate and exception flows instead.
- Handle validations by writing, in the "Basic Flow" section, "The system validates that...." Describe what happens when the validation fails in the alternate or exception flows.
- Merge data fields and use the merged data name in the use case. For example, use the merged field Contact Information rather than the individual fields Name, Address, and Phone Number. Describe merged fields elsewhere. (See the "Information Items" section of the template, which links to an external document, such as the data dictionary.)
- Do not describe the interface design within the use case. Describe the workflow only; document design details elsewhere.
- Document the sequencing of each step clearly and consistently. For example:
  - One step follows the other:
    1. User provides contact information.
    2. System validates user input.
  - A group of steps can be triggered in any sequence:
    - Steps 20 through 30 can happen in any order.

- ▪ A step is triggered at any time during a set of basic flow steps:

  At any time between Steps 7 and 9, the user may....

- ▪ Optional steps:

  - ▪ Steps 5 through 7 are optional.

  Alternatively, describe optional steps in the "Alternate Flow" section (recommended).

- ▪ Establish a standard for documenting repetitive steps. For example:

  1. User selects payee.

  2. System displays accounts and balances.

  3. User selects account and provides payment amount.

  4. System validates that funds are available.

  5. User repeats steps 1 through 4 until indicating end of session.

- ▪ Standardize triggers to external systems. For example:

  The user has the system query the account balance from Interac (and does not wait for a response).

- ▪ Label the requirements. Use a numbering scheme or text labels. (In the case study, you'll be using numbers to label the requirements.)

- ▪ Keep the focus on the flow. Exclude anything that would distract the reader from the narrative. Document other details elsewhere, and refer to them from the use case.

Basic Flow Example: CPP System/Review Case Report

Following is an example of some of the text that would appear in the Review Case Report system use case, a task that enables a user to review a case report and disburse funds against cases that qualify for payments.

2. Flow of Events

Basic Flow:

2.1 The system displays a list of resolved cases that have not been reviewed.

2.2. The user selects a case.

Note

Steps 2.3 and 2.4 refer the reader to 12.1, a decision table that describes the rules for making payments.

2.3 The system validates that the case is payable. (12.1)

2.4 The system determines the payment amount. (12.1)

2.5 The system marks the case as payable.

2.6 The system records the payment amount.

2.7 The system checks the Cash fund records to ensure that adequate funds exist.

2.8 The system records the fact that the case has been reviewed.

....

12. **Other Related Artifacts**

12.1 Case Payment Decision Table (link to table)

Documenting Alternate Flows

Document each scenario not covered in the basic flow as an *alternate flow* or as an *exception flow*. An alternate flow is a variation that does not lead to the abandonment of the user goal; an exception flow involves a non-recoverable error. If your team has trouble deciding whether to list a scenario in the "Alternate Flow" or "Exception Flow" section, merge the two sections into one and list both types of flows there.

What Is an Alternate Flow?

An alternate flow is a scenario other than the basic flow that leads to success. An alternate flow may deal with a user error as long as it is recoverable. Non-recoverable errors are handled as exception flows.

Typical Alternate Flows

There are many situations that may be documented as alternate flows. These include the following:

- The user selects an alternative option during a basic-flow step—for example, "User requests same-day delivery."

- The user selects a tool icon at any time during the use case—for example, "User selects spell-checking."

- A condition regarding the internal state of the system becomes true—for example, "Item out of stock."

- Recoverable data-entry errors are identified. For example, the basic flow states, "The System validates withdrawal amount"; the alternate flow reports, "Funds are low."

Alternate Flow Documentation

There are a number of issues you'll need to clarify for each flow you've identified. These are as follows:

- **Trigger:** The event or condition that causes the process to be diverted from the basic flow.
- **Divergence point:** The point within the basic flow from which the process jumps to the alternate flow.
- **Convergence point:** The point at which the process returns to the basic flow.

The following standard for naming alternate flows is advocated by Cockburn. It is not important that you use this particular standard, but it *is* important that you standardize the way you treat each of the issues described here.

Trigger: Use the triggering event to name the flow. For example: Inventory low.

Divergence point: If the flow diverges from a *specific* step of the basic flow, use the basic flow number and append "a" for the first alternate flow off of it, "b" for the second, and so on. For example:

Basic flow:

....

2.3 The system validates that the case is payable.

....

Alternate flow:

2.3a Cash funds low but sufficient:

   .1 The system marks the case as payable.

   .2 The system displays the low funds warning. (See "Prompts and Messages.")

If the flow may be triggered during a range of steps in the basic flow, specify the range and append an "a" for the first alternate flow off of the range, "b" for the second, and so on. For example:

Basic flow:

....

2.3 The system validates that the case is payable.

2.4 The system determines the payment amount.

2.5 The systems marks the case as payable.

....

Alternate flows:

2.3–2.5a   User selects option to add note:

.1 The user adds a note to the case.

If the flow may be triggered at any time during the basic flow, specify "*a" for the first such scenario, "*b" for the second, and so on. For example:

Alternate flow:

*a User selects save option:

.1 The system saves all updates made to the case in a draft folder.

Convergence point: Clearly indicate how the flow returns back to the basic flow. I use the following convention: If the flow returns to the step following the divergence point, I do not indicate a convergence point (it's understood); otherwise, I write "Continue at step x."

Example of Use Case with Alternate Flows: CPP System/Review Case Report

2. **Flow of Events**

Basic Flow:

.1 The system displays a list of resolved cases that have not been reviewed.

.2 The user selects a case.

.3 The system validates that the case is payable.

.4 The system determines the payment amount.

.5 The system marks the case as payable.

.6 The system records the payment amount.

.7 The system checks the Cash fund records to ensure that adequate funds exist.

.8 The system records the fact that the case has been reviewed.

Alternate flows:

2.3a Non-payable case:

.1 The system marks the case as non-payable.

.2 The user confirms the non-payable status of the case.

.3 Continue at step 8.

2.7a Cash funds low but sufficient:

.1 The system marks the case as payable.

.2 The system displays the low-funds warning. (See "Prompts and Messages.")

Documenting an Alternate of an Alternate

What if there are other ways that an alternate-flow step could play out? Document these the same way you documented the original alternate flows. For example, suppose that in the preceding case, you want to give the user the option of overriding the non-payable status at Step 3a.2. The system use case would now read:

2.   **Flow of Events**

   Basic Flow:

   .1 The system displays a list of resolved cases that have not been reviewed.

   .2 The user selects a case.

   .3 The system validates that the case is payable.

   .4 The system determines the payment amount.

   .5 The system marks the case as payable.

   .6 The system records the payment amount.

   .7 The system checks the cash-fund records to ensure that adequate funds exist.

   .8 The system records the fact that the case has been reviewed.

   Alternate flows:

   2.3a Non-payable case:

       .1 The system marks the case as non-payable.

       .2 The user confirms the non-payable status of the case.

       .3 Continue at step 8.

   2.3a.2a User overrides non-payable status:

       .1 The user indicates that the case is to be payable and enters a reason for the override.

....

   2.7a Cash funds low but sufficient:

       .1 The system marks the case as payable.

       .2 The system displays the low-funds warning. (See "Prompts and Messages.")

Documenting Exception Flows

List each error condition that leads to the abandonment of the user goal in the "Exception Flows" section. Typical exception flows include cancellation of a transaction by the user and system errors that force a transaction to be canceled. Documentation rules are the same as for the alternate flows except that there is often no convergence point, since the goal is abandoned. In that case, the last line of the flow should read, "The use case ends in failure."

Guidelines for Conducting System Use-Case Interviews

Now that you have a solid idea of what the flows look like, let's put it all together in the context of an interview:[3]

1. Ask interviewees to describe the basic flow.

2. Go through the basic flow, step by step, and ask if there is any other way each step could play out. List each of these as an alternate or exception flow—but don't let the interview veer off into the details of what happens within each of these flows. Your aim at this point is merely to list the flows.

3. Ask interviewees if there are any alternatives or errors that could happen at any time (as opposed to at a specific step) during the basic flow. Add these to the alternate or exception flows.

4. Now that you have a comprehensive list, ask interviewees to describe each flow in detail.

5. Finally, go over each of the steps in the alternate and exception flows, asking if there are any other ways those steps could play out.

Activity Diagrams for System Use Cases

The basic, alternate, and exception flows do an excellent job of describing scenarios—one at a time. If the flows connect to each other in complex ways, add an activity diagram as a supplement to the use-case description in order to clarify how all the flows fit together. You draw the diagram using the same conventions you used earlier when modeling the workflow of business use cases.

Related Artifacts

The template contains a number of sections that point the reader to other artifacts related to the use case. For example, there are sections titled "User Interface," "Prompts and Messages," "Business Rules," "Class Diagrams," "Information Items," and a catch-all "Related Artifacts" for anything else not included in the other sections. The point of these sections is to give you a convenient place to refer to details that are relevant to the use case, but that would distract from the overall flow. For example, at a particular point in a use case, the system may need to adjudicate a request for a credit limit increase. If the use case were to include the complex rules for doing that right in the flows, the details would distract from the narrative. The solution of the template is to describe these details in another artifact and refer to it from the use case. The flow step refers to the line number in the template where the artifact is described. For example, in the system use case Review Case Report, there were a couple of references to a decision table.

Basic flow:

....

2.3 The system validates that the case is payable. (12.1)

2.4 The system determines the payment amount. (12.1)

....

12. Related Artifacts

12.1 Case Payment Decision Table (link to decision table)

There is an added benefit to listing details separately from the use case when they apply across a number of use cases: Revisions to the documentation will have to be made in only one place should these details ever change. For example, if a data field has a valid range that applies wherever the field is referred to, document the rule in the class model or as an information item. If the valid range ever changes, you'll only have to change the documentation in one place.

Next, you'll look at examples of some of the artifacts that supplement the use case.

Are Use Cases All You Need?

People often ask me if the use cases are all of the requirements or whether they are all you need to create test cases. The answer to both questions is, "No." First of all, they are not all of the requirements because they only address the user requirements, omitting other requirements such as security requirements. Secondly, they focus on the *flow* of the conversation between the system and the actors—the storyboard of the interaction. Other issues, such as screen designs and data-validation rules, are defined in other artifacts that the use case links to. To fully document and test a system, you need use cases *and* these other artifacts.

Decision Tables

One of the useful artifacts to which you can link a use case is a *decision table*. (In the template, link to this document in the section "Related Artifacts.")

Decision Tables

Use a *decision table* to describe the system response to a number of interrelated factors. If each factor can be looked at separately, do not use a decision table; just use the alternate and exceptional flows or, alternatively, a condition/response table.

For example, the CPP use case Review Case Report referred to a decision table that describes the logic for validating whether a case is payable and for determining the payment amount. The rules for these steps could have been described in the use case proper, but that would have made the text harder to follow. Instead, the rules are extracted into an accompanying decision table, appended to the use case.

The Underlying Concept

Instead of explaining the logic that underlies a decision, you simply list every possible situation and document how the system treats it. The method for completing the table ensures that you have accounted for every mathematically possible combination of factors.

When Are Decision Tables Useful?

Use decision tables during the interview process to ensure that you have questioned the interviewee about all possible combinations of factors that affect the outcome of a use case. Document decision tables as appendices to system use cases or in an external document, for example, in a business rules folder. During testing, use decision tables to derive test cases that cover all combinations of related factors; each column of the table represents a test case. (You'll learn more about this in Chapter 10, "Designing Test Cases and Completing the Project.")

Example of a Use Case with a Decision Table

System Use Case: Process Life Insurance Application

2. **Flow of Events**

   Basic flow:

   .1 User enters application information.

   .2 System validates eligibility. (12.1)

   .3 System adds application to adjuster queue.

   Alternate flows:

   3a Referred application:

       .1 System adds application to referral queue.

       .2 The use case ends.

   Exception flows:

   3b Rejected application:

       .1 System adds application to rejection queue.

       .2 The use case ends in failure.

....

12. **Other Related Artifacts**

   12.1 Validate eligibility decision table (link to table)

A decision table, as shown in Figure 6.1, is appropriate here because all of the conditions are interrelated: You need to evaluate them together to determine how to process an application.

		1	2	3	4	5	6	7	8
CONDITION	Medical Condition (Poor/ Good/)	P	P	P	P	G	G	G	G
	Substance Abuse? (Y/N)	Y	Y	N	N	Y	Y	N	N
	Previous Rejections? (Y/N)	Y	N	Y	N	Y	N	Y	N
ACTION	Accept								X
	Reject	X	X	X		X		X	
	Refer				X		X		

Figure 6.1
Decision table: validate eligibility.

A Step-by-Step Procedure for Using a Decision Table During an Interview to Analyze System Behavior

One of the great things about decision tables is the way they simplify the interview process when dealing with the business's response to a complex and interrelated set of factors. Rather than getting bogged down trying to sort out the logic of the business response, the business analyst can break the interview up into a series of simple, easy-to-execute steps. Use the following guidelines when using decision tables to structure the interview:

1. Prompt interviewees for conditions (factors) that may affect the outcome. List each condition on a separate row in the top-left portion of the diagram. For example, in the previous decision-table example, the conditions are "Medical condition," "Substance abuse?" and "Previous rejections?"

2. Prompt interviewees for a complete list of possible values for each condition and list these next to the corresponding condition—for example, "Medical condition ('Poor,' 'Good')."

3. Prompt interviewees for a complete list of actions that the system may perform (regardless of the reason) and list each on a separate row in the bottom-left portion of the table—for example, "Reject." Do not let the interview wander into the issue of which actions are taken under what circumstances.

4. Calculate the number of cases by multiplying the number of values for condition 1 times the number of values for condition 2, and so on. This yields the number of columns you'll need to complete in the right portion of the table. For example, the preceding decision table has eight cases: two (for "Medical condition") times two (for "Substance abuse?") times two (for "Previous rejections?")

5. Start with the bottom row. Alternate possible condition values, moving from left to right until all cells are filled. For example, in Figure 6.1, the bottom row ("Previous rejections?") is Y N Y N Y N Y N.

6. Move one row up. Cover the first set of values appearing below with the first value for the condition on the current row. Cover the second set with the second value and repeat until all cells are filled. (If you run out of values, start again.) For example, in Figure 6.1, the second-to-last row ("Substance abuse?") is filled as follows:

> Y Y (covering one YN set of values for "Previous rejection?")
>
> N N (covering the next YN set)
>
> Y Y N N to finish off the row

7. Move one row up and repeat until all rows are filled.

8. Each column now describes a distinct scenario. Read down each column and ask the interviewee what actions the system should take for the case it describes. Make sure that you also verify which actions the system does *not* take.

Case Study F1: Decision Table

During an interview regarding the use case Review Case Report, the user describes the requirements as follows:

1. Payments depend on whether the Community Peace Project (CPP) code of good practice was followed, whether the steps and procedures (outlined by the CPP) have been followed, and how many Peace Committee (PC) members were involved in the case.

2. If there were fewer than three PC members present during the Peace Gathering, the case is marked "not payable."

3. If the code of good practice was not followed, the case is marked as "not payable."

4. If the steps and procedures were followed and three to five PC members were present, then mark the case "payable" and pay the standard amount unless there is another reason for marking it "not payable."

5. If the steps and procedures were followed and there were six or more PC members involved, mark the case as "payable" and pay double the standard amount. (This is the preferred number of PC members.)

6. If the steps and procedures were not followed and three or more PC members were present, mark as "payable" and pay half the standard amount.

You decide that the best way to deal with these requirements is with a decision table because a number of conditions need to be evaluated together in order to make a decision. Your plan is to create a decision table based on your notes and use this during a follow-up interview. In the follow-up, you'll go over each column with stakeholders and verify whether each scenario has been captured properly. Once verified, the decision table will be documented as a related artifact to which the use case links. The table will also act as a source document for designing test cases.

Suggestion

Create a decision table for validating a case and determining the amount paid against it based on the preceding interview notes for the use case Review Case Report. Use the following instructions to create the table:

1. First read through the interview notes looking for individual conditions and actions.

2. Use the procedure you've learned to fill in the upper portion of the columns.

3. Then pick a column and read through the interview notes to determine which actions apply. Continue until all columns are complete.

Case Study F1: Resulting Documentation

Figure F1.1 shows the resulting decision table.

		1	2	3	4	5	6	7	8	9	10	11	12
CONDITION	Code of Good Practice Followed (Y/N)	Y	Y	Y	Y	Y	Y	N	N	N	N	N	N
	Steps and Procedures Followed? (Y/N)	Y	Y	Y	N	N	N	Y	Y	Y	N	N	N
	# PC Members (<3,3–5,6+)	<3	3–5	6+	<3	3–5	6+	<3	3–5	6+	<3	3–5	6+
ACTION	Mark as Not Payable	X			X			X	X	X	X	X	X
	Mark as Payable		X	X		X	X						
	Pay ½ Standard Amount					X	X						
	Pay Standard Amount		X										
	Pay Double Amount			X									

Figure F1.1
Decision table: Validate case and determine payment amount.

Decision Trees

A *decision tree* is an alternative to a decision table.[4] Instead of a table, you use a picture to describe the system's behavior, as shown in Figure F1.2.

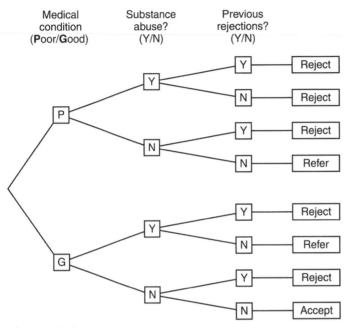

Figure F1.2
Decision tree example.

Creating a Decision Tree

Following are steps for creating a decision tree:

1. List conditions along the top. (Start a few inches to the right of the left edge.)
2. List actions down the right side of the drawing.
3. Draw an origin point at the left edge in the middle of the page.
4. From this point, draw one branch for each value of the first condition.
5. From each of these points (or tips), draw one branch for each value of the next condition.
6. Continue until you finish the last condition.
7. Connect each final tip to the appropriate action.
8. To avoid too many crossed lines, you may list the same action separately each time it is needed.

Case Study F2: Decision Tree

You decide to provide a decision tree for the previous case to accommodate stake-holders who prefer a pictorial presentation.

Case Study F2: Resulting Documentation

Figure F2.1 shows the resulting decision tree.

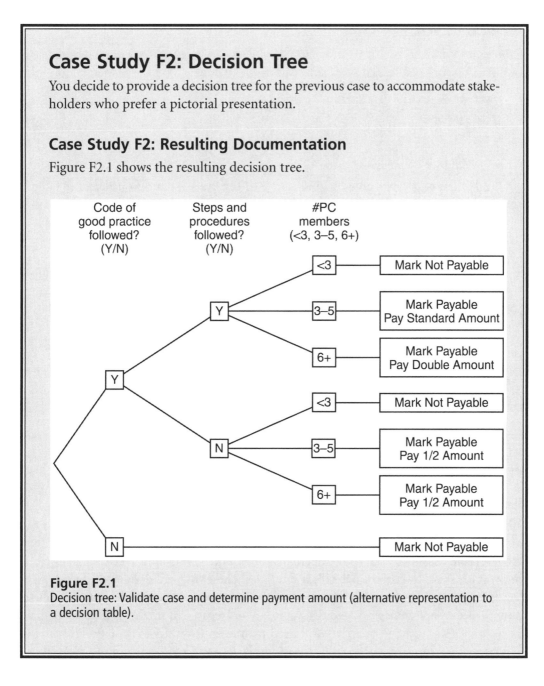

Figure F2.1
Decision tree: Validate case and determine payment amount (alternative representation to a decision table).

Condition/Response Table

If the input conditions contributing to a decision can be evaluated one by one, use a condition/response table instead of a decision table (or tree). Note the following example:

System use case: Prepare Taxes

Basic flow:

....

11. The user enters net income.

12. The system determines tax bracket. (See Tax Bracket condition/response table in Appendix A.)

13. The system displays tax bracket.

...

Appendix A:

Tax bracket condition/response table:

Condition	Response
Under minimum	No tax payable
Minimum–$18,000	Tax bracket A
$18,000.01–$60,000	Tax bracket B
$60,000.01–$500,000	Tax bracket C
Over $500,000	Tax bracket D

Business Rules

Other business rules (beyond those expressed in decision tables) represent another type of documentation that should be pulled from the use case proper and referred to in a dedicated section (Section 10 of the template: Business Rules). Business rules are rules from the business area that constrain business processes. These rules are documented separately because they would distract from the flow of the use case and because they often apply to more than one system use case. For example, an airline system might include a rule that the weight of an airplane must never exceed its maximum weight capacity. This rule is active during a number of use cases, for example, Check In Passenger and Load Cargo. Rather than restate this rule in every use case that it applies to, list it separately as a business rule and refer to the rule from the use cases.

Business rules may be stored the "low-tech" way—for example, in a book. At the other end of the spectrum are *rules engines*—software that manages and enforces business rules. Either way, it's not enough to record the rules; you must also specify which rules apply to which use cases. This makes it easy to identify which use cases need to be tested when a rule changes. When an automated rules engine is used, there is another advantage to linking use cases to a rule: It is inefficient to have the software, at run time, check all business rules for every use case when only some apply.

Advanced Use-Case Features

Once you have written up some system use cases, you may notice that certain steps appear in more than one use case. For example, the same steps for obtaining a valid policy may show up in the use cases Query Policy, Amend Policy, and Make a Claim Against a Policy. Keep an eye out for cases like this; they represent opportunities for reuse. Reuse is a good thing. It means that you only have to go through the effort of documenting the steps once; it means that if the steps ever change, you'll only have to change the documentation in one place; and it means that the steps will be treated consistently throughout the documentation. Often, these inconsistencies arise when, due to a change in requirements, one of the affected use cases is changed but the other is not.

The UML has provided some advanced use-case features to help you increase reuse in the use cases. Use the advanced features for internal documentation; don't show them to the users. For example, show business stakeholders use-case diagrams that include only the basic system use cases discussed up to this point; distribute diagrams with the added, advanced features to the internal team. Finally, don't go overboard. The addition of an advanced use-case feature adds complexity to the model; use it only when necessary. In some organizations, teams can get bogged down in theoretical discussions about whether to use this or that advanced feature. Rather than theoretically working out which feature to use, just write out the system use cases, as proscribed in B.O.O.M.[5]

The advanced use-case features have an impact on diagrams and on the written documentation. The purpose of the diagrams is to help the team organize (or structure) the requirements documentation. The diagrams later serve as a reference: They tell the reader which use-case documentation refers to other use-case documentation and the nature of the reference. These diagrams are also invaluable when changes are made to the textual documentation of a use case: The diagram clearly points out which other use cases are potentially affected.

Some organizations have a bias against use-case diagrams, especially when they contain advanced features. In my experience, this is often because they don't have a clear understanding of the purpose of the advanced diagramming features, mistakenly assuming, for example, that they are for the benefit of users rather than for organizing documentation. But if your organization is adamant about this issue, use the advanced features only for textual documentation and ignore the diagramming component.

The UML includes the following advanced use-case features:

- **Include:** Extract the common requirements into a "mini use case." The main use cases are said to *include* this mini use case. This approach is useful whenever a set of steps appears in more than one system use case.

- **Extend:** You leave one main system use case intact and create a new use case that *extends* the original one. The extending use case contains only the requirements that differ from the original. This approach is useful, for example, for enhanced versions of earlier software releases.

- **Generalization:** You create a new generalized use case that contains general rules. Other use cases are created as "specializations"; they contain the non-generic requirements. This approach is useful when a set of system use cases represents variations on a theme.

Now let's have a closer look at each of these options.

Include

Use this feature when a sequence of steps is performed *exactly* the same way in different use cases.

What They Say:

"An include relationship between two use cases means that the behavior defined in the including use case is included in the behavior of the base use case. The include relationship is intended to be used when there are common parts of the behavior of two or more use cases. This common part is then extracted to a separate use case, to be included by all the base use cases having this part in common. Since the primary use of the include relationship is for reuse of common parts, what is left in a base use case is usually not complete in itself but dependent on the included parts to be meaningful. This is reflected in the direction of the relationship, indicating that the base use case depends on the addition but not vice versa." [6] (UML)

What They Mean:

When the same set of steps appears in more than one use case, extract them into a separate use case—called an *included* use case—and refer to them from the main use cases—called base use cases. When modeling an *include* relationship between two use cases, draw a dashed arrow, pointing from the base use case to the included use case.

How It Works

You avoid repetition by extracting the common steps into a separate use case. (If you're a programmer, it helps to think of an included use case as a routine, called by the base use case.)

Terminology

- The original use cases are referred to as *base use cases* (also referred to as *including use cases*).
- The new use case is called the *included* (or *inclusion) use case*[7].
- Each of the other original use cases is said to *include* this new use case.

Examples of Included Use Cases

A Web-based banking system has two base use cases: Pay Bill and Transfer Funds. Each of these includes the use case Debit Account.

In an air-travel system, a Make Reservation use case and a Change Reservation use case both include the use case Check Available Seats.

How to Draw an Included Use Case

Figure 6.2 shows how to diagram an included use case.

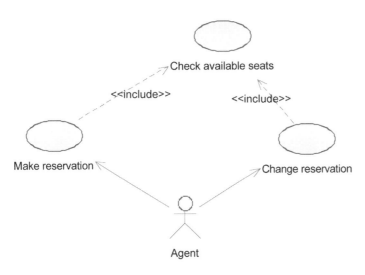

Figure 6.2
An included use case.

Inclusion Rules

- An included use case is triggered by a step in a base use case.
- An included use case does not have to be a complete task (and it usually isn't).
- A use case that appears in one context as an included use case may, in another context, act as a base use case triggered directly by an actor. (Be aware, however, that there is some controversy surrounding this issue.)[8]
- An included use case may include other included use cases for as many levels as necessary.
- The base use case may include as many included use cases as necessary.
- The inclusion does not have to be triggered *every* time the base use case is executed. (This issue also has some controversy associated with it.)[9] For example, the base use case may trigger the inclusion within an alternate flow scenario that is only conditionally executed.
- The included use case must not refer to the base use case; however, it should verify that the inclusion has completed successfully if there is any way the inclusion can fail.
- Write the inclusion so that it will apply regardless of which base use case triggers it.

How Does an Include Relationship Affect Use-Case Documentation?

To grasp the consequence of the include relationship, it is important to understand its effect on the textual documentation. The following example shows how a base use case refers to an included use case in the text, and how the included use case is written. (Keep in mind that the UML does not dictate a standard way to handle the text.)

In the example shown in Figure 6.2, a base use case, Make Reservation, includes the use case Check Available Seats. This is documented in the base use case Make Reservation as follows:

2. Flow of Events

Basic flow:

.1 The agent selects a trip.

.2 Include (Check Available Seats).

.3 The agent confirms the reservation.

Exception flows:

2.2a No available seats: (This flow handles the failure of the included use case)

   .1 Cancel the transaction.

The included use case Check Available Seats is documented as follows:

Description: Other reservation use cases reference this included use case.

2. Flow of Events

  Basic flow:

  .1 The system verifies that seats are available.

  .2 The system determines and displays the maximum number of seats for the trip.

  .3 The system determines and displays the number of seats currently reserved.

  .4 The system determines and displays the number of seats currently available.

  Exception flows:

  2.1a Seats not available: (This flow handles failure of step 2.1 of the basic flow.)

    .1 The system displays a "seats unavailable" warning message.

    .2 The use case ends in failure.

Extend

Use this feature whenever you need to add requirements to an existing use case *without changing the original text*. The following are some common reasons for an extension:

- **Seldom-used options that the user can choose at any time (known as *asynchronous interruptions*):** An extending use case will allow you to handle these options in separate extending use cases and keep the base use case free of the seldom-used requirements. Aside from the clarity this provides, it is also useful for planning software iterations: You may plan to implement the base use case in an early iteration and add the extending use cases later.
- **Customization of a generic product:** The generic product is described in the base use case. The extending use case describes the customization.

What They Say:

Extend: "This relationship specifies that the behavior of a use case may be extended by the behavior of another (usually supplementary) use case. The extension takes place at one or more specific extension points defined in the extended use case. Note, however, that the extended use case is defined independently of the extending use case and is meaningful independently of the extending use case. On the other hand, the extending use case typically defines behavior that may not necessarily be meaningful by itself. Instead, the extending use case defines a set of modular behavior increments that augment an execution of the extended use case under specific conditions."[10] (UML)

> **What They Mean:**
> You may extract a group of alternate flows that are triggered by the same conditions into a sep-
> arate use case, referred to as an extending use case. In the main (extended) use case, you define
> locations (extension points) where the flow may be interrupted; in the extending use case, you
> document the extracted flows, the conditions that trigger them, and the location where each alter-
> nate flow interrupts the extended use case.

How It Works

The base use case is written as a normal use case. It describes the interaction, except for the steps that are in the extension. (If you're a programmer, it helps to think of an extending use case as a "patch"[11] on the base use case.) The base use case does not contain any reference to the extending use case. However, it does contain labels within the textual documentation that mark points at which it might be extended. The extending use case contains all the steps that are inserted at these points.

Terminology

- The original use case is referred to as the *base use case*.
- The use case that is based on it is called the *extending (or extension)*[12] *use case*.
- A point at which the base use case might be extended is called an *extension point*.
- The circumstance that causes the extension to be activated is the *condition*.

Examples of Extending Use Cases

A word-processing system has a base use case Edit Document that is extended by the use case Check Spelling. The condition is User Selects Spell-Checking Option.

A school's tuition package has a base use case Assign Tuition Fee that is extended by Apply Subsidy. The extension point is Calculate Final Amount, a label that marks the point just before a final fee is calculated. The condition is Student Is Eligible for Subsidy.

Another Way to Think of Extending Use Cases

Recall that the system use-case template contains a "Basic Flow" section describing the normal success scenario, "Alternate Flows" for alternate pathways, and "Exception Flows" for paths that lead to abandonment of the goal. Instead of putting all the alternate and exception flows in one base system use case, you can extract some of them into an extending use case.

What You Need to Remember About an Extending Use Case

An *extending use case* represents one or more alternate or exception flows that are executed due to the same condition.

How to Draw an Extension

Figure 6.3 shows how to draw an extending use case.

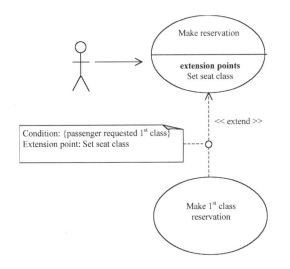

Figure 6.3
An extending use case.

The example in Figure 6.3 shows the following:

- The extended (base) use case is Make Reservation.
- The extending use case is Make 1st Class Reservation.
- The extension point is Set Seat Class.
- The condition is Passenger Requests 1st Class Seating.

Extension Rules

- The extended use case must be complete on its own.
- An extended base use case may have more than one extending use case.
- The extending use case interrupts the flow of the extended use case at defined extension points and under specified conditions.
- An extending use case may interrupt the extended use case at more than one extension point.
- The conditions attached to the extension are evaluated once, when the first extension point is reached inside the extended use case; the conditions are not reevaluated when subsequent points are reached.
- Once the system confirms that the extension applies, the extending use case will be invoked at all its extension points.
- The extended use case must not refer to the extending use case or even "know" that it is being extended. Exception: A section in the extended use case documentation may describe extension points.
- Connect actors to the extended use case; they automatically apply to the extension. Exception: If the extension introduces a new actor, connect the new actor to the extending use case.

How Does an Extend Relationship Affect Use-Case Documentation?

The extended (base) use case should not make any reference to the new extending use case. However, the extended use case must contain extension points—marked spots in the document to which the extending use case may refer.

The following example shows how the textual documentation of an extended use case indicates an extension point and how an extending use case refers to an extension point.

> **Extended Use Case:** Make Reservation
>
> **Extension Points:** Set Seat Class: Step 3
> **Basic flow:**
> ...
> 3. Assign coach seat.
> ...
>
> **Extending Use Case:** Make 1st Class Reservation
>
> **Description:** This use case extends the Make Reservation use case. It contains changes to the flow when the reservation is first-class.
> **Flows:**
>   **Set Seat Class:**
>   Assign first-class seat.

Generalized Use Case

Use this feature when a number of use cases represent variations on a theme. Common reasons for a generalized use case are the following:

- **Technology variations:** The same user goal is achieved using different technologies. Define a generalized use case to hold rules that apply regardless of technology; handle the technology variations as specialized use cases.

- **Similar process but different business artifacts:** The business has a standard process for handling different kinds of artifacts (for example, different kinds of application forms), but the process differs slightly depending on the artifact. Handle the generic rules in a generalized use case and describe the peculiarities in specialized use cases—one for each artifact.

What They Say:

Generalization [between use cases]: "A taxonomic relationship between a more general classifier [use case] and a more specific classifier [use case]. Each instance of the specific classifier [use case] is also an indirect instance of the general classifier [use cases]. Thus, the specific classifier [use case] indirectly has features of the more general classifier [use case]."[13] (UML)

What They Mean:

The UML does not have a specific definition for generalized use cases, but its broader definition applies to use cases. If one use case could be considered a specific type of another, the general one may be modeled as a generalized use case and the specific type as a specialized use case. For example, if there are three types of use cases for processing a transaction—a Canadian, a U.S., and a Mexican version—then the general interaction (non-specific to any country) may be modeled as the generalized use case Process Transaction, and the more specific interactions modeled as the specialized use cases Process Transaction (Canada), Process Transaction (U.S.), and Process Transaction (Mexico).

Anything true for the generalized use case is true for all of its specialized use cases. For example, if the model indicates that an actor is associated with the generalized use case Process Transaction, then this implies that the actor is associated with Process Transaction (Canada), Process Transaction (U.S.), and Process Transaction (Mexico).

How It Works

Write workflow steps that apply across a group of use cases in a generalized use case. Specify variations on how the steps are handled in the specialized use cases.

Terminology

- The generic use case is referred to as the *generalized use case*.
- Each variation is called a *specialized use case*.
- Each specialized use case has a *generalization* relationship with the generalized use case. The relationship points from the specialized use case to the generalized one.
- The specialized use cases *inherit* features of the generalized use case.

Examples of Generalized Use Cases

Following are examples of generalized and specialized use cases:

- A banking system that has a generalized use case Pay Bill and specialized use cases Pay Bill Through ATM, Pay Bill over the Web, and Pay Bill Through Teller
- A clinical research organization (CRO) that has a generalized use case File Documents and specialized use cases File Case Documents and File Regulatory Documents

How to Draw a Generalized Use Case

Figure 6.4 shows how to draw a generalized use case.

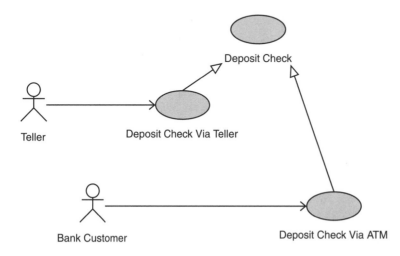

Figure 6.4
A generalized use case.

In Figure 6.4, Deposit Check is a generalized use case containing generic steps for depositing a check. Any overriding or additional steps are described in the specialized use cases Deposit Check via Teller and Deposit Check via ATM.

Rules for Generalized Use Cases

The UML does not provide much guidance regarding textual documentation. The following rules comply with the spirit of the UML generalization relationship and are useful extensions to the standard:

- The specialized use cases must comply with requirements documented in the generalized use case (including all sections: "Actors," "Flows," and so on).
- The specialized use case may not exclude any flows or steps inherited from the generalized use case. However, it may override them or add to them.
- The generalized use case should be *abstract*:
  - According to the UML, the generalized use case may be either abstract (conceptual) or concrete (real). An *abstract use case* is an invention used to pool together common requirements; a *concrete use case* is a full-blown, actual use case, containing everything necessary to describe the interaction. Since the extension relation is the widely accepted mechanism for creating a new use case from a concrete one, I suggest that all your generalized use cases be abstract.

How Does a Generalization Relationship Affect Use-Case Documentation?

One practice is to write generic steps in the generalized use case and write only the overriding and additional steps in the specialized use cases. Alternatively, you can write each specialized use case in its entirety, as long as it conforms to the rules set out in the generalized use case. The following example demonstrates the first approach.

In the diagram shown in Figure 6.4, a generalized use case Deposit Check holds generic rules for check deposits. The label (Hold check) marks the place it will be overridden with more specific steps. The specialized use cases contain the overriding or extra steps. The generalized use case, Deposit Check, is documented as follows:

Description: This generalized use case contains a generic workflow for depositing checks.

Basic flow:

The user identifies the deposit account and the amount of the check.

(Hold Check) The system places a hold on the check, blocking withdrawal of the check amount for the period of the hold.

The system credits the account with the check amount.

The specialized use case Deposit Check via ATM is documented as follows:

Description: This use case is a specialization of the use case Deposit Check. Only steps that override or are inserted into the generalized use case are documented herein.

Basic flow:

(Hold Check) Hold check for one business day.

The specialized use case Deposit Check via Teller is documented as follows:

Description: This use case is a specialization of the use case Deposit Check. Only steps that override or are inserted into the generalized use case are documented in Deposit Check via Teller.

Basic flow:

(Hold Check) Hold check for five business days.

Case Study F3: Advanced Use-Case Features

In this case study, you'll employ advanced use-case features to increase re-use and reduce redundancies in the requirements documentation.

Problem Statement

You can now examine the system use cases, looking for places where the same steps apply to more than one system use case. You will note that while carrying out the system use case Update Case, the user may become aware that the case involves a new Peace Committee or that information about an existing committee has changed. Users want the option of updating Peace Committee information without leaving the Update Case function. They also may want to add or update CPP Members without leaving the Update Case function. There is a redundancy here due to the fact that the Manage Administration package has already described both of these functions, Update Peace Committees and Update CPP Members, as system use cases.

Your Next Step

You review existing system use-case diagrams to restructure the use cases for maximum reuse. You'll be making changes to the use-case diagram for the Manage Case package.

Figures F3.1 and F3.2 are the existing diagrams relevant to Case Study F3.

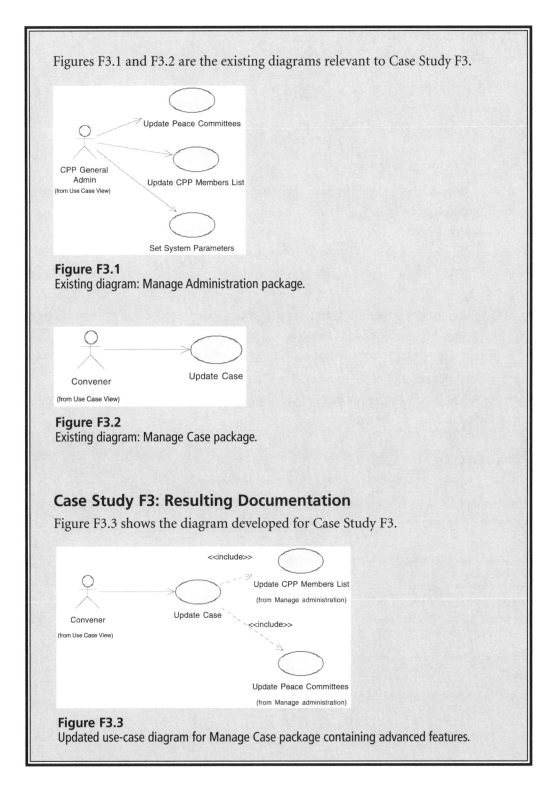

Figure F3.1
Existing diagram: Manage Administration package.

Figure F3.2
Existing diagram: Manage Case package.

Case Study F3: Resulting Documentation

Figure F3.3 shows the diagram developed for Case Study F3.

Figure F3.3
Updated use-case diagram for Manage Case package containing advanced features.

Chapter Summary

In this chapter, you performed the following B.O.O.M. steps:

2. Discovery

    2a) Behavioral analysis

        i) Describe system use cases (use-case description template)

You learned about the following new tools and concepts in this chapter:

- A *use-case description template* is a format for describing a system use case.
- A *decision table* is a table for describing requirements when conditions need to be evaluated together.
- A *decision tree* is a graphic alternative to a decision table.
- A *condition/response table* is a simpler table you can use to evaluate conditions one by one.
- Advanced use-case features include the following:
  - **Included use case:** For steps that occur the same way in more than one use case.
  - **Extending use case:** To add flows to an existing use case while leaving the original documentation intact.
  - **Generalized use case:** To be used when a number of use cases represent variations on a theme.

Endnotes

[1] Alistair Cockburn, *Writing Effective Use Cases*, Addison-Wesley, 2001.

[2] Some templates use named labels to avoid extensive renumbering every time the use case is amended.

[3] These guidelines are described by Alistair Cockburn in his book, *Writing Effective Use Cases*, Addison-Wesley Professional (October 15, 2000)

[4] An activity diagram may also be used for this purpose, but the format is different. On a decision tree, each possible value for an input condition is represented as a node; on an activity diagram, the values are represented as guards along the connecting lines. Many BAs and users find the decision tree format to be more intuitive than that of an activity diagram for requirements of this sort.

[5] Thanks to Brian Lyons for his contribution to the sequencing of B.O.O.M. steps on this and other issues.

[6] *UML Superstructure Specification*, v2.2, OMG, 2009, page 595.

[7] For use of the term *inclusion use case*, please see OMG, "UML 2.0: Infrastructure—Final Adopted Specification", 2003, page 10. The most recent specification, UML 2.2, uses the term *included use case*.

[8]Some analysts insist that an inclusion use case must *never* represent a complete user goal. Others allow it. (See Schneider and Winters, *Applying Use Cases*, 2nd edition, Addison Wesley, 2001.) I side with those who allow it because BAs often encounter processes that in one context are a side-goal and in others are main goals. For example, a licensing system has a Renew License use case. As a side-goal, the use case includes steps for changing the address if the licensee has moved. On the other hand, the system also has a Change Address use case to handle situations where the licensee calls a CSR specifically to report a move. This is most elegantly treated by defining a use case Change Address that is included by the Renew License use case but that also appears in the model as a base use case that interacts directly with the CSR actor.

[9]I have also seen this handled differently in different organizations. Some show an include relationship only if the base use case activates the inclusion every time. I don't see the benefit in restricting the use of such an effective feature in this way.

[10]*UML Superstructure Specification*, v2.2, OMG, 2009, page 591.

[11]This turn of phrase was coined by Rebecca Wirfs-Brock.

[12]For use of the term *extension use case*, please see OMG, "UML 2.0: Infrastructure—Final Adopted Specification", 2003, page 9. The most recent specification, UML 2.2, uses the term *extending use case*.

[13]The definition is written so that it applies to any generalization. I've added the phrase "use case" in brackets after each use of the term "classifier" so you can see how the rule applies to use cases.

CHAPTER 7

LIFECYCLE REQUIREMENTS FOR KEY BUSINESS OBJECTS

Chapter Objectives

In this chapter, you'll learn how to define the lifecycle of critical business objects.

You'll be able to carry out the following steps in bold:

    2a) Behavioral analysis

        i) Describe system use cases (use-case description)

        ii) Describe state behavior (state-machine diagram)

            1. Identify states of critical objects

            2. Identify state transitions

            3. Identify state activities

            4. Identify composite states

            5. Identify concurrent states

Tools and concepts that you'll learn to use in this chapter include the following:

- State-machine diagram
- State
- Transition
- Event
- Guard
- Activity
- Composite state
- Concurrent states

What Is a State-Machine Diagram?

A *state-machine diagram* is a picture that describes the different statuses (states) of an object and the events and conditions that cause an object to pass from one state to another. The diagram describes the life of a single object over a period of time—one that may span several system use cases.[1] For example, a state-machine diagram might show the different statuses of an insurance claim (Received, Validated, Under Adjustment, Adjusted, Paid, Not Paid, and so on).

What They Say:

State: "A state models a situation during which some (usually implicit) invariant condition holds. The invariant may represent a static situation such as an object waiting for some external event to occur. However, it can also model dynamic conditions such as the process of performing some behavior (i.e., the model element under consideration enters the state when the behavior commences and leaves it as soon as the behavior is completed)."[2] (UML)

What They Mean:

A state is a status that an object may have. The object may be in a dormant (static) state, which it exits once an event it is waiting for finally occurs; an example is the state Waiting for Receipt of Proposal, which ends once a proposal has been received. Alternatively, an object may be in an active state, which it exits once activities associated with the state have been completed; an example is the state Under Adjudication, which ends once adjudication activities have been completed.

What They Say:

State machine: "State machines can be used to express the behavior of part of a system. Behavior is modeled as a traversal of a graph of state nodes interconnected by one or more joined transition arcs that are triggered by the dispatching of series of (event) occurrences. During this traversal, the state machine executes a series of activities associated with various elements of the state machine."[3] (UML)

State-machine diagram: "State machine diagrams specify state machines."[4] (UML)

What They Mean:

A state machine is a model of the statuses through which an object passes; the model describes the events and conditions that cause it to move from state to state and the activities associated with each state. The model may be depicted as a state-machine diagram.

The terms *state machine* and *state-machine diagram* are almost synonymous: The state machine is the behavior, and the state-machine diagram depicts it. Other names for the diagram are *state diagram* and *statechart diagram.* The diagram was originally developed by David Harel.

Why Draw a State-Machine Diagram?

The behavior of an object over time *could* be surmised by analyzing system use-case descriptions, activity diagrams, and so on. For example, one could gain an understanding of an Insurance Claim object by noting how it is handled during the system use cases Receive Claim, Validate Claim, Adjust Claim, and Pay Claim. But if the state of the object is critical to the system, it is helpful to be able to get the full picture for the object as it passes through the system.

State-Machine Diagram Example: Credit-Card Application

In the next steps, we'll walk through the creation of a state-machine diagram. To give you an idea of where we're headed, Figure 7.1 shows an example derived from a credit-card system.

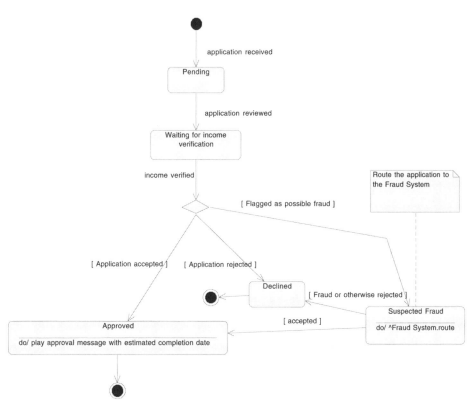

Figure 7.1
A state-machine diagram for a credit-card system.

Step 2aii: 1. Identify States of Critical Objects

Define a new state for the object if the system treats the object differently because of a change or if the object itself behaves differently. If there is no difference, then only a piece of information about the object has changed. You can modify a piece of information about the object by using attributes (which you'll learn about in Chapter 9, "Optimizing Consistency and Reuse in the Requirements Documentation," in the section "Step 2bviii: Add Attributes").

Examples of states and attributes include the following:

- Red and Blue are not two states of a Product object, but merely indicate different values of a color attribute.

- However, Sold and Unsold may be considered states because they affect how the product is handled.

Other examples of states include the following:

- Telephone line states: Busy, Off-the-Hook, Not-in-Use

- Invoice states: Entered, Paid, Unpaid, Canceled

- Student registrant states: Wait-Listed, Pre-Screened, Accepted, Attending, Graduated, On Leave, Left Institution

Types of States

Many of the elements that appear on a state-machine diagram fall into one of the following categories, which are shown in Figure 7.2. Thinking in terms of these categories will help you discover states.

- **Initial pseudostate:** This is shown as a dot on the diagram. It is the start point for the object. The UML classifies this, as well as some other modeling elements, as *pseudostates* rather than *states*. *Pseudostates* mark points that transitions may leave from or go to, but they do not represent actual states of the object.

- **Final state:** This appears as a bulls-eye. It represents the final state of the object. The final state may be named, and there may be more than one final state for an object. There are a number of restrictions on how you can use the final state: It may not have any outgoing transitions, and you cannot associate specific behaviors, such as entry, exit, or ongoing activities. (You'll learn how to specify these activities for other kinds of states in the section "Step 2aii: 3. Identify State Activities.")

Other states are shown as a rounded rectangle. These typically fall into one of the following categories:

- **Wait state:** The object isn't doing anything important; it is simply waiting for an event to happen or a condition to become true. In the credit-card example in Figure 7.1, the state Waiting for Income Verification is of this type.
- **Ongoing state:** The object is performing some ongoing process and stays in this state until some event interrupts the process. For example, a system to manage the work of health inspectors has an inspector state Monitoring Compliance that ends only when management instructs the inspector to discontinue.
- **Finite state:** The object is performing some work that has a definite end. Once the work is over, the object passes out of the state.

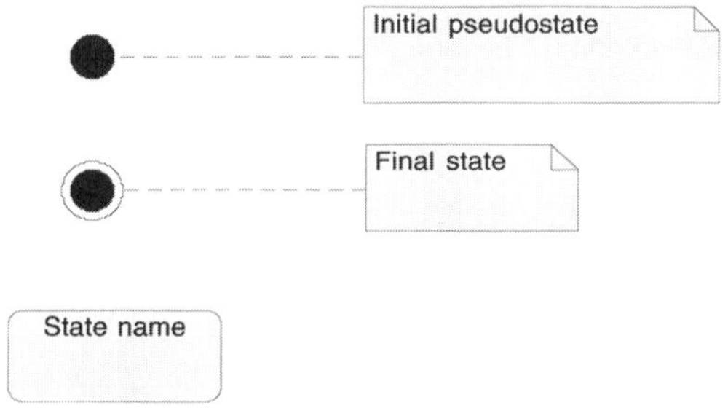

Figure 7.2
Drawing states in UML.

Case Study G1: States

During interviews with the CPP, you've identified a case (a dispute handled by the CPP) as a critical business object tracked by the system. You ask the interviewees what states a case can be in, and learn that they are as follows:

- Initiated: When the initial report has been made.
- Scheduled for Gathering: Once a Peace Gathering has been scheduled.
- Gathering Held: Once a Peace Gathering has been held.
- Monitored: While it is being monitored.
- Resolved/No Gathering
- Referred to Police

- Awaiting Review: Indicating the case has been resolved and is awaiting a review to determine whether it is payable.
- Under Review: While it is being reviewed.
- Payable: Once the case has been reviewed and deemed payable.
- Not Payable: Once the case has been reviewed and deemed not payable.
- Paid: Once all payments for the case have been made.
- Final State

Your next step is to begin the drawing of a state-machine diagram by depicting these states.

Case Study G1: Resulting Diagram

Figure G1.1 shows the diagram that results from these interviews.

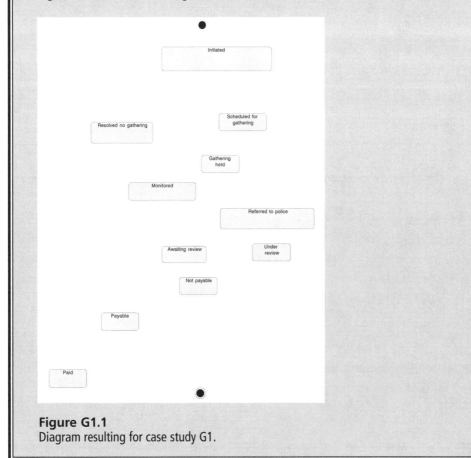

Figure G1.1
Diagram resulting for case study G1.

Step 2aii: 2. Identify State Transitions

The next step is to establish what causes the object to pass—or *transition*—from one state to another. There are two ways that this transition may occur.

Transition

A *transition* is a change of state.

A transition may occur automatically when activities taking place while the object was in a previous state have been completed. For example, while an insurance claim is in the state Under Adjustment, it is evaluated by an adjuster. As soon as the adjuster completes the evaluation, the object automatically transitions out of the state. This type of transition is called a *completion transition*.

Alternatively, a transition may occur because an event *interrupts* the previous state. For example, an application in the state Waiting for Income Verification stays there indefinitely until it receives the event Income Verified. This type of transition is a *labeled transition*.

Depicting State Transitions in UML

Figure 7.3 shows a first draft of a diagram showing state transitions for the Case object. The example shows a number of elements involved in documenting a transition.

The model elements that appear on this diagram are the following:

- **Transition:** A change of state, indicated with an arrow.
- **Event:** A trigger that fires—or forces—a transition. To document an event, simply write the event name beside the transition symbol.
- **Transition activity:** A quick, uninterruptible activity that happens whenever the transition occurs. To document an activity, precede the activity name with a slash, as in /Assign Temporary Case Number.
- **Send event:** A message that is sent to *another* object whenever the transition occurs. To document a send event, identify the target (the object receiving the request) and the event (or message) that is sent as follows: ^Target.Event. For example, ^Convener.Notify Central Office means "Tell the convener to notify the central office." You can also identify any information (parameters) that you need to send to the object. For example, if the convener needs to know the temporary case number, then specify ^Convener.Notify Central Office(Temporary Case Number).

If you find the notation of a send event cumbersome, or if the diagram is to be presented to business stakeholders, don't use this feature. Document it as a regular event and clarify who performs the job with a note if necessary.

▪ **Guard:** A condition that must be true for the transition to occur. A guard is somewhat like an event in that both determine whether a transition may occur. The difference is that an event *forces* the previous state to end; a guard is only checked once the previous state has already ended for some other reason. Show a guard in square brackets, as in [Consensus Reached].

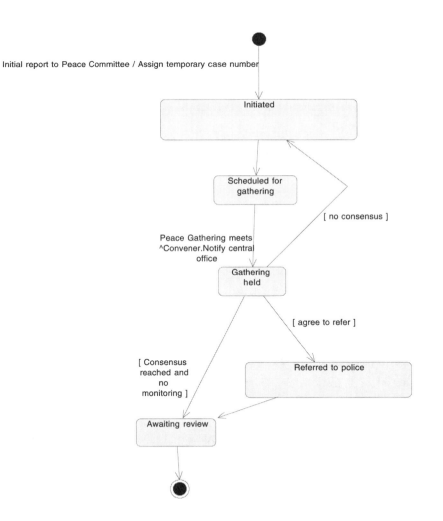

Figure 7.3
Draft of a diagram depicting state transitions for the Case object.

You can also use the diamond decision symbol the same way you used it in activity diagrams, as shown in Figure 7.4. The official UML term for this is *choice pseudostate*.

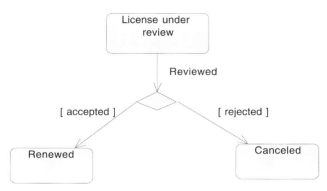

Figure 7.4
Using a choice pseudostate when documenting state transitions.

Mapping State-Machine Diagrams to System Use Cases

You can use state-machine diagrams to compile a comprehensive picture of how system use cases change the states of objects. To do this, use the names of the system use cases for events and the names of flows for guards. For example, a transition labeled Review Report [Not Payable] means that the transition occurs when the Not Payable flow of the system use case Review Report is executed.

This naming convention can also lead to pre-conditions and post-conditions for the relevant use case. For example, in Figure 7.5, the system use case Review Application is used to name the transition of an application from Pending to Waiting for Income Verification. A pre-condition for this use case is that the application is in the Pending state. A post-condition is that the application is in the state Waiting for Income Verification. You can also explicitly document other use-case pre-conditions and post-conditions right on the transition label. These look like regular guards but are distinguished by where they appear relative to the use-case name. Use the form [pre-condition] use-case name/[post-condition]. For example, if the transition in Figure 7.5 were labeled [valid reviewer has been identified] review application/[request for income sent], the implication is that, for the use case Review Application, the following interpretations apply:

- The pre-conditions are that a valid reviewer has been identified and that the application is pending.
- The post-conditions are that a request for income had been sent and the application is waiting for income verification.

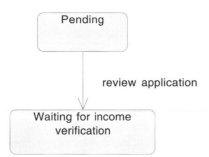

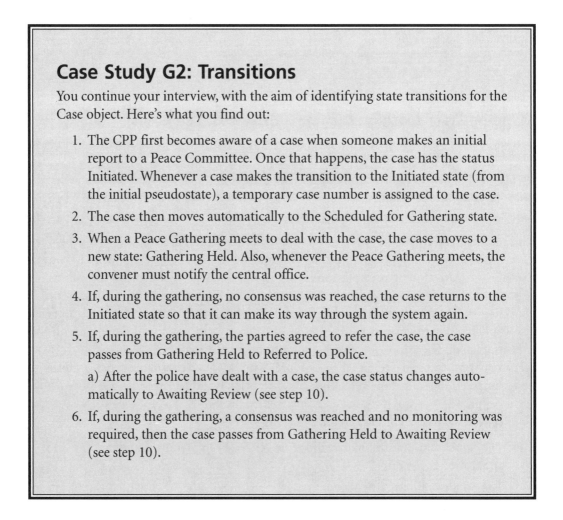

Figure 7.5
Naming a transition as a use case.

Case Study G2: Transitions

You continue your interview, with the aim of identifying state transitions for the Case object. Here's what you find out:

1. The CPP first becomes aware of a case when someone makes an initial report to a Peace Committee. Once that happens, the case has the status Initiated. Whenever a case makes the transition to the Initiated state (from the initial pseudostate), a temporary case number is assigned to the case.

2. The case then moves automatically to the Scheduled for Gathering state.

3. When a Peace Gathering meets to deal with the case, the case moves to a new state: Gathering Held. Also, whenever the Peace Gathering meets, the convener must notify the central office.

4. If, during the gathering, no consensus was reached, the case returns to the Initiated state so that it can make its way through the system again.

5. If, during the gathering, the parties agreed to refer the case, the case passes from Gathering Held to Referred to Police.

   a) After the police have dealt with a case, the case status changes automatically to Awaiting Review (see step 10).

6. If, during the gathering, a consensus was reached and no monitoring was required, then the case passes from Gathering Held to Awaiting Review (see step 10).

7. If a consensus was reached during the gathering and monitoring is required, then the case status moves from Gathering Held to Monitoring.

8. While a case is being monitored, when the deadline for compliance comes up, the case transitions out of the Monitoring state.

   a) If the monitoring conditions have not been met, the case is put back into the system, returning to the Initiated state.

   b) If the monitoring conditions have been met, the case passes from Monitoring to Awaiting Review.

9. A case remains in the Awaiting Review state until the case report is selected for review, at which time it is placed in the Under Review state.

10. At the end of the review, the case will have been deemed either payable or non-payable:

    a) If the case was deemed payable (as a result of the review), the case state becomes Payable.

    b) On the other hand, if the case was deemed non-payable, its status becomes Not Payable. From there it moves to its final state.

11. Once a check has been issued for a Payable case, it becomes Paid. From there, it moves to its final state.

12. If, at any time while a case is Initiated or Scheduled for a Gathering, the parties agree to dismiss the case, then its status is recorded as Resolved/No Gathering. From there it moves to its final state.

Your next step is to document these transitions on the state-machine diagram you began earlier.

Case Study G2: Resulting Documentation

Figure G2.1 shows the state-machine diagram you've developed for the Case object.

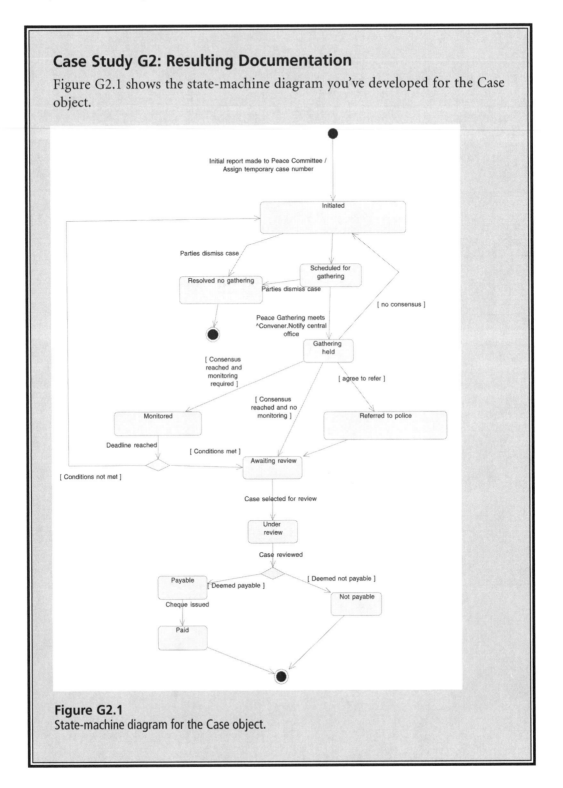

Figure G2.1
State-machine diagram for the Case object.

Step 2aii: 3. Identify State Activities

The next step is to identify what activities occur while the object is in each state.

State Activity

A *state activity* is a process that occurs while an object is in a certain state. An activity within a state may take some time. (This is in contrast to an activity on a state transition, which always occurs quickly.)

List activities inside the state symbol. You'll need to identify when each activity occurs with a prefix, as follows (the UML keywords are in bold):

entry/ activity	The activity occurs whenever the object enters this state.
do/ activity	The activity occurs while the object is in this state.
eventname/ activity	The activity occurs in response to an external event. (Deviating from the UML standard, Rational Rose uses the keyword event before this phrase. Some of the diagrams in this book were produced from Rose and use this keyword inside the state symbol.)
exit/ activity	The activity occurs whenever the object leaves the state.

Name the activity informally, such as Monitor Case. If you want to specify that a different object carries out the activity, handle it as a send event, as in ^Monitor.Monitor Case. (As before, if you find the notation of a send event cumbersome, don't use it. Document it as a regular event and clarify who performs the job with a note if necessary.) Figure 7.6 shows the various types of activities associated with the Monitored state of a Case object in the CPP system.

Figure 7.6
Documenting the Monitored state.

Case Study G3: State Activities

Further interviews with the users reveal that the following activities are carried out for a case based upon its state:

- **Initiated:** While a case is in this state, the Peace Committee interviews the parties to the dispute and sets a date for the Peace Gathering.

- **Referred to Police:** When a case enters this state, the Peace Gathering escorts the parties to the police station.

- **Resolved no Gathering:** As soon as a case enters this state, a case report must be entered.

- **Under Review:** While a case is in this state, the convener reviews the case.

- **Monitored:** Whenever a case enters this state, the convener is asked to appoint a monitor. While the case is in this state, the monitor provides ongoing monitoring. If the monitor becomes ill while the case is in this state, the convener is to appoint a temporary monitor. Whenever the case leaves this state, the monitor is to submit a monitoring report.

Case Study G3: Resulting Diagram

Your next step is to add these activities to the state-machine diagram you have been developing, as shown in Figure G3.1. Please note that this diagram was produced using Rational Rose and, therefore, uses the Event keyword for activities in a state that are triggered by an external event. As noted earlier, the UML does not advise the use of the Event keyword in this context.

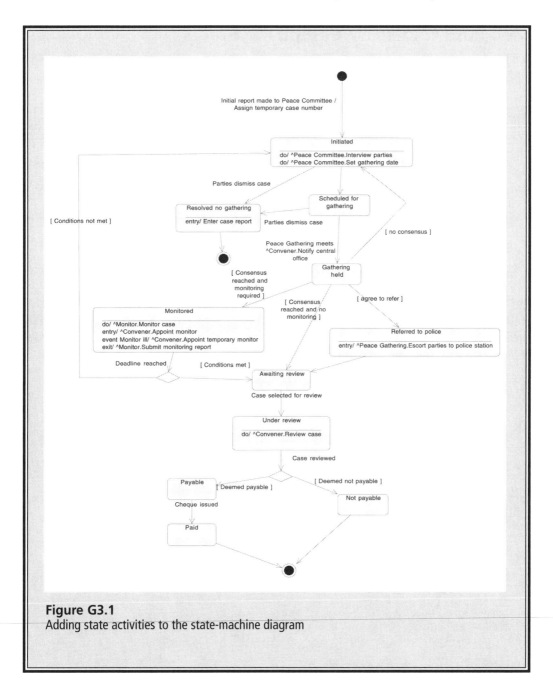

Figure G3.1
Adding state activities to the state-machine diagram

Step 2aii: 4. Identify Composite States

If a number of states share one or more transitions, you can simplify the drawing by using composite states.

Composite State

A *composite state* is a state that contains other states. It represents a general state for an object that encompasses any number of more specific states, called *substates*. A *substate* inherits the transitions of its composite state. Place an initial pseudostate inside the composite state so that you can indicate the first state that the object moves to as it enters the composite state.

For example, an ATM transaction initially passes through the states Checking Access, Getting Input, and Checking Balance. If the user cancels the transaction while it is any of these states, the transaction immediately changes to a Cancelled state. Rather than show three transitions, you invent a composite state, In Progress, and use it as shown in Figure 7.7.

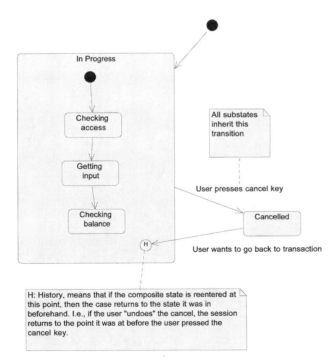

Figure 7.7
Adding a composite state to the state-machine diagram.

Case Study G4: Composite States

You examine the state diagram you have developed so far, looking for an opportunity to simplify it through the use of composite states.

Suggestion

Look for two transitions that have the same label and that go to the same state. Model the states at the origin of these transitions as substates.

Case Study G4: Resulting Documentation

Figure G4.1 shows the state-machine diagram after you've incorporated composite states.

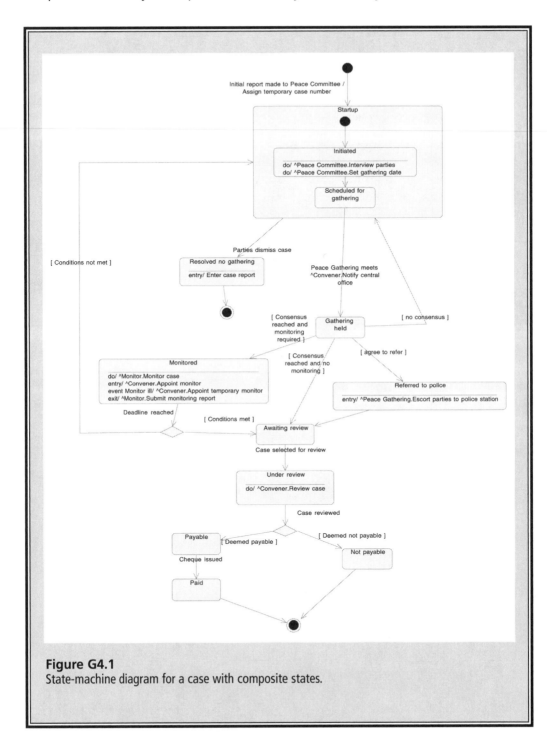

Figure G4.1
State-machine diagram for a case with composite states.

Step 2aii: 5. Identify Concurrent States

If, according to one criterion, an object can be in one of a set of states and, according to another criterion, can be in another state at the same time, use concurrent states to model the object.

Concurrent States

An object is in concurrent states when it is considered to be in more than one state at the same time.

The UML refers to the state that holds the concurrent states as an *orthogonal* state. An *orthogonal* state contains more than one region; each region holds states that can vary independently of the states in the other regions.

Concurrent State Example

If the payment on an insurance claim is large, it is not paid right away. Rather, it is scheduled for payment, during which payments are made at regular intervals. At the same time, the claim also undergoes monitoring for a specified period. One way to model this is with concurrent states, as shown in Figure 7.8.

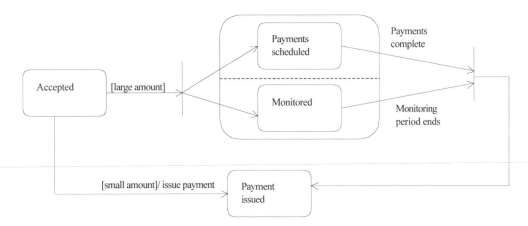

Figure 7.8
State-machine diagram with concurrent states

In Figure 7.8, the claim object moves from the Accepted state into the concurrent states if the amount of the claim is large. In this case, the vertical bar indicates a *fork*—a point after which the following transitions occur in any order: a transition to Payments Scheduled and a transition to Monitored. Once all payments have been completed, the case makes the transition out of the Payments Scheduled state. When the monitoring period is over, it makes the transition out of the Monitored state. When *both* these transitions have occurred (indicated by the second vertical bar, or a *join*), the object moves into the Payment Issued state. On the other hand, if the amount of an accepted payment is small, it immediately goes into the Payment Issued state.

This is a simple example to introduce the concept of concurrent states. Concurrent states can get much more complicated. For example, each half of the diagram typically depicts a *series* of state transitions.

Chapter Summary

In this chapter, you performed the following B.O.O.M. steps:

2. Discovery

    2a) Behavioral analysis

        i) Describe use cases (use-case description)

        ii) Describe state behavior (state-machine diagram)

            1. Identify states of critical objects

            2. Identify state transitions

            3. Identify state activities

            4. Identify composite states

            5. Identify concurrent states

New tools and concepts you learned in this chapter include the following:

- A *state-machine diagram* is a picture indicating how an object changes from one state to another.
- *State* refers to the status that an object may have at any given time. The state of the object determines what activities are performed, how the object responds to events, and so on.
- A *transition* is a change of state.
- An *event* is something that happens, causing the state of an object to change.
- A *guard* is a condition.
- A *state activity* is a process that occurs while an object is in a given state. It may be specified as Entry, Do, Exit, and so on.

- A *composite state* is a general state that encompasses more precise substates. *Substates* inherit the transitions of the composite state.

- *Concurrent states* are states that may occur or may apply to an object at the same time. The state holding the concurrent states is referred to by the UML as an *orthogonal* state.

Endnotes

[1]Unlike many of the other concepts in the UML, there is no single programming equivalent to a state—but they can be programmed. An object's state is often tracked with a state attribute; the object's operations can then be written so that they depend upon this state attribute. Other programming mechanisms involve design patterns that use a combination of associations and generalizations to model states.

[2]*UML Superstructure Specification*, v2.2, OMG, 2009, page 550.

[3]*UML Superstructure Specification*, v2.2, OMG, 2009, page 554.

[4]*UML Superstructure Specification*, v2.2, OMG, 2009, page 582.

CHAPTER 8

GATHERING ACROSS-THE-BOARD BUSINESS RULES WITH CLASS DIAGRAMS

Chapter Objectives

In this chapter, you will do the following:

- Learn a step-by-step interviewing process for uncovering business rules regarding the precise relationships between business classes.
- Document these relationships in accordance with the UML.
- Through this process, decrease the likelihood that the developers will introduce database and screen-design errors.

B.O.O.M. steps covered in this chapter include the following:

2b) Structural analysis
  i)   Identify entity classes
  ii) Model generalizations
  iii) Model transient roles
  iv) Model whole/part relationships
  v)   Analyze associations
  vi) Analyze multiplicity

You'll learn to use the following tools/concepts in this chapter:

- Entity class
- Class diagram
- Inheritance
- Aggregation
- Composite aggregation
- Association
- Multiplicity
- Object diagram
- Link

Step 2b: Structural Analysis

In Chapter 7, "Lifecycle Requirements for Key Business Objects," you worked with state-machine diagrams. You looked at state-machine diagrams together with activity diagrams because those are your main options for describing the dynamic nature of the business—the sequencing of business events and activities. If you want to highlight activities, use activity diagrams; if you want to shine the spotlight on a specific object and how it changes in response to conditions and events, use the state-machine diagram.

The state-machine diagram started you thinking about the dynamic nature of business objects. Objects are the fundamental "atoms" that make up a business system. In this chapter, you'll learn to analyze the static, structural nature of business objects—the rules that apply *irrespective of time*. An example of such a rule is the maximum number of Peace Committees that can handle a case. The rule about this maximum does not change over time and is, therefore, part of the structural model.

Structural Model

A *structural model* is an abstract representation of what the system is. It represents the aspects of a system that are not related to time, such as the kinds of subjects tracked by the system, how these subjects are related to each other, and the information and business rules that relate to each one. The main diagram you'll be using for structural modeling is the *class diagram*.

Output from this step consists of the following:

- Class diagram
- Package diagram
- Composite structure diagram
- Object diagram

FAQs about Structural Analysis

You may be wondering why the business analyst should bother with structural modeling when business stakeholders are primarily concerned with what they can do with the system—an issue that is addressed in the behavioral model. In this section, we'll look at this and other frequently asked questions.

Why Isn't the Business Analyst's Job Over after Behavioral Analysis?

The dynamic, behavioral requirements lack a complete description of the "nouns" of the business. Also, the precise numerical relationship between the nouns is undefined. For example, in Chapter 2, "The BA's Perspective on Object Orientation," you read about a municipality with a human-resources (HR) system. Because they had not worked out the numerical relationship between employees and unions, they ended up purchasing an HR system that allowed an employee to belong to only one union when in fact some employees belonged to more than one. As a result, the software could make only a single deduction of union dues for each paycheck, the data tables were set up incorrectly, and the input screens used to assign employees to unions were incorrect. Guess who had to pay for all those corrections? (Answer: the municipality.) Had the BAs performed a proper structural analysis, they would have included the employee-union rule in the requirements documentation, diminishing the chances that it would be missed in the software and ensuring that, at the very least, the cost of the fix would be borne by the developers.

Aren't These Issues Addressed in the Behavioral Analysis?

It is true that many of these issues are contained within the system use-case descriptions. For example, in a banking system, the relationship between customers and accounts might be found in an Open New Account system use case. However, because behavioral analysis does not include a rigorous approach to examining the "nouns," it is likely that some important requirements will be missed. Also, because these rules are dispersed throughout the use cases, there is the possibility for internal inconsistency within the BRD. For example, a system use case Open New Account might allow up to three people to co-own an account, while a system use case Query Account Activity allows for only one owner. In addition, future requirements for enhancements to the system may add new inconsistencies.

What Does Structural Analysis Have to Do with This?

Structural analysis focuses on the "nouns" of the system. It provides a rigorous method for ensuring that all of these nouns are fully analyzed and documented. Requirements that cut across system use cases but relate to the same classes of objects (nouns) are centralized in a set of diagrams and accompanying documentation. This makes it easier to ensure internal consistency within the BRD. Each system use-case description is verified against the structural model. As future system use cases are added, these too are checked against the structural model, ensuring that business rules are obeyed in future enhancements.

What Is the Context for Structural Modeling?

Use the structure diagrams as a guide for asking questions and as a form of shorthand during interviews. Later, include the diagrams in the BRD. They enable a seamless transition to development, since they present the business model in a form widely understood by OO developers.

What Issues Are Addressed During Structural Analysis?

OO structural analysis provides a step-by-step procedure for documenting the attributes and operations that apply to each type of business object and the numerical relationships between business objects, such as the fact that many customers may co-own a particular account.

Step 2bi: Identify Entity Classes

In this step, you identify the categories of business objects that must be tracked by the IT solution. These categories are referred to as entity classes.

Entity Class

An *entity class* is a *category* of business object, tracked by the system.

Rules about Objects and Classes

All objects of the same class must share the same operations, methods, and attributes.

FAQs about Entity Classes

Following are some frequently asked questions about entity classes and how they are analyzed by the business analyst.

Why Use the Term Entity Class? Why Not Just Class?

The term *entity* is used to differentiate these classes from other types of classes introduced into the system during the development stage.[1] An *entity class* describes objects that are tracked by the business. Since all the classes we'll be interested in as BAs are entity classes, I will sometimes just use the simpler term *class*.

What Are Some Examples of Entity Classes?

Some examples of entity classes are Payment and Customer.

What Attributes Are Specified for a Class?

The attributes specified for an entity class are information items typically stored by the business for a long period, such as the date and amount of a payment, the name and address of a customer, and the price of a product. Attributes usually show up in the user interface as field names on screens and reports. In the database, they show up as data fields (also called *columns*).

How Do You Come Up with a List of Entity Classes?

Review the system use-case documentation and human-interface requirements (screen mock-ups, report layouts, and so on). Any noun phrase appearing in these, such as Wholesale Customer, is a candidate class. (I use the term *candidate class* because the noun may represent something else, such as an attribute.) Consider also conducting interviews specifically for the purposes of structural analysis. Interview questions for finding classes and other structural modeling elements are interspersed throughout this chapter.

Indicating a Class in the UML

Figure 8.1 shows how to indicate classes in the UML.

Naming Conventions

Name a class with a singular noun phrase, such as Invoice or Retail Customer. Although the UML includes more formal naming conventions, these are more relevant to developers than to business analysts. As a BA, your prime interest is to enhance communication between business stakeholders and the technical team, and an informal naming convention works best for this purpose.[2]

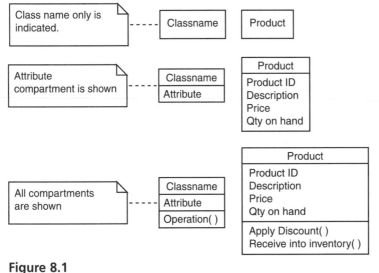

Figure 8.1
Classes in UML.

Grouping Classes into Packages

If the model contains a large number of classes, it's worth grouping them so they'll be easier to manage. The UML provides the package symbol to stand for a container. We've seen this before with respect to use cases. Here, we will use the package to contain classes and class diagrams. Class packages may contain other packages for as many levels as necessary.

It's helpful to depict all of the packages on a single diagram—a simple form of the class diagram. When using a modeling tool such as Rational Rose, it is a good practice to make this the top-level *main* diagram. Used this way, the diagram acts as a navigation map—each package icon links to the class diagram that depicts all of the classes in the package.

There is no rule (although there are suggestions[3]) for how to group the classes into packages. One recommended approach, applicable to many business contexts, is to define packages according to the common "flavors" of business classes: People and Organizations, Products and Services, and Events/Transactions. Figure 8.2 shows this approach, which you'll use in the case study.

Figure 8.2
Example: Class packages for business entities in the CPP system.

The Package Diagram

A *package diagram* is simply a large package symbol with the package's classes drawn inside it. This form of diagram was valid in previous versions of the UML standard, but the name for the diagram, *package diagram*, is new to UML 2.[4] Figure 8.3 is an example of an early draft of the package diagram for the Product and Services package for a telecommunications company.

Figure 8.3
A package diagram for a telecommunications company.

The best way to organize the diagrams is to use the package diagram to show only classes, their attributes, and operations; show relationships between the classes on separate diagrams. (An exception may be made for generalization relationships, which are often shown on the package diagram.) Don't try to say too much on any one diagram. Instead, draw a new diagram to highlight a specific aspect of the system, such as a particular inheritance hierarchy. This way, each diagram gets across one main idea, making it easy to interpret.

Why It's Worth Pausing to Do Some Structural Modeling When Stakeholders Introduce New Terms

I once worked on the model for a telecommunications system. My contacts in the company kept talking about "product groups." It was only after I began to develop the structural model that it became apparent there was no consensus on the meaning of this business term. Half the people on the project thought it referred to a group of products and services marketed together under one package price; others thought it referred to a particular telephone line and all the services attached to it. This type of ambiguity often crops up in the requirements and can lead to serious errors in the software. By creating a structural model, you'll ensure that there is a clear understanding of each business noun that appears in the requirements.

Tip

Dedicate interview time specifically for the purpose of structural modeling. This helps you learn the business terminology relevant to the project.

Interview Questions for Finding Classes

The first step of structural modeling is to identify the classes of objects that comprise the business. These may be found through a review of existing documentation (for example, by searching for business nouns in the use-case model) and through direct interview questions.

To discover candidate classes, ask stakeholders:

- What people and organizations does the system keep track of? Examples include customer, card holder, and board member.
- What events and transactions does the system keep a record of? An example is a sale.
- What products and services does the system keep a record of? Examples include checking accounts (products) and check returns (services).

Challenge Questions

Ask these follow-up questions about candidate classes:

- Is it important that the business track this class? If not, exclude it from the list of classes. For example, in a point-of-sale system for a corner grocery store, you would exclude the class Customer because the store doesn't keep track of its customers.
- If two candidate classes appear similar, is there any attribute, operation, method, or relationship that applies to one class but not the other? If the answer is yes, treat each candidate as a separate class.[5] Otherwise list one class only for both. For example, Digital Cell Phone and Analog Cell Phone each have specialized attributes, although they also share others. List them as two separate classes.[6] On the other hand, Green Cell Phone and Blue Cell Phone share the same attributes and operations and do not represent distinct classes. (A Color attribute in the Cell Phone class will suffice to distinguish between them.)
- Is the candidate class merely a piece of information about something else? If the answer is yes, you are not dealing with a class at all, but an attribute. For example, Customer Name is not a class; it's an attribute of the Customer class.
- Is the candidate class an alias for a previously recorded class? Sometimes, business stakeholders use two names for the same thing. If this is the case, ask them to settle on one phrase as the main name; document this as the *class name*. Treat the other one as an *alias*—an alternative name for the class.[7] For example, Client is an alias for Customer. If your BRD includes a business glossary (a dictionary of business terms), then add the alias to this glossary.

For Now, Focus on the Classes

The goal of this step is to produce a simple list of classes. Anything else you pick up at this stage is gravy. For example, if you pick up any attributes now, by all means record them, but don't spend too much time on them.

Here are some follow-up questions to ask users about selected classes:

- Could you provide a brief description of the class? (The description should be one paragraph.)
- Could you provide a couple of examples of the class?
- Could you tell me a few pieces of information (attributes) that you'd track about each example (object)?

Supporting Class Documentation

Document the following for each class:

- Class (use a singular noun phrase to name the class)
- Alias
- Description
- Examples
- Sample attributes

Here is an example:

Class:	Customer
Alias:	Client
Description:	Person or company that does business with us
Examples:	Stan Plotnick, Minelli Enterprises
Sample Attributes:	Name, Mailing Address, Credit Rating

Case Study H1: Entity Classes

Seeking to define the nouns used within the CPP, you conduct an interview with business subject matter experts. You ask them what types of people and organizations are tracked by the CPP, what types of events or transactions occur, and what products and services are offered by the CPP. Here's what you learn:

- The organization consists of CPP members who work for the head office. It administers a network of Peace Committees throughout South Africa.

- When a Peace Committee member is informed about a case (dispute), he or she alerts the Peace Committee, which then meets with each party to the dispute and organizes a Peace Gathering.

- Various attendees participate in the Peace Gathering. An attendee may be a person or may represent an agency involved in the case.

- All attendees at a gathering must be recorded. Extra information is kept about attendees who are there as observers (for example, information about an observer's relationship to the parties involved in the dispute is recorded).

- When a case has been dealt with, various payments are disbursed to the personnel involved in dealing with the case and to various community funds. (The next several items explain the disbursement of funds.) Payments are not made to the parties involved in the dispute.

- The Peace Committee members involved with the case are paid a standard amount.

- Also, payments are made into three fund accounts, which the system tracks internally: Admin Fund Account, Peace Building Fund Account, and Microenterprise Fund Account. The same fields are tracked for each of these funds.[8]

- Payments are also deposited into Peace Committee (PC) member accounts for each PC member involved in the case.

- Internal accounts are kept so that the CPP is aware of the current balances and payments for all fund accounts, Peace Committee member accounts, and the cash account.

Your Next Step

Start developing the structural model, showing only the classes you've derived from the notes.

Suggestions

First, create a main diagram showing only the People and Organizations, Products and Services, and Events/Transactions packages. Then create a package diagram for each package. Use the aforementioned interview questions and challenge questions to pick out the classes mentioned in the preceding notes. When you discover a class, add it to the appropriate package diagram.

Case Study H1: Resulting Documentation

Figure H1.1 shows the diagrams that you've developed after determining the entity classes.

Events/ Transactions		
Payment	Peace Gathering	Case

Figure H1.1
Diagrams reflecting the entity classes for the CPP system.

Notes on the Model

The model includes classes such as Person and Agency because they came up during the interviews, and it seems likely that they will each have special attributes. For example, every person in the system is likely to be tracked with attributes (such as name and address) that stay with the person, whether that person is a CPP member, a party in the dispute, or so on.

Only one Fund Account class is included, because the system treats all fund accounts the same way: a single process for calculating payments to a fund could be described, the attributes kept on each fund are the same, and so on. Cash Account is treated as a separate class because it is different from other funds and accounts. For example, payments are *not* deposited to a cash account when a case is processed, whereas payments may be deposited to all the other accounts and funds.

A PC member and his or her corresponding account could have been modeled with a single class, but two classes were used because the organization often treats them separately. There are many instances where account information is irrelevant and only biographical information and operations should be accessible.

Step 2bii: Model Generalizations

The upcoming steps deal with the issue of subtyping.[9] Subtypes allow you to model business objects that share some things in common but have other, distinguishing characteristics.

Subtyping

A *subtype* is a smaller category within a larger category. Subtyping is useful because it allows the business analyst to make statements about general types that automatically apply to all subtypes. You'll need to distinguish between two kinds of subtypes: full-time and part-time.

Full-Time Subtypes

A general category can be split into a number of full-time subtypes if objects cannot change from one subtype to the other over their lifetime. For example, in a non-coed dormitory where dormers are processed differently according to their sex, Male Dormer and Female Dormer are two full-time subtypes of Dormer. Use the generalization relationship to describe full-time subtypes.

Part-Time Subtypes

Part-time subtypes are unstable. Use part-time subtypes to model objects that may change from subtype to subtype during their lifespan. For example, in a welfare system, there are two subtypes of Client: Employed Client and Unemployed Client. Because a client might change from one to the other, the two subtypes are part-time. The UML does not have a specific relationship icon for part-time subtypes. B.O.O.M. uses the UML *association* relationship, stereotyped as Plays Role, and refers to the relationship as a *transient role*. (More on this relationship in the section "Step 2biii: Model Transient Roles" later in this chapter.)

Generalization

Use the generalization relationship to model full-time subtypes. The relationship points from the subtype (specialized class) to the more general type (generalized class).

> ### Memory Jog: Generalization
>
> If class *x* is a kind of class *y*, then class *x* is said to be a *specialized class* (or specialization) of the generalized class *y*. Objects of class *x* inherit all the features of class *y*, such as attributes, operations, and relationships. To this definition, we now add the following: For proper use of generalization, the subtypes must be full-time. An object cannot change from one specialized class to another during its lifetime.[10]

Why Model Generalizations?

Use of generalization reduces redundancy in the requirements; requirements that apply across a number of classes may be stated only once. Also, generalization allows you to specify rules that extend into the future; rules stated for a generalized class apply to all current and *future* specialized classes.

Sources of Information for Finding Generalizations

Ask leading questions during your interviews:

- Use the initial class diagrams of classes you drew in the previous step as a guide for questions. Ask interviewees if any of the classes are variations on others. (A more detailed guide to questions follows in this section.)
- Review the system use-case documentation. Anywhere the documentation indicates that there is more than one "kind of" something (for example, two kinds of accounts), generalization may be indicated.

Rules Regarding Generalization

- The specialized class inherits all the attributes, operations, and relationships of the generalized class.
- The specialized class may have additional attributes, operations, and relationships beyond those inherited from the generalized class.
- The specialized class may have a unique *polymorphic*[11] method for carrying out an operation it inherits from the generalized class.
- According to the UML, a specialized class may inherit from more than one generalized class. This is called *multiple inheritance*. Many IT organizations limit the use of multiple inheritance because it can lead to ambiguities. For example, if a specialized class inherits two methods for the same operation from two generalized classes, which one applies? Check with your organization before using multiple inheritance.

Generalization Example from the Case Study

An observer is an (that is, a kind of) attendee. The specialized class is Observer; the generalized class is Attendee. The specialized class Observer inherits all the attributes, operations, and relationships of the generalized class Attendee. Observer may also have additional attributes, operations, and relationships. Also, through polymorphism, an object belonging to the class Observer may perform an operation inherited from the generalized Attendee class in its own unique way.

Don't Go Overboard

Remember that the use of generalization is meant to make life easier for the BA (ultimately). If the addition of a generalized class doesn't buy you anything, there is no reason to model it.

If you are unsure whether to list a generalized class, include it for now and reassess your decision later. If, toward the end of analysis, there are no generic attributes, operations, or relationships that you can specify for the generalized class, you may discard it then.

Remember that the specializations must be full-time: An object of a specialized class cannot change into a different specialization. For example, a Fund Account does not turn into a Peace Committee Member Account. (Part-time subtypes are dealt with in the next step.)

Indicating Generalization in the UML

Figure 8.4 demonstrates how you express generalization in a diagram.

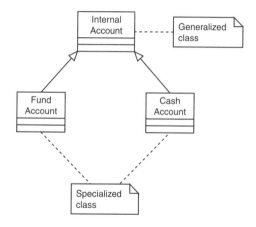

Figure 8.4
Indicating generalization in the UML.

Interview Questions for Finding Generalizations

Use the following list of questions during an interview to identify possible cases of generalization. (Verify any decision made at this point using the challenge questions that follow.)

- Can the following statement be made about any two classes? "Class A *is a kind of* class B." If the answer is yes, model class A as a specialized class of B. Model B as the generalized class. For example, a Cash Account is a kind of Internal Account.
- Are any classes the same in some respects but different in others? If the answer is yes, the two classes are specializations of a generalized class. For example, Peace Committee Member Account and Fund Account are similar but different. Both are specializations of Internal Account.

■ Is there any point where the business treats two otherwise distinct classes in a generic fashion? If the answer is yes, the two classes are specializations of a generalized class. For example, a report on account activity for all objects of the generalized class Internal Account prints the same information about all kinds of accounts, regardless of whether they are of subtype Fund Account, Cash Account, or Peace Committee Member Account.

Challenge Questions

■ Can you substitute a specialized class wherever the generalized class is used in the requirements and still have valid specs? (This is called the *rule of substitution*.) If the answer is no, then don't use generalization.

■ Is there at least one generic rule (an attribute, operation, or relationship) that can be stated for the generalized class? If not, it may not be a worthwhile generalization. For example, Telephone Line and Gas Line are two kinds of lines but they're treated as *specialized classes* of the Line class only if they have some things in common. If you think that you may uncover some commonalities later in the analysis, keep the generalization for now and reassess your decision later.

Advanced Challenge Questions

With generalization, the subtype of an object must be full-time—that is, stable during its lifetime—otherwise, a transient role is indicated. The following challenge questions can help determine whether the subtyping can be treated through generalization:

■ Can the object change its subtype during its lifetime? If it can, then don't use generalization or specialization to describe the relationship between the classes. For example, an Employee changes from being On Leave to Working. These are not considered as specializations of Employee.[12]

■ Can an object be more than one subtype at the same time? If it can, don't use generalization or specialization. For example, a person might be a CPP member and a Peace Committee member at the same time. CPP Member and Peace Committee Member are *not* treated as specialized classes of Person.[13]

■ Can an object act as more than one instance of the subtype? If it can, then don't use generalization. For example, a person might be classified as a Party to a Dispute twice, once for each involvement; you cannot use generalization to describe the relationship between Person and Party to Dispute.[14]

Case Study H2: Generalizations

Interviews to identify generalizations yield the following notes:

1. An observer is a special kind of attendee (at a gathering). Extra data is tracked about observers over and above that kept for other attendees.

2. A person may be a CPP member as well as a Peace Committee member. The person may become a CPP member or a Peace Committee member at any time.

3. A party to dispute is a person or an agency. One person may be viewed as many parties to dispute. For example, if one person were a party to five disputes in five different cases, that person would be considered as five separate instances of a party to a dispute. One record of biographical information is kept for the person and one for *each* involvement.

4. All internal accounts are identified with a generic account number, and some common information is kept for all accounts (account balance and so on). However, additional information is kept on an account based on its type, which would be either Cash Account, Fund Account, or Peace Committee Member Account.

Your next step is to model the generalization relationships that these notes imply.

Suggestions

Create a new diagram for each grouping of full-time subtypes. Use the challenge questions to ensure that you've used generalization properly. If you discover any part-time subtypes, make a note about them; you'll add them to the model later.

Case Study H2: Resulting Documentation

Figure H2.1 shows the resulting diagrams for each group of full-time subtypes.

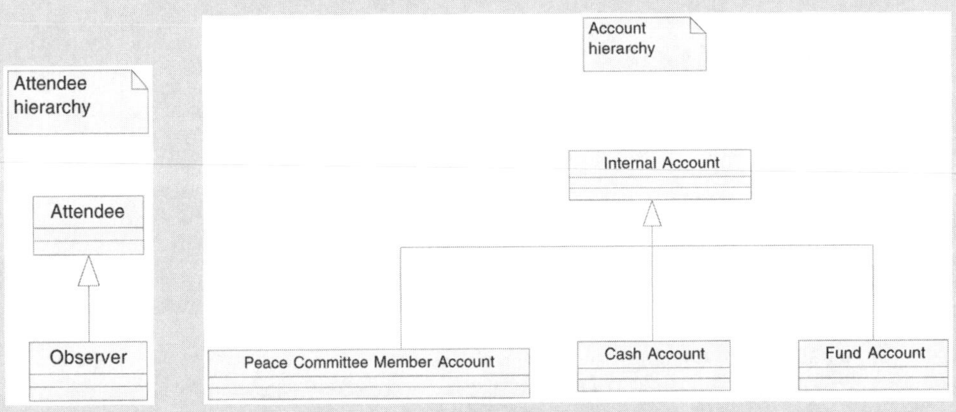

Figure H2.1
Full-time subtypes.

Notes on the Model

The numbers in the following list correspond to those used earlier for the interview notes:

1. Observer is a specialized class of Attendee.

2. CPP Member is not a specialized class of Person because the same person may also be classified as Peace Committee Member[15] and because the subtype is not full-time.

3. Generalization does not apply. To be a specialization, a particular person could only be viewed as at most one party to a dispute, which is clearly not the case here.

4. Generalization applies. Internal Account is the generalized class, with each Account type being a specialization.

Step 2biii: Model Transient Roles

Next, you model the part-time subtypes that you skipped over in the previous step. A *transient role* is a part-time subtype representing a role that an object may play at one time or another during its existence—but may not play at other times.[16] (The term is not part of the UML.)

Is It a *State* or a *Transient Role*?

You may be wondering if you can handle part-time subtypes as *states* on a state-machine diagram. The answer is that, in fact, a part-time subtype can be modeled both ways—in the state-machine diagrams as a state and on class diagrams as a transient role. It's a question of what you want to communicate. If you want to get across how the object changes in response to events, use the state diagram; if you want to communicate the rules that govern how an object, acting in a given role, is related to other objects, use the class diagram with transient roles.

For example, in the case study, it is important to describe the lifecycle of a Case object as it goes from the Initiated state through its intermediate states, and all the way to Paid and Not Payable in response to events and conditions. The state-machine diagram explains this best. On the other hand, it is not important to explain how a Case object's relationships to other classes change based on its evolving states—so there is little value in treating these states as transient roles in the structural model.

The situation is different for a Participant object. Here, there isn't much to be gained by explaining the lifecycle of a Participant object as he or she changes from being in the state CPP Member to Peace Committee Member and so on, since the events that cause these changes are fairly self-evident. (For example, a participant becomes a Peace Committee member by joining a Peace Committee.) For that reason, a state-machine diagram of a participant adds little value. However, it *is* important to nail down exactly how the various Participant object roles—such as CPP Member, Peace Committee Member, Attendee, and so on—are related to other classes, such as Case, Peace Committee, and Peace Gathering. This is best explained by including these roles in the class diagrams.

Example of Transient Role

An employee is assigned the role of a business analyst when hired but later changes roles to become a systems analyst. Business Analyst and Systems Analyst are *transient roles* of an Employee object.

How Does a Transient Role Differ from a Specialization?

- An object's specialization cannot change during its lifetime; an object's transient role may.
- Objects of a specialized class *inherit* properties from the generalized class. Inheritance does not apply, however, to transient roles.

Some Terminology

If objects belonging to class A have a part-time role, B, then:

- A is the primary class
- B is the transient role
- The relationship between A and B is "plays a role."

(These terms are not part of the UML.[17])

Why Indicate Transient Roles?

The developers need to know whether the subtyping you indicate is full-time (generalization) or part-time (transient role). Different design and coding solutions apply in each case.[18] The only people who really know how stable the relationship is are the users—and as their ombudsperson, you are in the best position to find this out.

Also, by indicating a subtype as a transient role rather than as a specialization, you are signaling to yourself that you need to follow up with extra questions that do not apply to specializations. (These involve *multiplicity*, discussed in the section "Step 2bvi: Analyze Multiplicity" later in this chapter.)

Rules about Transient Roles

- It is possible (though not necessary) for objects of the primary class to have more than one transient role at a time.
- An object may change its transient role during its lifetime.
- By indicating that a primary class plays a role, you are not specifying that every object of the primary class *has* to play this role—only that it might do so.

Indicating Transient Roles

The concept of a transient role is not part of the UML. However, the UML allows for extensions to the language through specialized use of its symbols, referred to as *stereotyping*. We'll invent a <<plays role>> association stereotype to convey this relationship, as shown in Figure 8.5.

Sources of Information for Finding Transient Roles

Interview the stakeholders regarding the classes that you discovered in the previous steps. A guide to questions follows.

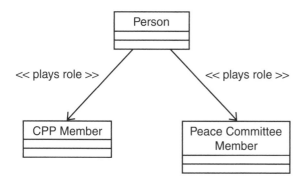

Figure 8.5
Indicating a transient role as an association stereotype.

Interview Questions for Determining Transient Roles

To find transient roles, ask the following questions:

- Can an object wear many hats? If the answer is yes, each "hat" is a transient role. For example, can an employee have more than one role in the organization? If so, create a new class for each transient role, and draw a Plays Role relationship between the primary class and the roles.

- Can an object of a given class change its subtype during its lifespan? If the answer is yes, the subtype is a transient role. For example, any person in the CPP organization may change from being a CPP member to a Peace Committee member, so these are considered transient roles of Person.

What If a Group of Specialized Classes Can All Play the Same Role?

If *all* specializations of a generalized class can play the same role, indicate the generalized class as the primary class.[19] For example, if members of the classes Person and Agency (two specializations of Participant[20]) may attend a Peace Gathering, indicate that Participant (generalized class) plays the role of Attendee. It is understood that this means that a person can be an attendee and that an agency can be an attendee.

Case Study H3: Transient Roles

You continue your interviews, intending to elicit requirements about transient roles. You review the classes in the People and Organization package that relate to a role that a person or agency plays when involved with the CPP. You verify that there are no additional roles. Your next objective in the interview is to find out whether each role can be played only by a person, only by an agency—or either a person or an agency. To simplify the next series of questions, you work with stakeholders on defining a term that means "either a person or an agency." You settle on the term *participant*. To record and explain this new class, you draw a new class diagram. (Hint: The diagram should treat Person and Agency as two kinds of Participant objects.) Next, referring to the existing People and Organization package, you select each class that represents a role and ask stakeholders whether it can be played only by a person, only by an agency, or by any participant. You record each answer on the model as you get it by drawing the appropriate transient role relationship. Here's what you learn in response to your questions:

- Any participant (that is, a person or an agency) may be a party to a dispute. Each time a participant acts as a party to a dispute, separate statistics and data are recorded about the involvement.

- Any participant (that is, a person or an agency) may be an attendee at a Peace Gathering. Each time a participant is an attendee at a gathering, separate statistics and information are tracked.

- Only a person may be a CPP member or a Peace Committee member (that is, an agency may not be a member). Furthermore, a person may cease being a CPP member at any time and become a Peace Committee member. A person may also be a member of both organizations at the same time.

Your next step is to finalize the class diagrams describing the new class, Participant, and the new transient roles.

Case Study H3: Resulting Documentation

Figure H3.1 shows the diagrams that describe the transient roles that you identified.

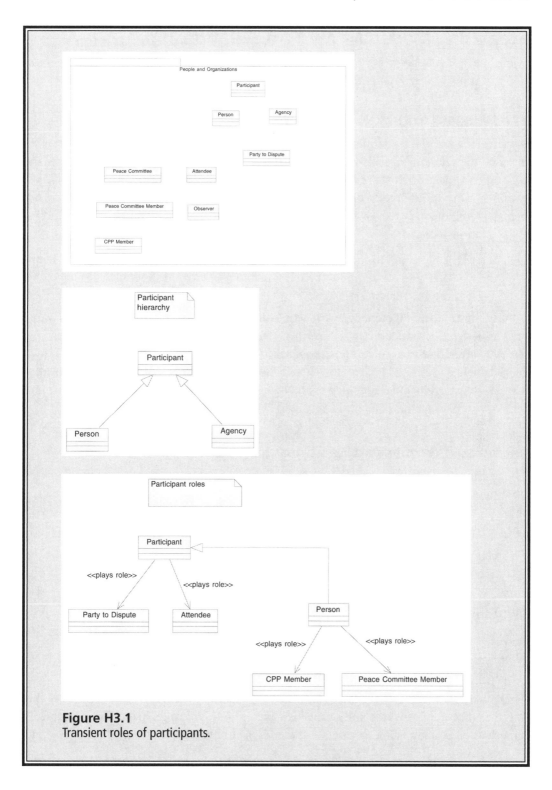

Figure H3.1
Transient roles of participants.

Step 2biv: Model Whole/Part Relationships

Some objects consist of other objects. In OO, you model these relationships using *aggregation* and *composite aggregation*.

The "Whole" Truth

Aggregation (without a qualifier) and *composite aggregation* (also known as *composition*)[21] describe the relationship between a whole and its parts. Aggregation is the more general term: It just means that there is *some* kind of whole/part relationship. Composite aggregation is more specific: It means that the whole owns the part entirely; the part may not belong simultaneously to any other whole. Use the following guidelines to decide which of these relationships to use:

- If a part can belong to more than one whole and the part continues to exist when the whole is destroyed, model the relationship as Aggregation. Words that suggest aggregation include *collection*, *list*, and *group*.

- If a part is totally "owned" by the whole and the part ceases to exist when the whole is destroyed, model the relationship as Composite Aggregation. (Keep in mind, however, that even in composite aggregation, a part can be preserved if it is detached and saved before the whole is destroyed.) Words that suggest composite aggregation include *composed of* and *component*.

- If you are not sure, specify Aggregation.

Examples of Whole/Part Relationships

The relationship between a catalog and the products that it includes is aggregation. On the other hand, the relationship between the catalog and the catalog line items (that refer to these products) is composite aggregation because, if the catalog is discontinued, so are its line items.

The relationship between a travel booking and its flight, hotel, and car-rental reservations is composite aggregation, since the cancellation of a booking also removes its reservations.

Why Indicate Whole/Part Relationships?

Aggregation is a strategy for reuse. If the same kind of part is used in more than one whole, the requirements for the part's class only need to be written once. Later, if requirements for the part change, they need to be specified only once to apply throughout the project.

These relationships also help the business analyst to distinguish between properties that are important for the whole and properties that are relevant to the parts. For example, in a mechanic's garage system, requirements that apply to a vehicle might include the attribute

Assembly Date and the rule that each vehicle may be owned by one or more owners; requirements that apply to vehicle's part might include the attributes Replacement Date and Part #.

How Far Should You Decompose a Whole into Its Parts?

Take things as far as the business requires. For example, a used-car lot might have only a Vehicle class to describe its inventory, whereas a service garage might require a Vehicle class as well as a Vehicle Component class. The difference is that only the service garage needs to keep track of the components of a vehicle.

Sources of Information for Finding Aggregation and Composite Aggregation

Conduct interviews with stakeholders. Base your interview questions on the list of classes you compiled in the previous steps. A guide to questions follows. You can also discover whole/part relationships by reviewing screens, reports, layouts, and so on. Parts are often displayed along with the whole to which they belong. Also, review the system use-case descriptions; if you discover any reference to parts, part attributes, or business operations related to parts, include the parts in the model. For example, a system for an auto-repair shop may include a system use case Service Vehicle that refers to the next inspection dates for various parts of an automobile.

Rules Regarding Aggregation and Composite Aggregation

- Parts do not inherit attributes, operations, or relationships from the whole—or vice versa.[22]

- Aggregation and composite aggregation do not imply full-time links between objects. The whole can drop or add parts during its lifetime.

- If a part dies when the whole dies, model the relationship between them as composite aggregation. For example, the relationship between a policy and the riders attached to a policy is a composite-aggregation relationship.

- Specify any other whole/part relationship, for which the preceding rule does not apply, as aggregation.

- Don't lose too much sleep over whether a whole/part relationship is aggregation or composite aggregation. If you're not sure, specify aggregation.

Indicating Aggregation and Composite Aggregation in the UML

Figure 8.6 shows how to indicate aggregation and composite aggregation in a UML diagram.

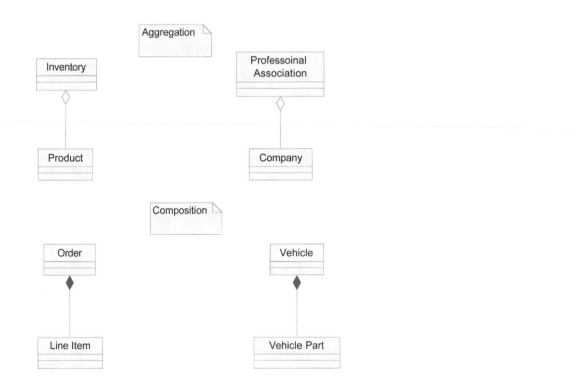

Figure 8.6
Aggregation and composite aggregation.

The Composite Structure Diagram

UML 2 has introduced a new diagram for indicating composite aggregation, the *composite structure diagram*,[23] which gives a more intuitive view of a composite. The idea is simply to show the component parts inside the icon representing the whole, as shown in Figure 8.7.

Figure 8.7
Composite structure diagram.

This type of diagram is useful for describing the connections between component parts. For example, Figure 8.8 shows some of the component parts of a Vehicle object.

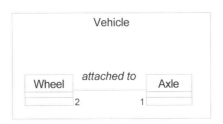

Figure 8.8
Showing component parts.

The lines between the components indicate that the parts are connected. The numbers in the diagram are *multiplicities*, which are covered in the section "Step 2bvi: Analyze Multiplicity" later in this chapter. The diagram in Figure 8.8, for example, specifies that each wheel is attached to one axle, and each axle to two wheels.

Interview Questions for Determining Aggregation and Composite Aggregation

- Is one object a part of another object? If the answer is yes, indicate either composite aggregation or aggregation.

- Is one object a collection or list of other objects? If the answer is yes, then a whole/part relationship is indicated. The last two questions in this list will help you decide whether to use aggregation or composite aggregation. As a rule of thumb, in most cases a list or collection is handled with aggregation. For example, an inventory is a collection—that is, an aggregation—of products.

- Is one object an organization consisting of individual members? If the answer is yes, then indicate a whole/part relationship. Whether you use aggregation or composite aggregation depends on the precise nature of the two classes involved. If you are specifying the relationship between the organization and a membership in the organization, use composite aggregation. If you are specifying the relationship between the organization and the independent bodies that belong to it, specify aggregation. If you're not sure, use aggregation.

- When you destroy the whole, do you destroy its parts? If the answer is yes, use composite aggregation. For example, when an invoice is removed from the system, all line items must also be removed.

- Can one object be a part of more than one group? If the answer is yes, then indicate aggregation. For example, a passenger might be part of two passenger manifests (lists)—one for each flight. Passenger List is an aggregate of Passengers.

Remember: If you are still not sure what to specify for a whole/part relationship, specify aggregation.

Challenge Question

- Does it really make sense to say that A is a part of B? If the answer is no, then you may not be dealing with aggregation or composite aggregation but with a more general relationship called an *association* (which is discussed later). For example, an Insurance Policy object is linked to a Customer object, but one is not part of the other.

Keep This in Mind

It is not a "big mistake" to confuse aggregation and another relationship you'll soon learn about, *association*. In fact, sometimes it's just a matter of semantics.

Case Study H4: Whole/Part Relationships

You continue your structural modeling session with subject matter experts, now focusing on whole/part relationships. First, you examine your model for organizations and notice the Peace Committee class. You ask stakeholders if it is important for the CPP to track the Peace Committee members who belong to each Peace Committee. Next, you look for objects that might be composed of other objects. Noting that a case is a record of everything that happens with respect to a dispute, you ask stakeholders to identify what its components might be—using existing classes as your guide. You also note that a Peace Gathering is a collection of attendees and ask stakeholders if it is important for the CPP to track which attendees showed up at which gatherings. This is what you find out:

1. The Peace Committee is an organization composed of Peace Committee members.

2. A case is a conglomerate of everything that is known and all actions taken with respect to a dispute. This includes Peace Gathering events, which are held as many times as necessary for a case. Each case also consists of a number of parties to the dispute.

3. Every time a Peace Gathering event is held, the CPP must keep track of all the attendees who made up the gathering.

4. One case may require many Peace Gatherings. Only one case is ever discussed during a Peace Gathering.

Your next step is to create a draft of the diagrams required to document your findings. Consider creating a separate diagram to describe each whole object's relationship to its parts.

Case Study H4: Resulting Documentation

Figure H4.1 shows the diagrams resulting from the information your interviews uncovered about whole/part relationships.

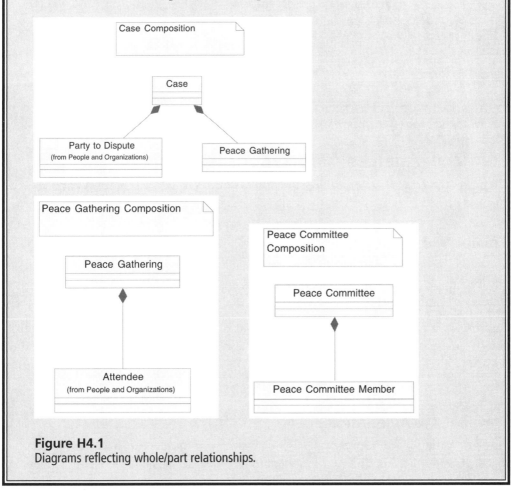

Figure H4.1
Diagrams reflecting whole/part relationships.

> **Notes on the Model**
> - When a Peace Committee disbands, all of its memberships are meaningless. Consequently, composite aggregation was used between Peace Committee and Peace Committee Member.
> - A Case object is a record of everything that happened with respect to the dispute. This includes actions taken to deal with the dispute, such as Peace Gatherings. Since without a case there is no Peace Gathering, and a Peace Gathering object cannot be a component of more than one Case object, composite aggregation was used. This situation is similar to the composite aggregation relationship between a call taken in a call center and all of the actions resulting from the call.
> - If there is no case, there are no parties to it. Consequently, the Case object is a composite aggregation of Party to Dispute.
> - There is no meaning to an Attendee object unless there is a Peace Gathering event to attend; consequently, composite aggregation was used.

Step 2bv: Analyze Associations

The next step is to discover all the remaining ways that the system tracks one class of business objects against another. Each of these relationships is called an association.

Examples of Association

Information about one object refers to information about another object. For example, invoice data refers to product information (such as description and price), so Invoice is associated with Product.

To carry out a business operation relating to one object, an operation relating to another object must be performed. For example, when a booking is canceled (an operation of Booking), flights must be updated to reflect the newly available seat. Booking is thus associated with Flight.

Why Indicate Association?

First, associations become part of the user's contract with the developers, ensuring that the software supports the business requirement to link business objects. Second, the modeling of associations is a necessary preliminary step toward getting more detailed requirements (known as *multiplicities*, discussed later in this chapter). Finally, associations are an important input for design. In the design phase, associations are implemented both in the code (as pointers) and in the database (as foreign keys). Keep in mind, though, that you are not dictating to the developers *how* to design the software; you are merely instructing them, through the associations you model, that the software needs to support the relationships— for example, that the software needs to track a case to the payments made against it.

Why Isn't It the Developers' Job to Find Associations?

You can't know what the associations are without knowing the way the business works. For example, only the business side knows whether payments are made against individual bills or against an account. It is the *BA's* role—not the developers'—to discover and document the rules that govern the business.

Discovering Associations

- Conduct interviews focused on the issue. Use the class diagrams you compiled in the previous steps for this purpose. Starting with key classes, interview users about possible associations to other classes.

- Review the system use-case model. A requirement of the form *[noun] [verb] [noun]*—where both nouns represent classes—often suggests an association. For example, Customer Makes Claim implies an association between Customer and Claim; the association is labeled Makes.

Rules Regarding Associations

- Most associations are *binary*—an object of one class is related to an object (or objects) in a different class. For example, each Case object is associated with Payment objects.

- An association may be *reflexive*, meaning that an object of the class is associated with another object of the same class. For example, one employee (the manager) manages other employees (team members).

- An association does not have to be named—but it is a good idea to do so in order to clarify its meaning. If you do name the association, make sure the name is not already used by any other association or class in the package. You may also add a small triangular arrowhead, shown in Figure 8.9, after the association name to indicate to the reader the direction in which to read the association.[24] This arrowhead is not required by the UML. It is often omitted by business analysts because the associations usually only make sense when read in one direction and because, by convention, the associations are read from left to right and top to bottom.

(Keep in mind, though, that the UML standard does not attach any formal significance to the relative placement—left, right, etc.—of an element on a diagram.) It is recommended that you use the arrowhead wherever you feel there might be any confusion about how to read the association.

Figure 8.9
This triangular arrowhead, placed after the association name,
indicates to the reader the direction in which to read the association.

- As an alternative (or in addition) to an association name, you may specify role names,[25] such as manager and team member (see Figure 8.10).
- Indicate associations as far up an inheritance hierarchy as possible. For example, if a transaction log were kept for all internal accounts, indicate an association from Transaction Log to the generalized class Internal Account, not to the specialized classes Fund Account, Peace Committee Member Account, and so on.
- If you are not sure if something is an aggregation or association, specify it as an association.

Figure 8.10 shows how to indicate associations in the UML.

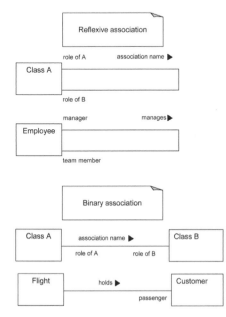

Figure 8.10
Indicating associations in the UML.

The Association Must Reflect the Business Reality

It all sounds so easy! And it often is. However, be careful; sometimes there are subtleties. For example, Figure 8.11 shows a diagram modeling a system that manages credit-card accounts.

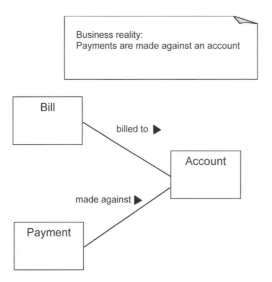

Figure 8.11
Bills and payments for credit-card accounts.

In Figure 8.11, a payment is made against an account, not against a bill. One consequence is that the system will not be able to track which bills have been paid and how much was paid on each bill. This may be adequate for credit-card payments, since they are not targeted to specific bills. Contrast this with Figure 8.12, which shows the model for a small business's accounts-receivable system.

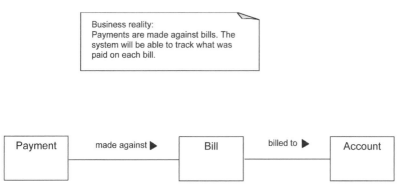

Figure 8.12
A small business's accounts-receivable system.

In Figure 8.12, the tracking of payments is more detailed; each payment is linked to a specific bill (or to specific bills). This type of tracking is usually required in an accounts-receivable system.

Redundant Association Rule of Thumb

As a rule of thumb, if your model includes an indirect way to get from class A to class B and a shortcut that goes right from A to B, throw out the shortcut. Figure 8.13 illustrates this type of redundancy.

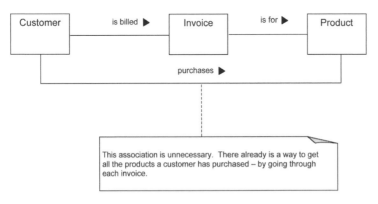

Figure 8.13
An example of redundant association

In Figure 8.13, the associations that run along the top of the diagram require the system to track all the invoices billed to a customer and for each invoice, to track all the products appearing on it. This implies that the system is required to track the products purchased by each customer. The shortcut adds nothing new, so it is removed.

Exception to the Rule of Thumb

Don't throw out the shortcut if it adds a new rule. Figure 8.14 shows an example.

In Figure 8.14, the top path requires that the system track all of the sales made by a salesperson, and for each sale the customer to whom it was billed. This implies that the system is required to track all the customers to whom a salesperson has made sales. But that's not what the shortcut says. It requires the system to associate salespeople with the customers for whom they are the prime contact. This is not the same as the first rule. For example, a salesperson may make sales to customers for whom he or she is *not* the prime contact—perhaps because the prime contact was away that day. As well, a salesperson may be the prime contact for a customer, yet not have made any sales to that customer—perhaps because the customer was only recently assigned to the salesperson. Since the two rules are distinct, the shortcut is retained.

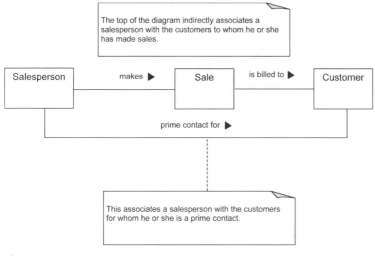

Figure 8.14
An example of a non-redundant association.

Modeling Object Links with Object Diagrams

Sometimes, you can get an idea across better by diagramming a connection between objects rather than a connection between classes. For example, suppose you wanted to show that a transfer is debited from a From Account and credited to a To Account. You could show the requirement using classes and associations as shown in Figure 8.15.

Figure 8.15
Showing requirements using classes and associations.

However, since From Account and To Account belong to the same class but play quite different roles, it might be clearer to diagram the business rule as shown in Figure 8.16.

Because the diagram in Figure 8.16 shows objects rather than classes, it is not a class diagram but another UML structure diagram called an *object diagram*. Note the following ways that this diagram differs from a class diagram:

- The names inside the boxes are names of objects, not classes. The following rules apply to object names:
  - Object names are underlined.
    - The full format of an object name is *object-name: class-name*. An example is *from account: Account*.
    - You may omit the object name, as in *:Transfer*.
    - Alternatively, you may omit the class name, as in *to account*.
- The relationship between the objects is referred to as a *link* (as opposed to an association, which relates classes). The link name should be underlined.

Tip

Use an object diagram instead of a class diagram if the situation you are trying to describe involves two objects that belong to the same class but act in different roles.

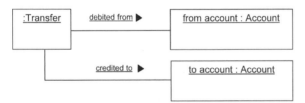

Figure 8.16
Diagramming objects of the same class with different roles.

How to Discover Associations

- During system use-case interviews, look out for statements of the form *X* [*verb*] *Y*, where *X* and *Y* represent business objects. They often reveal associations. For example, in the sentence "A Peace Committee supervises a case," Peace Committee is associated with Case; the association name is Supervises.
- Conduct interviews focused on associations using existing class diagrams. Try to match each class symbol with each of the other classes. Ask interviewees, "Do you need to be able to track one of these [objects] against one of those?" If the answer is yes, model the connection as an association on the diagram. Although this can be tedious when there are many classes, it does ensure that no associations slip through the cracks. For example, looking at Payment, you ask, "Do you need to match up a payment to a Peace Gathering, a case, a Peace Committee member account, an observer...?" From the answers, you note that Payment is associated with Case, since each payment must be tracked to a specific case. You also find out that Payment is associated with Peace Committee Member Account, since a payment

will be deposited into the account of each Peace Committee member who worked on a case. There is no direct association, however, between Payment and Peace Gathering, because a payment is not tracked to each Peace Gathering of a case.

- Examine screens, report layouts, and so on. If a screen or report ties together information about two objects, the objects are probably associated with each other.[26] For example, an invoice form includes a box for customer information: Customer is associated with Invoice.

- Look out for redundant associations. Use the rule of thumb you learned in this chapter: If there is a long, indirect route to get from one class to another and a shortcut, the shortcut is probably redundant. Just to be sure, ask whether the shortcut expresses anything new. If it does, keep it; if not, remove it.

- If there is a fine point about an association that you can't get across with the notations you've learned, add a note to explain the issue and attach it to the association. For example, in the following case study, a payment may be associated with either a Peace Committee member account or a fund account—but not both at the same time. There are sophisticated UML features, such as the Object Constraint Language (OCL), that allow the modeler to formally make these kinds of distinctions. These UML features are of great value to developers, particularly if they intend to generate code from UML design diagrams. However, features such as OCL are of limited use to the business analyst, who can best get across these distinctions to his or her audience with simple, informal notes.

Case Study H5: Associations

Next, you try to elicit from stakeholders the associations the CPP needs to keep track of. To do this, you use the existing class diagrams as your guide, asking stakeholders to identify any time one object needs to be tracked against another. For example, you ask, "Does the CPP need to keep track of what payments go with each case?" If the answer is yes, you draw an association line between the classes and prompt stakeholders for a meaningful verb to use as its name. At this point, you may learn that a case *generates* payments, providing the association name Generates. Based on this line of questioning, you learn the following:

- Each case generates a number of payments (subject to certain conditions).
- Each payment is withdrawn from the cash account and deposited into one of the fund accounts or into a Peace Committee member account. Each Peace Committee member owns a Peace Committee member account so that these deposits can be made.

Follow-up interviews regarding the system use case Update Cases results in the following notes:

- A Peace Committee handles a case throughout its lifespan.
- There is a special requirement for observers who attend a Peace Gathering: Each observer must be related in some way to one of the parties to the dispute.

Your Next Step

Create a draft of these associations (with descriptive text, if necessary) so they can be distributed to and verified by stakeholders.

Case Study H5: Resulting Documentation

Figure H5.1 shows the diagrams you've developed in determining the associations for the CPP.

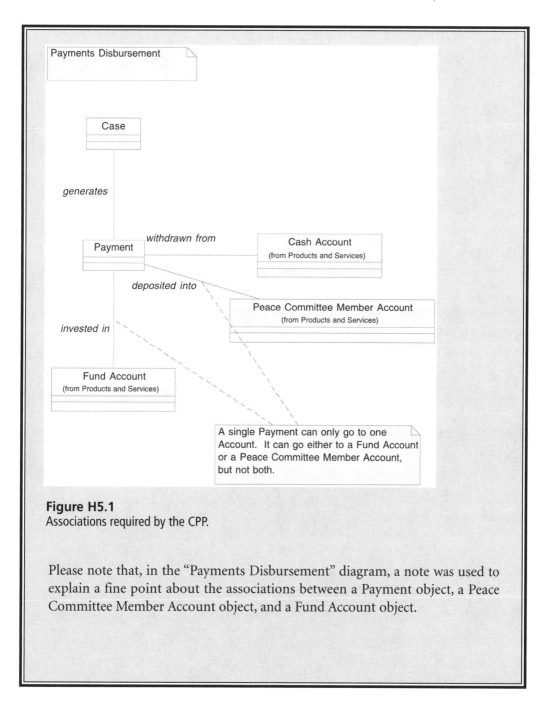

Figure H5.1
Associations required by the CPP.

Please note that, in the "Payments Disbursement" diagram, a note was used to explain a fine point about the associations between a Payment object, a Peace Committee Member Account object, and a Fund Account object.

Step 2bvi: Analyze Multiplicity

In this step, you model business rules that deal with the number of business objects that may be linked to each other.

Multiplicity

An indication of the number of objects that may participate in a transient role,[27] association, aggregation, or composite aggregation.

Example of Multiplicity

In the CPP, each Case object generates zero or more Payment objects. Each Payment object is generated by one and only one Case object.

Why Indicate Multiplicity?

If you don't specify multiplicity, the software may not support important business rules, such as the number of customers who can co-own an account or the number of beneficiaries who can be listed for an insurance policy.

Indicating Multiplicity in the UML

Figure 8.17 shows how to indicate multiplicity in the UML.

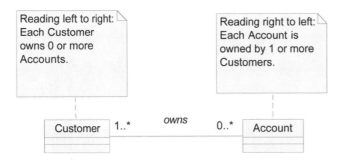

Figure 8.17
Multiplicity in UML.

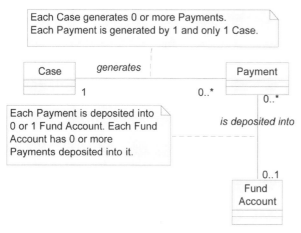

Figure 8.17
Multiplicity in UML (continued).

Rules Regarding Multiplicity

- Indicate multiplicity at every tip of every UML symbol indicating a transient role, association, aggregation, or composite aggregation.
- Indicate a multiplicity as follows:

    0..1   Zero or one

    0..*   Zero or more

    *   Zero or more (an alternative to 0..*)

    1..*   One or more

    1   One and only one

    a..b   From a through b, as in 1..5

- Each association generates two different sentences, one in each direction. When reading an association from class A to class B, ignore the multiplicity next to class A. When reading from left to right, piece together the sentence as follows: "Each [*class name on left side of association*] [*association name*] [*multiplicity on right side*] [*class name on right side*]." For example, "Each Case generates 0 or more Payments." When reading from right to left, reverse the process. For example, "Each Payment is generated by one and only one Case."
- Do not specify multiplicity along a generalization arrow.
- In a composite aggregation, the multiplicity adjacent to the class representing the whole must not be greater than one. (This is just the diagramming implication of the rule that, in a composite aggregation relationship, a part may not belong to more than one whole.)

Sources of Information for Finding Multiplicity

Conduct interviews, using your class diagrams as a guide for interviewing. A guide for questioning follows.

The Four Interview Questions for Determining Multiplicity

Conduct an interview using all your existing class diagrams as source documents. The interview is over when you have answered all the following questions for *each* transient role, association, aggregation, or composite aggregation in the model:

- Consider one object belonging to class A. What is the minimum number of class B objects to which it could be tied? (Common answers are zero and one.) Just to be sure, follow up with, "Is there any way it could be zero?" For example, looking at one case, "What is the minimum number of payments that might be posted against it? Is there any way there might be no payments on a case?" (The answer is that there may be zero payments for two reasons: The case may not have advanced to the payment stage yet, or the case was deemed Not Payable.)

- Consider one object belonging to class A. What is the maximum number of class B objects to which it could be tied? (Common answers are one and many.) For example, looking at one case, ask, "What is the maximum number of payments that might be posted against it?" (The answer is many.)

- Consider one object belonging to class B. What is the minimum number of class A objects to which it could be tied? (Common answers are zero and one.) Just to be sure, follow up with, "Is there any way it could be zero?" For example, looking at one payment, ask, "What is the minimum number of cases that it is generated by? Could a payment exist that was not generated by a case?" (Answer: A Payment object *must* be generated by a Case object, so the minimum multiplicity is one.)

- Consider one object belonging to class B. What is the maximum number of class A objects to which it could be tied? (Common answers are one and many.) For example, looking at one payment, ask "What is the maximum number of cases that might have generated it?" (The answer is one.)

Case Study H6: Multiplicity

You conduct interviews with users in order to work out the business rules governing the numerical relationships between business objects. With your class diagrams to guide you, you inquire about the multiplicities of the associations, aggregations, composite aggregations, and transient roles that appear in the diagrams. For example, you ask, "How many participants constitute a party to a dispute? Could two participants be considered a single party if, for example, they were part of the same group? How many times can a participant be involved as a party to a dispute?" In this manner, you ask your stakeholders about every single relationship other than generalization that appears in the class diagrams. Here's what your interviewees may tell you:

- Some participants are never involved as a party to a dispute. Some participants play the role of party to a dispute once. Others play the role many times—once for each time they are involved in a dispute. (Considering each involvement as a separate occurrence of Party to Dispute allows for a new set of business information—for example, the party's testimony—to be tracked for each involvement.)

- Any party to a dispute must be listed with the CPP as a Participant (either Agency or Person).

- A person can take out only one CPP membership.

- A person may be a member of more than one Peace Committee at the same time.

- Each case generates zero or more payments (one for each fund and one for each Peace Committee member). Each payment must be for one and only one case.

- A case must involve two or more parties to the dispute. Each involvement as party to a dispute refers to one and only one case.

- An observer must be related to at least one party in a dispute. There is no limit to the number of parties to which the observer can be related. A party to a dispute does not have to have any observers present on his or her behalf; there is no limit to the number of observers that may be related to a party.

- If a case is deemed payable, then payments are made to various accounts. Each payment is withdrawn from the one cash account in the system and is deposited into one of the fund accounts (such as Microenterprise) or to one Peace Committee member account.

- A Peace Committee may be set up without any members. As members join, they are added to the committee.

- There must be at least one attendee at a Peace Gathering. (This excludes parties to the dispute, who are expected to be at each Peace Gathering and are not considered attendees.)

- Every Peace Committee member owns one Peace Committee member account. Every Peace Committee member account is owned by one and only one Peace Committee member.

- A case may have no Peace Gatherings either because it has not progressed to that point yet or because it has been resolved without a gathering. A case is typically dealt with in one gathering; however, more than one gathering may be required if the first fails to resolve the problem. A Peace Gathering always discusses one and only one case.

- A Peace Committee handles zero or more cases. Every case is handled by one and only one Peace Committee.

Your Next Step

Document the preceding notes as multiplicities on the existing class diagrams.

Case Study H6: Resulting Documentation

Figure H6.1 shows the diagrams resulting from your examination of the preceding multiplicities.

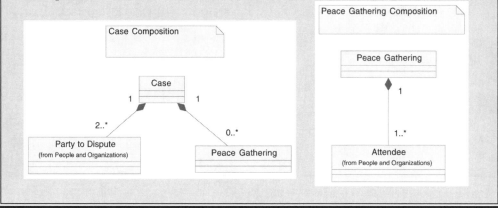

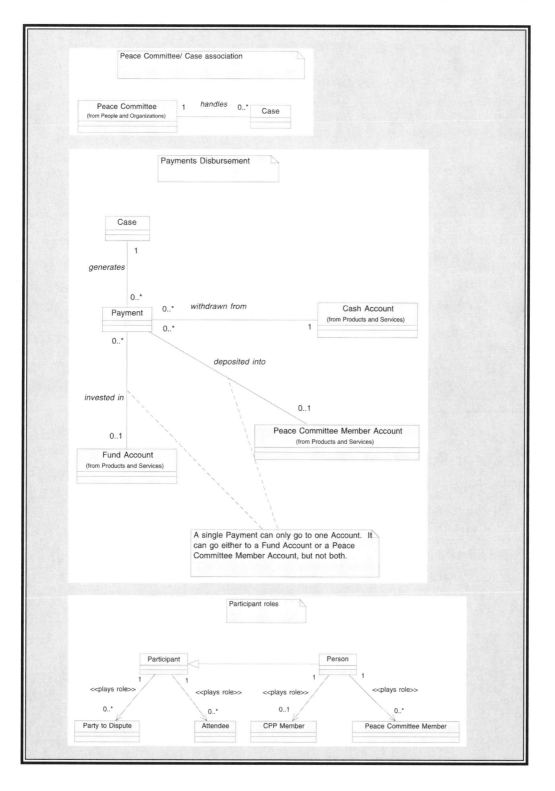

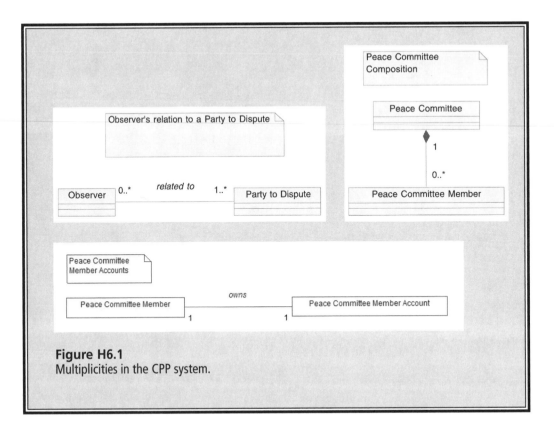

Figure H6.1
Multiplicities in the CPP system.

Chapter Summary

In this chapter, you learned to complete the following B.O.O.M. steps:

    2b)   Structural analysis

      i)   Identify entity classes

      ii)   Model generalizations

      iii)   Model transient roles

      iv)   Model whole/part relationships

      v)   Analyze associations

      vi)   Analyze multiplicity

By following these steps, you were able to elicit from stakeholders the precise meaning of business nouns and the ways that the business needs to be able to relate business objects to each other.

New tools and concepts you learned in this chapter include the following:

- An *entity class* is a category of business object tracked by the business.
- A *class diagram* describes classes and the relationships between classes.
- *Inheritance* is a property related to generalization. The specialized class is said to inherit all the attributes, operations, and relationships of the generalized class.
- *Aggregation* is a relationship between a whole and its parts.
- *Composite aggregation* is a special kind of whole/part relationship, where a part cannot belong to more than one whole at the same time and where the destruction of the whole causes the destruction of its parts.
- An *object diagram* can be used in place of a class diagram to describe situations that involve more than one object of the same class acting in different roles, as in a payment that is withdrawn from a From Account and deposited into a To Account. In an object diagram, a connection between the objects is called a *link*.

Endnotes

[1] These include control classes, which encapsulate process logic; boundary classes that act as interfaces; utility classes, like Date; special design classes to support multi-tiered architecture; and so on. In the UML, the kind of class can be shown with a *stereotype*. The stereotype may be shown as <<Control>>, <<Entity>>, and so on, when the class appears on a class diagram, or special symbols may be used.

[2] The UML does include other naming conventions for classes, attributes, and operations. I use these during the design stage. These standards include the following:

- For a class name: Begin the name with an uppercase letter.
- For an attribute name: Begin the name with a lowercase letter.
- For an operation name: Begin the name with a lowercase letter. Follow the name with parentheses; these will be used to surround parameters and help identify the name as an operation.
- For any name: If there are two or more words to the name, join the words into a single name; mark the beginning of each new name with an uppercase letter.

[3] Some methodologies use a package for each group of classes within an inheritance or aggregation arrangement. Others design packages so that collaboration between classes in separate packages will be at a minimum and/or unidirectional.

[4] Previously, the diagram was treated as a form of the class diagram.

[5] You may also add a new class to act as a generalized class for common attributes, though you will focus on this later.

[6] A new class Cell Phone may also be added to contain rules applying to all cell phones. More on this when we discuss inheritance.

[7]There must be a one-to-one association between two terms or they are not aliases but separate classes. For example, Account and Customer cannot be considered aliases if a customer can have more than one account. Additionally, if different operations apply to each or they are used in different contexts, they must be considered as separate classes rather than aliases.

[8]Note that while the Fund Manager actor referred to elsewhere represents an external software system, the listed fund accounts (Admin Fund Account, Peace Building Fund Account, and so on) refer to the internal records of the accounts.

[9]I use the word *subtype* here instead of *subclass* because I don't yet want to dictate the OO relationship to be used.

[10]Some object-oriented languages do, in fact, allow an object to change its type during its lifetime, but even in these cases, you'll need to let the developers know whether a subtype is full-time or part-time. By distinguishing between these kinds of subtypes, as described in this book, you'll be able to clarify this issue to the developers.

[11]The quality whereby a number of classes can have different implementations of the same operations is called *polymorphism*.

[12]They might be viewed as transient roles or merely distinguished by a Status attribute.

[13]They would be viewed as transient roles of a person.

[14]Party to Dispute is a transient role of a Person object and of an Agency object.

[15]An object may not belong to two specialized classes simultaneously. Another mechanism (role) must be used to model the relationship.

[16]Booch, Rumbaugh, and Jacobson, in their book *The Unified Modeling Language User Guide* (Addison-Wesley, 1999, page 165), refer to this concept as a *dynamic type*. They suggest modeling this situation by showing the primary class (in their example, Person) as a specialized class and the roles as generalized classes. The important thing is not *how* you model part-time subtypes, but that you have a consistent and clear way of indicating them. B.O.O.M. uses transient roles because they lend easily to the analysis of associations, multiplicities, etc. right on the class diagram.

[17]Formally, this relationship is modeled as a UML association, stereotyped as Plays Role.

[18]Technical note: In the code, transient roles may be handled as aggregations; the aggregate object is composed of an object of the primary class plus objects representing each of its roles. Inheritance does not apply, but special operations (referred to as *wrapper* operations) may be written to allow public access to role operations.

[19]If only some of the specialized classes can play the role, indicate those specializations as primary classes.

[20]Recall that the term *participant* used in this context is a project-specific term that refers to any body (person or organization) that may have standing at a Peace Gathering. It is not to be confused with the UML term *participant* (meaning any person or system that interacts with a use case).

[21]In UML 2.0, this relationship was named *composition*. In the current version, UML 2.2, it is named *composite aggregation*, though the previous term, *composition*, is sometimes used to describe the relationship.

[22]To make component (part) operations usable at the aggregate (whole) level, you need to define special operations, called *wrapper operations*, for the aggregate. A wrapper operation may have the same name as that used by the component(s). The wrapper asks the components to execute their version of the operation.

[23]Prior to UML 2, an equivalent diagram could have been constructed using context diagramming.

[24]At the time of this writing, many modeling tools, such as Rational Rose, do not support this feature.

[25]Don't confuse the UML role name—which defines the role an object plays in an association—with Plays Role—a B.O.O.M. stereotype.

[26]Be careful not to include redundant associations—that is, ones that can already be derived indirectly.

[27]Recall that in B.O.O.M., a transient role is an association stereotype. Multiplicity applies to transient roles because an object may, in theory, play any number of roles—even if they are of the same type. For example, a person may be playing many attendee roles, one for each Peace Gathering. Consequently, you'd indicate: "Each person may play the role of zero or more attendees. Each attendee role is played by one and only one person."

CHAPTER 9

OPTIMIZING CONSISTENCY AND REUSE IN THE REQUIREMENTS DOCUMENTATION

Chapter Objectives

In this chapter, you will do the following:

- Connect system use cases to the structural model.
- Promote consistency and reuse of requirements by adding rules about attributes, operations, and lookup tables to the model.

B.O.O.M. steps covered in this chapter include the following:

2b) Structural analysis
  vii)   Link system use cases to the structural model
  viii) Add attributes
  ix)   Add lookup tables
  x)   Distribute operations
  xi)   Revise class structure

Tools and concepts that you'll learn to use in this chapter include the following:

- Association classes
- Attribute
- Meta-attribute
- Operation
- Pre-condition
- Post-condition

Where Do You Go from Here?

At this point, your structural model identifies the classes of objects that are used within the business domain as well as the business rules dictating the relationships between them.[1] You also have documented some system use cases—a result of the behavioral modeling going on prior to and concurrently with the structural modeling. This is a good time to consider the issue of traceability between the behavioral and structural model. You should be able to *trace* (link) any system use case to elements of the structural model because the structural model contains details that apply to the use case but are not explicitly mentioned in it—for example, data-validation rules.[2] The upcoming B.O.O.M. step walks you through this.

Next, you'll be adding detail to your structural model by documenting rules about the attributes and operations related to each class. By adding each rule to the structural model, you're giving it one centralized place to reside in the documentation, ensuring it will be consistently applied. You'll also learn to carry out this step in this chapter.

Once the structural model has been set up, make sure that you actively use it. Every time a system use case is added or revised, check to see if the changes are consistent with the structural model and resolve any differences.

Does the Business Analyst Need to Put Every Attribute and Operation in the Structural Model?

No. Focus on elements and that have the broadest application and that, if not included in the model, carry a risk that they will not be implemented properly in the solution. Here are some guidelines to help you make that judgment call:

- What is the lifespan of the software and how stable are the requirements? If the software is to be short-lived or the business requirements are deemed to be fairly stable, you lose some of the benefit of structural modeling: reduced time to identify and make changes to the business requirements documentation. Such cases would lean you toward doing less structural modeling.

- Is the software going to be bought *off the shelf* (OTS)? If so, concentrate on high-priority attributes and operations.

- And, of course, how much time do you have? If you haven't been given enough time to do a complete model, concentrate on the high-priority attributes and operations described next.

The following considerations will help you pick out the high-priority attributes and operations to concentrate on during structural modeling if time is tight. Time spent documenting these in the structural model will give you the highest payback. Concentrate on attributes and operations that

- Apply across a number of system use cases.

- Have a high risk of being *inappropriately* handled in the software. For example, focus on non–industry-standard attributes when buying an OTS system.

- Will have a large negative impact on the outcome of the project if incorrectly handled.

Step 2bvii: Link System Use Cases to the Structural Model

In this step, you review any existing system use-case documentation for references to structural modeling elements, such as classes and associations.

How Do You Find the Modeling Elements Involved in a System Use Case?

Look for nouns that represent categories of business objects, such as *customer* and *invoice*; these are often classes. Next, pick out the verbs linking these nouns. For example, a salesperson *makes* a sale; these are often the relationships. (In the section "Step 2bviii: Add Attributes" later in this chapter, you'll also learn to look for fields; these correspond to attributes in the structural model.)

How Do You Document the Links Between System Use Cases and the Structural Model?

If you have a requirements-tracing tool, use it to tie each system use case to the structural modeling elements to which it refers. The approach used in this book documents the link in a special section of the system use-case documentation. This section appears in the template as follows.

6. Class Diagram

Include all classes that participate in the system use case. If any of the classes are part of an inheritance hierarchy, describe the related generalizations and specializations in the diagram or add another diagram depicting them.

If you're using a drawing tool, such as Rational Rose, a recommended approach is to create a dedicated class diagram within the tool for classes that participate in the system use case. Then add a macro in the system use-case text document to retrieve this diagram from the drawing tool when the document is opened. (If using Rational Rose, you'll need to investigate a product called SoDa for this purpose.) A second-best option is to manually copy and paste the diagram right into the text document.

There are many good reasons for providing traceability between the behavioral and structural models. As mentioned at the beginning of this chapter, one reason is to be able to direct the reader to the appropriate parts of the structural model that contain additional rules relevant to the system use case. Another reason is so that you will be able to identify which system use cases are affected by a change in the structural model; these are the system use cases that might need to be revised and retested if rules about the affected classes are updated in the structural model. Traceability also makes it easier for you to verify that any rules that appear in the system use case comply with the across-the-board rules expressed in the structural model.

Case Study I1:
Link System Use Cases to the Structural Model

You analyze the system use case, Review Case Report, documented below, looking for structural modeling elements so that you can cross-check the models to see if there are any discrepancies between the system use-case documentation and the class diagrams.

Suggestions

1. Begin by scanning the document for noun phrases. These are often classes. Verify that each class you've identified appears in the structural model. If it doesn't, add it to the structural model.

2. Next, scan the document for phrases of the form <<class>> <<verb phrase>> <<class>>, for example, "A Peace Committee is assigned to a case." The verb phrase is often a relationship—typically an association. Verify that each relationship you've identified is currently present in the model. Be careful not to add an association if there already is an indirect but equivalent association. If you discover a relationship that is not handled in any way in the structural model, add it.

3. Next, scan the documentation for any rules regarding multiplicity. For example, a system use case might presume that there is only one Peace Committee assigned to a case. Verify that these multiplicities are consistent with those in the structural model and resolve any inconsistencies.

4. Based on your analysis, create a draft of the class diagram that depicts only the classes that participate in the system use case, and then insert it into section 6 of the use-case documentation. If you needed to make any assumptions, document them in the "Assumptions" section of the template so that you will remember to verify them with stakeholders.

Following is your source document:

System use case: Disburse Payments

...

    1.3 Triggers: Convener selects disburse payments option.

    1.4 Pre-conditions

        1.4.1 The case is in the payable state and a payment amount for the case has been determined.

    1.5 Post-conditions

        1.5.1 Post-conditions on Success

            1.5.1.1 Payments are made into the accounts of all Peace Committee members involved in the case and into the fund accounts.

            1.5.1.2 The case is in the Paid state.

2. Flow of Events

Basic Flow:

    2.1 The system displays a list of payable cases.

    2.2 The user selects a case.

    2.3 The system displays the amount payable for the case.

    2.4 The system displays each Peace Committee member assigned to the case.

    2.5 The system displays the Peace Committee member account owned by each of the displayed Peace Committee members.

    2.6 The system displays the payment amounts to be deposited into each Peace Committee member account and invested into each fund.

        2.6.1 TBD (To be determined): The formula for disbursing payments to the various accounts.

    2.7 The user approves the disbursement.

    2.8 The system creates payments for the case.

        2.8.1 Each payment invests a specified amount from the cash account into one of the fund accounts or deposits an amount into one Peace Committee member account.

        2.8.2 The system sends a notice letter to a Peace Committee member whenever a deposit is made to the member's account.

    2.9 The system marks the case as Paid.

Alternate Flows:

    2.7a User does not approve disbursement amounts:

        .1 The user overrides the disbursement amounts.

        .2 The system confirms that the total payable for the case has not changed.

    2.7a.2a Total payable has changed:

        .1 The system displays a message indicating the amount of the discrepancy.

        .2 Continue at step 2.7a.1.

    2.8a Payment causes a withdrawal from cash that pushes balance below a specified trigger point:

        .1 The system sends a notice to Admin requesting new cash funds.

...

6. Class Diagram

(Include class diagram depicting business classes, relationships, and multiplicities of all objects participating in this use case.)

7. Assumptions

(List any assumptions made when writing the use case. Verify all assumptions with stakeholders before sign-off.)

Case Study I1: Resulting Documentation

1. Upon reviewing the system use case, you listed the following classes:

- Case
- Peace Committee Member
- Payment
- Peace Committee Member Account
- Fund Account
- Cash Account

Checking the structural model, you happily noted that it includes all of these classes.

2. Next, searching for relationships, you scanned the textual documentation for verbs connecting the classes. At this point, you discovered that the following relationship did not appear to be anywhere in the model:

   ▪ A Peace Committee member is assigned to a case.

   You checked to see if there were any indirect associations between the classes but nothing hit the mark. For example, although the model showed that each Peace Committee handles a case and each Peace Committee is composed of Peace Committee members, the model did not indicate a requirement to track which of these members is assigned to each case. Based on this analysis, you added these two associations to the model.

3. Next, you attempted to assign multiplicities to the associations. You guessed that each case may have zero or more assigned Peace Committee members because some cases are resolved without a Peace Gathering. You included your best guesses for the multiplicities but made a note in the "Assumptions" section to verify them with stakeholders.

4. Finally, you created a class diagram describing the classes involved in this system use case, incorporating the newly discovered relationships. Because the account classes belong to an inheritance hierarchy, you included a diagram depicting the hierarchy as well. Figure I1.1 shows the diagrams that you inserted into section 6 ("Class Diagram") of the use-case documentation.

5. Based on the analysis above, you have added the following to the use-case documentation:

   7. Assumptions

      7.1 Minimum Peace Committee members assigned to a case is zero.

      7.2 Maximum Peace Committee members assigned to a case is many. (There is no upper limit.)

      7.3 Each Peace Committee member owns exactly one Peace Committee member account.

      7.3 Each Peace Committee member account is owned by exactly one Peace Committee member.

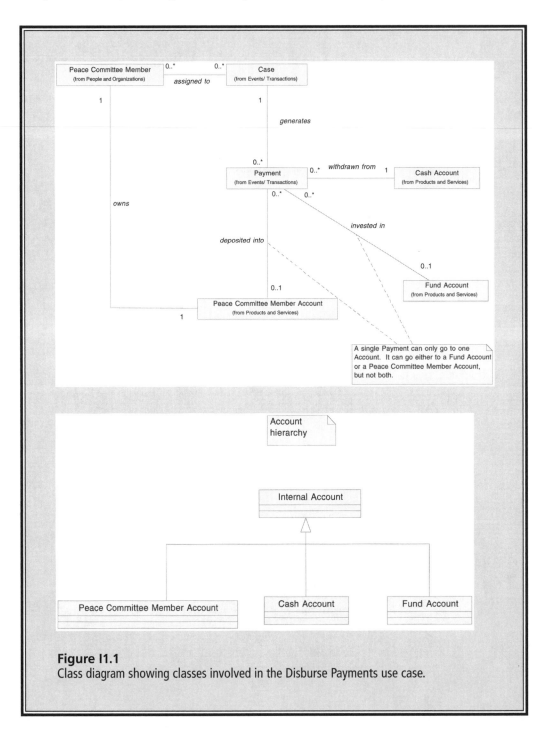

Figure I1.1
Class diagram showing classes involved in the Disburse Payments use case.

Step 2bviii: Add Attributes

The next step is to find out and document the attributes that are kept by the business for each class.

Attribute

An *attribute* is an item of information about an object that is tracked by the business. An attribute is specified at the class level. All objects of that class have the same attributes, but the value of the attributes may differ from object to object.[3]

Example

Some of the attributes the CPP might need to keep track of include the following:

- *Peace Gathering* class: The date that the gathering was held
- *Party to Dispute* class: The testimony given by the party

Why Indicate Attributes?

Attributes are part of the user's contract with the developers. If you miss an attribute in your model, you run the risk that the system will not track that attribute. Another reason to indicate attributes is that you then have a place in your model to "hang" rules about each attribute, such as valid ranges and other verifications.

Don't Verification Rules about Attributes Belong with the System Use-Case Documentation?

Generally, no. The best place to put an attribute rule is right in the structural model, since it gives the rule greater scope: The class diagrams in the OO model apply across the board[4]. On the other hand, if a rule applies to the attribute only within the context of a specific system use case, include the rule with the system use-case documentation. Yet another option for documenting these rules is along with the screens that are developed to handle the graphical user interface (GUI) for the system use case. Use this option if the rule only applies whenever the screen is used but does not apply across the board. As discussed in point 3 in the next section, screens are not considered a business-analysis artifact as they relate to the solution design, but you may request the designer to add in rules you've identified.

Sources of Information for Finding Attributes

■ Using the class diagrams as a guide, interview the user about each class.

■ Inspect existing system use cases for references to attributes. For example, the system use case Disburse Payments refers to a Payment Amount—an attribute of a Payment.

■ Inspect artifacts created by other members of the project. These include screens, reports, forms, and interfaces to external computer systems. Artifacts such as these are not formally within the scope of the BA because they deal with invention (the "how"), whereas the BA is concerned with discovery (the "what"). However, the BA should inspect them as they become available because they provide a rich source of attributes: The fields in these artifacts typically represent attributes in the structural model.

■ Inspect business rules expressed in the system use cases or in a separate business rules document. (These rules are sometimes stored electronically in a rules engine.) Sometimes they require new attributes. For example, the Disburse Funds system use case contains a rule that whenever the cash balance falls below a trigger point, a message is to be sent to administration. This rule requires that the Cash Account class have a Trigger Point attribute and a Current Balance attribute.

Rules for Assigning Attributes

■ Check each candidate attribute to ensure that it isn't already listed as a class. For example, you might be tempted to list Peace Committee Member Account as an attribute of Peace Committee Member because it represents information tied to a member. However, there is no need to do so, since this requirement is already in the model in another form: the Peace Committee Member Account class is associated with Peace Committee Member.

■ Take care to assign the attribute to the right class. The attribute should describe a property of objects in the class. Also, the attribute should be a property that the system tracks individually for each object in the class. For example, Dispute Date is not listed as an attribute of Peace Gathering because it is constant for all gatherings related to the same case; rather, Dispute Date is listed as a Case attribute. An attribute for Peace Gathering is one that is kept for *each* gathering, like Gathering Date.

■ List an attribute as far up an inheritance hierarchy as possible. (Keep in mind that if you list an attribute in a generalized class, it must apply to *all* specialized classes.)

■ For aggregations and compositions, take care to differentiate between an attribute that is related to the whole and an attribute that is tracked at the part level.

■ Attributes that the business tracks about an object regardless of the role are listed with the primary class. Attributes that are kept once for each role are listed with the role. For example, a person's name is kept regardless of one's role, but the date that person became a member of a Peace Committee is recorded once for each Peace Committee membership.

Derived Attributes

A *derived attribute* is one whose values can be derived in more than one way from the model. If an attribute can be derived from other attributes in the model, either do not include it or document it as a derived attribute. In the UML, you mark a derived attribute with a slash (/)—for example, /extended price. The documentation for a derived attribute should explain how the attribute value is determined from other aspects of the model. For example, /extended price is a derived attribute of an invoice line item that can be calculated from other attributes as follows: /extended price = unit price × quantity.

Why Is It Important for the BA to Indicate Which Attributes Are Derived?

Derived attributes can lead to data integrity problems if they pass unnoticed from the requirements into the database design. For example, consider a student final average that can be derived directly by querying a Final Mark attribute and, indirectly, by calculating it from the student's individual marks. Since there are two ways to derive this mark, there is always the possibility that they will yield different results. One solution (referred to as *normalization*) prevents the problem by eliminating the Final Mark attribute entirely from the model. If there is no duplication, there is no inconsistency. Eliminating the redundancy also means less storage requirements, since the Final Mark attribute of each student is no longer kept on file but is recalculated as needed. On the other hand, this recalculation uses up system resources at run-time. The decision on how to handle a derived attribute is up to the database designer. But for that person to do his or her job properly, the BA needs to clearly mark which attributes are derived and how they are derived.

Indicating Attributes in the UML

Figure 9.1 shows how to indicate attributes in the UML by listing them in an attribute compartment (or box) that sits just below the class name. (The empty box below it is the operation compartment.) In the figure, /Number Members is marked as derived because it can be determined by counting the number of Peace Committee members in the Peace Committee.

```
┌─────────────────────────────────┐
│                                 │
│         Peace Committee         │
│                                 │
├─────────────────────────────────┤
│  PC name                        │
│  date founded                   │
│  /number members                │
├─────────────────────────────────┤
│                                 │
│                                 │
└─────────────────────────────────┘
```

Figure 9.1
Indicating attributes in the UML.

For business-analysis purposes, this notation, along with supporting text, is usually suffi-cient. The UML does offer, however, a more formal way of declaring attributes. I'll describe it here for completeness, but you probably won't need to be this formal:

attributeName: AttributeType [Multiplicity] = default

For example:

contactNumber: PhoneNumber [0..2] = "(416) - "

where

- attributeName is the name of the attribute—for example, contactNumber. During analysis, use informal names. Later, in design, use the formal format: one term (no spaces) beginning with a lowercase letter, with each subsequent word beginning in uppercase.
- AttributeType characterizes the attribute—for example, PhoneNumber. Use one of the following approaches to naming the AttributeType (listed in order of preference from a BA perspective):
  - A user-defined type, formally defined elsewhere as another class. For example: PhoneNumber is defined as a class with its own attributes of AreaCode and Number.
  - Units of measurement[5], such as Inches.
  - A data-type supported by the programming environment. For example:
    - Integer: A whole number (no fractions)
    - Boolean: A yes/no field
    - String: Text (any string of characters). Use this for free-form text and for codes even if they are numeric.
    - Double: A decimal number.
    - Date

- Multiplicity is the number of times the attribute appears. Use the same notation you used when describing multiplicities for associations. For example, contactNumber: PhoneNumber [0..2] means that zero through two contact numbers may appear.
- Default is the attribute's initial value.

Once you've added the attributes and their rules to classes in the structural model, ideally, you should remove these details anywhere they appear in the system use cases. For example, once you've added a rule to the Date Founded attribute (that is, the date the committee was established) of a Peace Committee, this rule should be removed from the Manage Peace Committees system use case. The reader will be referred to the rule because the "Class Diagram" section of the use-case documentation will have included the Peace Committee class. This approach ensures consistent treatment and makes it easier to change rules if circumstances require it. Many organizations balk at this point, however, partly because this approach requires too much cross-referencing on the part of the reader. A second-best approach is to add the rule to the structural model, include a reference from the system use case to the model, but leave the explicit rule itself in place in the system use case. While this approach means that some requirements will reside in more than one place, it still provides the benefit of a centralized reference (the structural model) for verifying that each system use case is consistent with project-wide rules. Similar considerations will apply when you look at pulling operation rules out of the system use cases.

Meta-Attributes

A *meta-attribute* is an attribute of an attribute—a fancy way of referring to the verification rules and other properties of an attribute. To document an attribute fully, you need to describe its meta-attributes. In the previous discussion on the UML declaration of attributes, you read about the following:

- Attribute type
- Multiplicity
- Default value

These are examples of meta-attributes. You also learned to document that an attribute is derived by including a slash before its name. Other meta-attributes worth documenting include the following

- Unique?: A "yes" indicates that the value of the attribute is unique for each object in the class—in other words, no two objects may have the same value for this attribute.
- Range of acceptable values, such as:
  - Quantity on Hand: Range is 0–10.
  - Invoice Date: Range is (any past date) through (current date).

- List of acceptable values, such as:
  - Gender: Values are Male and Female.[6] However, if the list of acceptable values is subject to change, define the whole attribute as a lookup table (described in the section "Step 2bix: Add Lookup Tables" later in this chapter).
- Accuracy such as:
  - Balance: 9,999.99 (stored to nearest cent).
- Length: The length of the field, such as:
  - Name (maximum 30 characters long).
- Dependencies on other attributes, such as:
  - Date Resolved (must be on or after date reported).

Document these meta-attributes using an informal style.

Case Study 12: Add Attributes

You ask stakeholders about the items of information the business tracks about each class that appears in your model. Also, you examine screen mockups and report layouts that have been created by the designers. You list each field you find and verify with stakeholders what class they describe. Through your interviews, you discover the following.

People/Organizations

- A unique participant ID (PID) must be given to each person or agency involved with the CPP.
- The date that a person was first entered into the system must be recorded. The system must also record the following for each person: mailing address, last name, sex, and date of birth.
- The date that an agency was first entered into the system must be recorded. The system must record the following for each agency: mailing address and name. Some reports need to indicate whether an agency is a government agency.
- The testimony of each party to a dispute appears on case reports.
- Descriptive information about each Peace Committee includes township and ward number.

- For each Peace Committee member, the system must record the date the person joined and a status indicating whether the person is active.

- For each CPP member, the system must record the date the person joined and a status indicating whether the person is active.

- The system must track the type of relationship (such as neighbor, family member, and so on) each observer has to a party to the dispute. If the observer has a relationship with more than one party, then each relationship must be tracked.

Events/Transactions

- A payment report shows one line per payment with a unique payment sequence number, payment date, amount, and the account to which it was paid.

- The meeting date of each Peace Gathering for a case appears on the case report.

- The case report also shows the date of the dispute, the conflict type (a predefined code), a status code describing the progress of the case, an indication of whether the rules were followed, a predefined reason code describing why a gathering was not held (if applicable), and whether monitoring was required for the case.

- If monitoring was required, the conditions imposed appear on the case report, as well as the deadline for monitoring and whether the monitoring conditions have been met.

- Payable cases appear on a separate report.

Products and Services

- All accounts are identified by a unique account number.

- For Peace Committee member accounts, information items are Balance, Date Last Accessed, and Overdraft Limit.

- For fund accounts, information items are Balance, Date Last Accessed, and Access Code.

- For cash accounts, information items are Balance, Date Last Accessed, and Low Trigger—the balance below which new cash funds are requested.

Your Next Step

Based on these notes, you aim to discover the attributes and assign them to the appropriate classes.

Suggestions

- If an attribute applies to all specializations of a generalized class, assign the attribute to the generalized class.
- For any generalization hierarchy, show attributes of the classes involved on the same diagram that shows the generalization relationships. That way, the reader will be able to see which attributes are inherited by specialization classes.

Case Study I2: Resulting Documentation

Your analysis of the CPP system's attributes results in the diagrams shown in Figure I2.1.

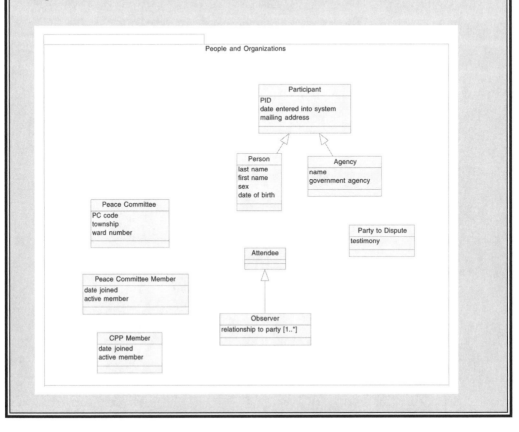

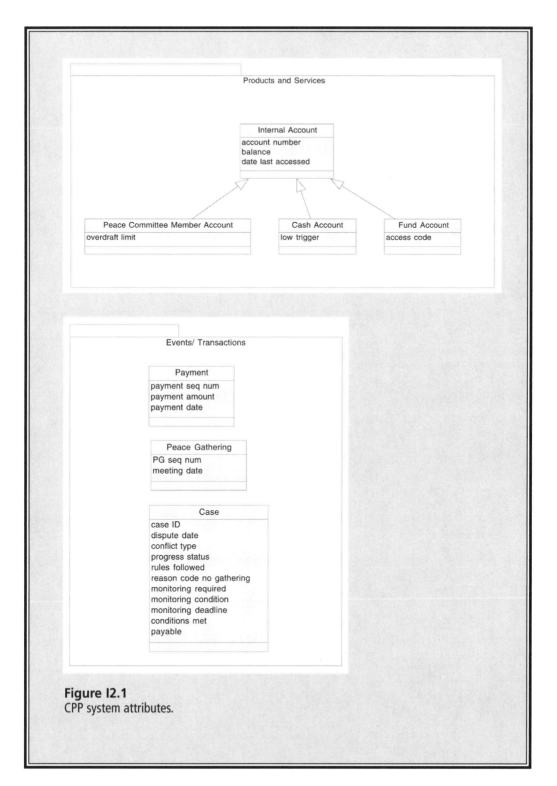

Figure I2.1
CPP system attributes.

Association Classes

The UML offers another way to treat the attribute Relationship to Party, specified for the Observer class. Rather than treat it as an attribute of Observer, you could consider it to be an attribute of the association between Observer and Party to Dispute. The rationale for this is that the value of the Relationship to Party attribute changes for each instance of an association between one observer and one party. To handle the attribute this way, you need to introduce a new kind of class to the model called an *association class*. An association class is considered by the UML to be both an association and a class. Each instance of the class describes one link between an object on one association end and an object at the other end. Association classes are useful at design time but are confusing during business analysis, as they are not likely to be readily understood by business stakeholders. They are mentioned in this book just in case you run into them and wonder what they're all about.

Figure I2.2 shows an example of an association class between Observer and Party to Dispute. Note how the Relationship to Party attribute has been removed from Observer and added to the class, Observer Related to Party. The multiplicity of the attribute has changed from [1..*] to [1] because each Observer Related to Party object represents a single link between the objects at both ends; each link only requires one value of the attribute.

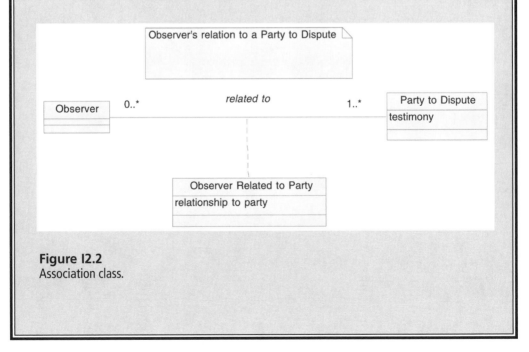

Figure I2.2
Association class.

Step 2bix: Add Lookup Tables

A *lookup table* is a file that lists the allowable values of an attribute. The term is not part of UML. An example is a relation code describing a relationship between two individuals, where PC = Parent/Child, EE = Employer/Employee, and so on.

Why Analyze Lookup Tables?

Analyzing lookup tables leads to enormous savings in future modifications to the system. When implemented, lookup tables enable the user to add new acceptable values without calling on a programmer. How? For each lookup table that you identify, the developers will create data-entry screens to add, change, and delete standardized codes. These screens allow users to modify codes interactively without programmer intervention.

Example

While you've been analyzing the CPP system, you've noticed that stakeholders have revised the list of allowable relationship codes (Spouse, Neighbor, and so on) a number of times. You verify that these codes are, in fact, subject to change, so you define a lookup table.

Rules for Analyzing Lookup Tables

- Look for candidate lookup tables:
    - If a screen uses pull-down menus to allow the user to select the value of an attribute, the attribute is a candidate lookup table. (That said, see the upcoming challenge question to determine whether the table is worth defining.) For example, the attribute Relationship to Party to Dispute includes a pull-down menu of relationship codes.
    - If any statistics are compiled based on the number of objects that match a particular attribute value, that attribute is a candidate lookup table. For example, statistics based on conflict type are candidates for a table.
    - If the attribute appears in more than one context, and standardization of its values makes business sense, the attribute is a candidate for a lookup table. For example, in a later enhancement to the CPP system, a relationship code is used to describe the relationship of one party to another party involved in a dispute (in addition to its current use to describe Observer Relation to a Party). It makes sense to standardize the relationship codes so that the same ones are used throughout the system.
    - If you have any lookup tables to add, create a package called Lookup Tables and add the tables to this package. For example, add the new classes Dispute Parameter and Relation Parameter to a Lookup Table package. Another recommendation is to declare the stereotype for this new class to be <<Lookup Table>> to clarify its purpose to the reader.

- For each new class you've added:
  - Add attributes. For example, add the following attributes to Dispute Parameter: Description and Criminal Offense. (The Criminal Offense attribute would be defined as a Boolean attribute, meaning it can take on the values of Yes or No.)
  - Indicate associations to each of the classes that use the lookup table. For example, Dispute Parameter is associated with Case.
  - Indicate multiplicities for each of the associations. For example, each dispute parameter is associated with zero or more cases. Each case is associated with one and only one dispute parameter.
  - Make sure that no other attributes related to the lookup table appear in any of the associated classes. For example, Conflict Type should no longer appear as an attribute of Case; the requirement is captured through an association with a dispute parameter.

Challenge Question

- Can you be sure that these codes will always stay the same? If the answer is yes, you don't need to define the attribute they describe as a lookup table. For example, a Sex code (M/F) does not require a lookup table.

Indicating Lookup Tables in the UML

Figure 9.2 shows how to indicate a lookup table in the UML.

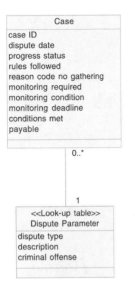

Figure 9.2
Indicating a lookup table in the UML.

Case Study 13: Analyze Lookup Tables

You analyze the following report layouts, looking for opportunities to define a lookup table.

Peace Gathering Report

There is a section filled out by each observer at a Peace Gathering that includes the following:

Which party are you related to? _____

How are you related? (Please select one: ____)

1. Married

2. Relative/near

3. Relative/far

4. Neighbor

5. Friend

6. Lover: boyfriend/girlfriend

7. Acquaintance

8. Stranger

9. Professional: employer/employee

10. Client/service provider

11. Tenant/landlord

12. Other agency

Governmental Report

- Percentage of cases where no gathering was held because the dispute was resolved in the meantime: ____%.

- Percentage of cases where no gathering was held because the relationship between the parties improved: ____%.

- Percentage of cases where no gathering was held because someone rejected the process: ____%.

- Percentage of cases where no gathering was held because the case was taken over by another agency: ____%.

- Percentage of cases where no gathering was held because the case was referred to another agency by the CPP: ____%.

Dispute Frequency Report

- Money lending % cases: _____
- Theft (burglary of dwelling) % cases: _____
- Failure to make payments on goods received % cases: _____
- Assault without weapon % cases: _____
- Assault with sharp object % cases: _____
- Assault with blunt object % cases: _____
- Assault with gun % cases: _____
- Robbery with violence % cases: _____
- Spatial dispute urination, encroachment % cases: _____
- Loan of goods % cases: _____
- Extramarital affair % cases: _____
- Other sexual affair % cases: _____
- Spousal abuse % cases: _____
- Child abuse % cases: _____
- Insult (direct disrespect or damage to identity and reputation) % cases: _____
- Housing dispute—ownership, head of house % cases: _____
- Moral issues—e.g., sister living with boyfriend % cases: _____
- Attempted rape/indecent assault % cases: _____
- Rape % cases: _____
- Gossip % cases: _____
- Drunkenness % cases: _____
- Child/spouse % cases: _____
- Witchcraft % cases: _____
- Percentage of cases involving disputes representing criminally indictable offenses: _____

Case Study I3: Resulting Documentation

Figure I3.1 shows the diagrams resulting from your analysis of lookup tables.

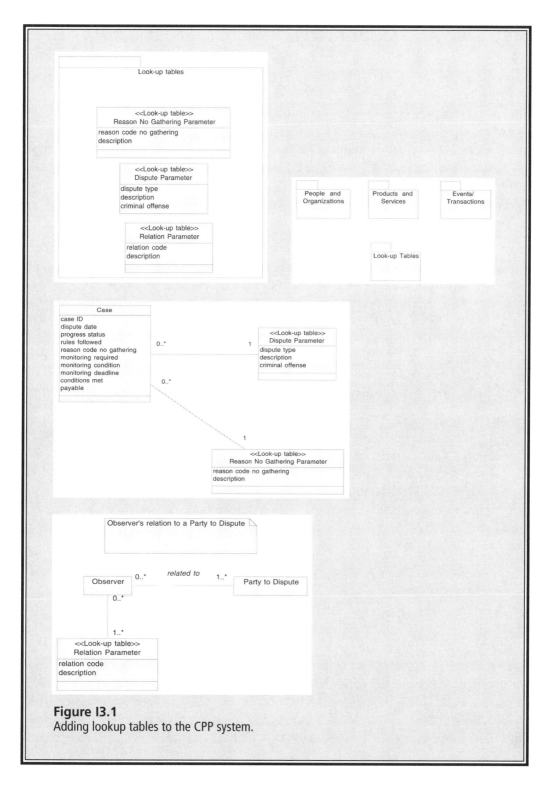

Figure I3.1
Adding lookup tables to the CPP system.

Step 2bx: Add Operations

Recall that a class can hold both attributes and operations. You added attributes to the structural model's classes in order to ensure that the rules for these attributes are treated consistently in the requirements. Also, by encapsulating attribute rules within the class's documentation, you created a self-contained unit of documentation that can be easily reused in other contexts. The same arguments apply to a class's operations. On the other hand, while there is a good argument for modeling the operations of a class, in practice, few business analysts currently carry out this step—so check with your organization before including operations in your model.

An Example from the Case Study

The CPP has a business rule stating that whenever a withdrawal from cash pushes the current balance below a certain minimum (a trigger point), a notice must be sent to the admin requesting new cash funds. This requirement now resides in the Disburse Payments use case. But what if this rule about the cash account must be applied to all other systems that withdraw from this account? Your solution is to add the operation Withdraw Funds to the Cash Account class. You attach the rule about sending a notice to the admin to this operation. In the future, any BA documenting requirements for any other system that involves the cash account will be able to include the Cash Account class documentation that you created, ensuring consistent handling of withdrawals and other Cash Account rules.

As discussed earlier in this chapter, the generally preferred approach is to remove the rule from the system use case once it's been added to the structural model in order to avoid duplication. At one extreme, this would mean removing the entire alternate flow describing the low cash balance situation. However, this may place too heavy a burden on the reader—in particular a stakeholder from the business side not accustomed to this sort of cross-referencing. A workable solution is to keep the alternate flow condition but refer the reader to the Cash Account class for details on the system's response to the condition. For example:

> 2.8a Payment causes a withdrawal from cash that pushes balance below a specified trigger point:
>
> > .1   The system responds as described in the Withdraw operation of the Cash Fund specifications. (See structural model.)

This allows you to clearly describe the condition that is checked while leaving the documentation of the response in one place. If the required response changes later, it will still be easy to revise. If even this degree of cross-referencing is too much for your readers, then update the Withdraw operation in the Cash Fund class but leave the entire rule in place (including the response) in the system use case. This, at least, gives you a central place to return to when writing other use cases that involve the cash account so that you can verify that withdrawals are consistently handled.

How to Distribute Operations

Use the following guidelines to model operations and distribute them amongst the classes in the structural model:

- Examine the flow steps that appear in the system use-case documentation. If you find an activity that pertains to a class and needs to be handled consistently regardless of the system use case, add it as an operation of the class. For example, add Withdraw Funds to Cash Account. Then attach any relevant rules to the operation, such as "When funds fall below trigger point, send notice to the admin."

- If the operation applies to all subtypes, list the operation with the generalized class. For example, if the rule about sending a notice to the admin applies to withdrawals from all kinds of accounts, list the operation Withdraw Funds and its requirements with the generalized class Account. Each specialized class inherits this operation from the generalized class, but it may have its own method (procedure) for carrying it out (due to polymorphism). If it does, attach documentation about the new method to the specialized class.

Figure 9.3 shows how to indicate operations in the UML. The operations are placed in a special operations compartment—a box below the attribute compartment in the class icon. Each operation is followed by parentheses.

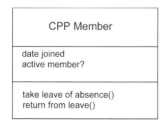

Figure 9.3
Indicating operations in UML.

This informal naming of operations is sufficient for most BA purposes. The UML offers the following formal format for declaring operations:

operationName (argument1:Argument1Type, argument2:Argument2Type, ...): ReturnType

Example: takeLeaveOfAbsence (EffectiveDate: Date): Boolean

The preceding operation, takeLeaveOfAbsence, requires an effective date, whose type is Date. The operation returns a Boolean answer (True or False) indicating success or failure.

Also, you can document a pre-condition and post-condition for each operation. A pre-condition is something that must be true before the operation begins. A post-condition is something that must be true once it has been completed.

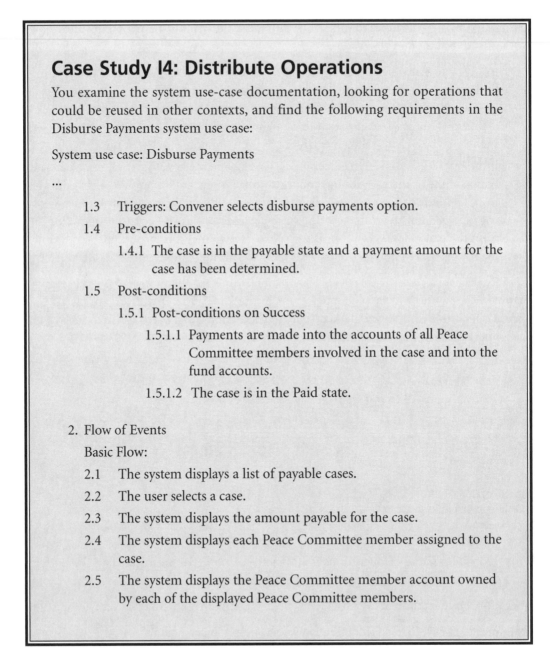

Case Study 14: Distribute Operations

You examine the system use-case documentation, looking for operations that could be reused in other contexts, and find the following requirements in the Disburse Payments system use case:

System use case: Disburse Payments

...

    1.3   Triggers: Convener selects disburse payments option.

    1.4   Pre-conditions

        1.4.1 The case is in the payable state and a payment amount for the case has been determined.

    1.5   Post-conditions

        1.5.1 Post-conditions on Success

            1.5.1.1 Payments are made into the accounts of all Peace Committee members involved in the case and into the fund accounts.

            1.5.1.2 The case is in the Paid state.

  2. Flow of Events

    Basic Flow:

    2.1   The system displays a list of payable cases.

    2.2   The user selects a case.

    2.3   The system displays the amount payable for the case.

    2.4   The system displays each Peace Committee member assigned to the case.

    2.5   The system displays the Peace Committee member account owned by each of the displayed Peace Committee members.

2.6   The system displays the payment amount to be deposited into each Peace Committee member account and invested into each fund.

    2.6.1 To be determined (TBD): The formula for disbursing payments to the various accounts.

2.7   The user approves the disbursement.

2.8   The system creates payments for the case. Each payment deposits a specified amount from the cash account into one of the fund accounts or into one Peace Committee member account. The system sends a notice letter to a Peace Committee member whenever a deposit is made to the member's account.

2.9   The system marks the case as Paid.

Alternate Flows:

2.7a   User does not approve disbursement amounts:

    .1 The user overrides the disbursement amounts.

    .2 The system confirms that the total payable for the case has not changed.

2.7a.2a Total payable has changed:

    .1 The system displays a message indicating the amount of the discrepancy.

    .2 Continue at step 2.7a.1.

2.8a   Payment causes a withdrawal from cash that pushes balance below a specified trigger point:

    .1 The system sends a notice to admin requesting new cash funds.

...

6. Class Diagram: See Figure I4.1

7. Assumptions:

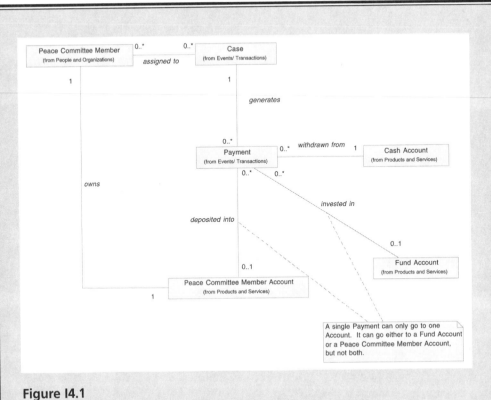

Figure I4.1
Classes participating in the system use case Disburse Payments.

Your Next Step

You look for rules applying to the classes mentioned in this use case that might apply to other system use cases and/or systems. You add these as annotated operations of the appropriate classes.

Case Study I4: Resulting Documentation

Figure I4.2 shows the diagram that results from your addition of operations to the structural model. To illustrate your options for documenting operations, the withdraw() operation has been documented using the formal format; the deposit() operation has been documented informally.

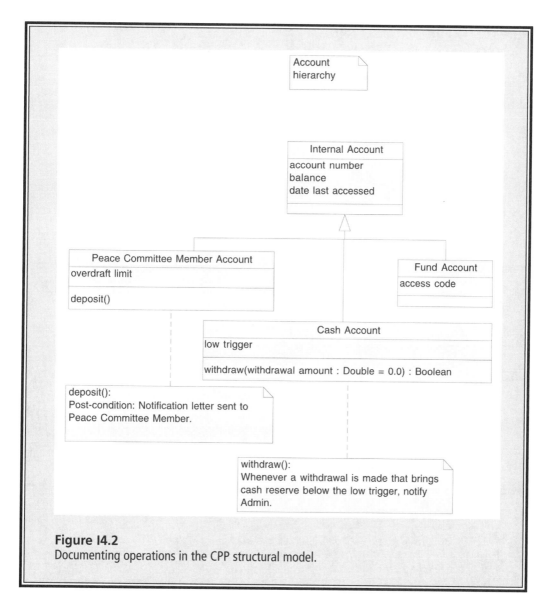

Figure I4.2
Documenting operations in the CPP structural model.

Step 2bxi: Revise Class Structure

As a last step, make a final review of the model and revise it if necessary. You may need to add some generalizations and drop some others. For example, you may find a generalized class with no requirements (attributes, operations, or relationships) and decide to discard it because it's simply cluttering up the model and not adding value. On the other hand, you may discover classes with shared attributes, operations, or relationships. In such cases, you'll want to consider adding a generalized class.

Rules for Reviewing Structure

- Look for any classes that have the same associations to other classes. Consider adding a generalized class for them.

- Look for any classes that have the same attributes or operations as other classes. Consider adding a generalized class to hold the common attributes.

- Whenever you add a generalized class, move the common associations, attributes, and operations from the specialized classes to the generalized class.

- Can you justify every generalized class in the model? The point of introducing a generalized class is to provide a convenient, single place to put rules that affect a number of specialized classes. There should be at least one attribute, operation, or relationship that can be ascribed to the generalized class.

- As rule of thumb, each generalized class should have at least two specializations. There are two exceptions to this rule, however:

  - The generalized class is concrete. For example, in the case study, Attendee is a concrete generalized class of Observer.

  - You anticipate that you will need to add more specializations in the future.

Challenge Question

- Are any of the subtypes already specializations of some other generalized class? If so, you have a case of multiple inheritance. Some companies do not allow this type of structure, or do so only if certain rules are followed. Make sure your model complies with your company's policy on this.[7]

Case Study I5: Revise Structure

You review the existing class diagrams looking for generalized classes that can be discarded due to a lack of attributes, associations, and so on. Also, you are looking for classes with common attributes, operations, and/or associations.

Suggestions

Notice that that there are properties common to all members, regardless of the organization to which they belong.

Case Study I5: Resulting Documentation

Figure I5.1 shows the diagram that results from your review of the CPP system's class structure. You've added a Member class as a generalized class of Peace Committee Member and CPP Member and moved the common attributes to it. This left no attributes or operations in the specialized member classes; however, you've retained these classes because they have special multiplicities and associations.

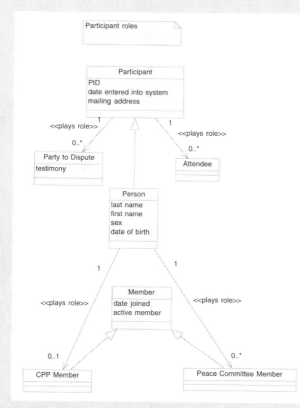

Figure I5.1
The CPP system's revised class structure.

Notes on the Model

A new generalized class, Member, has been added to the People and Organizations package. The common attributes Date Joined and Active Member have been moved from the specialized classes Peace Committee Member and CPP Member to the new class, Member.

Chapter Summary

In this chapter, you completed the structural model of the system. You linked the system use cases to the structural model and you added detail to the structural model by including attributes and operations. Finally, you revised the structural model, adding classes to promote reuse and removing unused classes.

Tools and concepts introduced in this chapter for the first time or in a new context include the following:

- An *attribute* is a piece of information that the business tracks about a class of objects.
- A *meta-attribute* is a property of an attribute, such as a valid range.
- An *association class* is a class that describes an association. Each object represents one link between instances of the classes at both ends of the association.
- A *lookup table* is a table of codes for an attribute. The user can change the table's list of allowable values and their meanings.
- An *operation* is an activity that all objects of a class can perform.
- An *operation pre-condition* is a condition that must be true before the operation is performed.
- An *operation post-condition* is a condition that will be true after the operation has completed.

Endnotes

[1]The structural model in this state is sometimes referred to as the *conceptual* structural model.

[2]Tracing in the opposite direction—from the structural model to the behavioral model—is also useful as it makes it easy to identify which system use cases are affected when changes are made to the structural model.

[3]You may also specify a special kind of attribute that allows one value only to be shared by all objects of the class. Such an attribute is termed a *class attribute*.

[4]Another option that provides the same coverage is to place the rule in a data dictionary.

[5]This approach is particularly useful during analysis, but during design, it will be converted to one of the options listed here.

[6]This can also be defined by declaring an enumeration data type, which is not covered in this book.

[7]Multiple inheritance can lead to ambiguities about attributes if the same attribute is inherited from two generalizations, particularly if there is a *diamond inheritance*—that is, both parent classes inherit from the same grandparent.

CHAPTER 10

DESIGNING TEST CASES AND COMPLETING THE PROJECT

Chapter Objectives

In this chapter, you'll learn how to design test cases that are most likely to uncover errors—an activity that should begin during the Discovery phase, before the Construction phase (design and coding). By specifying these tests up front, you add *measurable* quality requirements to your contract with the developers—clear-cut criteria that will be used to judge the acceptability of the software.

Steps covered in this chapter include the following (highlighted in bold):

2. The Discovery phase
   a) Behavioral analysis
   b) Structural analysis (object/data model) (class diagram)
   c) **Specify testing (test plan/decision tables)**
       i)   **Specify white-box testing quality level**
       ii) **Specify black-box test cases**
       iii) **Specify system tests**
   d) **Specify implementation plan**
   e) **Prepare BRD/Discovery**
   f) Set baseline for development

Tools and concepts that you'll learn about in this chapter include the following:

- Structured testing principles
- Structured walkthroughs for testing
- White-box testing criteria (statement coverage, decision coverage, condition coverage, and multiple-condition coverage)
- Black-box testing
- Use-case scenario testing
- Decision tables
- Unit testing
- Boundary-value analysis
- System tests
- Regression testing
- Volume testing
- Stress testing
- Usability testing
- Security testing
- Performance testing
- Storage testing
- Configuration testing
- Compatibility testing
- Reliability testing
- Recovery testing
- Implementation plan

Step 2c: Specify Testing

The testing process includes technical tests of the software's components and architecture (white-box tests), tests to see if it works as advertised (requirements-based tests), and tests that see whether the software does these things "well enough" (system tests).

Who Does These Tests and How Does the BA Fit In?

The BA's responsibility is to support testing. What this means, exactly, depends on the organization. Some organizations have a quality-assurance (QA) team responsible for testing. The BA is often a member of this team. In fact, many organizations have people with a BA title who do nothing *but* testing. Business analysts are particularly well suited to this work due to their role as representatives of the business stakeholders, and because they are often the authors of the business requirements against which the software is being measured.

If you're a BA involved in testing, most of your testing time will be absorbed by requirements-based testing. If your organization does not have specifically trained usability testers, you may also be asked to specify and/or run usability tests (discussed later in this chapter under the section "System Tests"). You'll need to know how to design effective tests and how to write them up. This chapter will give you techniques and templates to help you do that.

In general, the rest of the tests (white-box and most system tests) are too "techie" for the business analyst. You still need to know enough about them to know what to ask for and to be able to understand the significance of the results, however. You'll learn about these tests later in this chapter.

What Is Testing?

Testing is any activity aimed at proving that the software system does not do what it is supposed to. The negative phrasing is intentional. Each time a test uncovers a bug, it has proven itself—it means the bug won't be released to the end-user. The term *quality assurance* is sometimes used because it suggests that more than the physical testing of the software may be required. For example, verifying a draft of a system use-case description with stakeholders is a testing activity.

> ### What Exactly Is a Bug?
>
> We'll take the broad view. A *bug* is any variance between what the system is supposed to do and what it actually does. Some of these bugs are going to be introduced by the programmers. But others are introduced earlier on by business analysts through inaccurate, ambiguous, or missing requirements. It's your job to eliminate as many of these bugs as possible.

General Guidelines

Ivar Jacobson, a founder of OO, advises that you derive test cases from system use cases as follows:

- Test scenarios that cover the basic flow of each use case
- Tests scenarios that cover the alternate and exception flows[1] of each use case
- Tests of line-item requirements[2] in the BRD, where the requirements are traced to use case(s)
- Tests of features in the user documentation, where the documentation is traced to use case(s)

You'll need more than these suggestions to plan appropriate testing. Fortunately, much groundwork regarding testing has been done prior to OO. This pre-OO approach is called *structured testing*. In this chapter, we'll look at how structured testing can be integrated with UML techniques and applied to a UML project.

Structured Testing

In 1976, Glenford Myers pioneered the field of testing with his book *The Art of Software Testing*. He laid out a discipline he termed *structured testing*. His work remains the basis for testing to this day.

Structured Testing

Structured testing is the process of using standardized techniques to locate flaws (bugs). Flaws detected by structured testing include those introduced during business analysis, design, and programming.

When Is Testing Performed?

Different activities occur at various phases of project development:

- Structured walkthroughs are performed throughout the project.
- During the Discovery phase, the test cases are designed. On an iterative project, architectural proofs of concept are implemented and tested as well during this phase.
- During the Construction phase, unit testing (tests of the individual software components) is carried out.
- As system use-case scenarios are implemented during the Construction phase, requirements-based (black-box) tests are performed to verify compliance with the requirements.
- Before acceptance of the product, the developers or technical testers perform system tests.
- During the Closeout phase, the user performs and supervises user acceptance testing (UAT).

Principles of Structured Testing (Adapted for UML)

You begin by establishing some principles, adapted from structured testing to OO projects. Why not go directly to the techniques? A sound understanding of basic principles helps avoid the kinds of institutional problems that lead to buggy systems. (The real-life story in the accompanying sidebar helps illustrate this point.)

Why Testers Need to Have Good Principles

One of my first jobs in IT was a programming stint for a company that designed and built nuclear reactors. I was working on a computer program that simulated a loss-of-coolant accident at a nuclear power plant. I found it odd that even though I had not yet graduated from university, the company relied on me to test my own programs. Sure enough, in my first programming assignment, I introduced a bug into the system—one that was found out only once the program had been put into production. (Fortunately, the error was minor.)

This incident suggested a systemic flaw in the way the organization handled quality assurance. This was borne out a number of years later when the company released a software-controlled medical device to deliver radiation to brain tumors. The device occasionally malfunctioned, causing a number of deaths. A testing specialist was eventually called in to determine the source of the problem. He found the bug—but he also warned of systemic problems that would continue to result in new bugs unless corrected.

The principles of structured testing are as follows:

- The purpose of testing is to locate bugs.
  - A *bug* is any aspect of a system that does not meet the requirements of the business and of users.
  - A bug can be introduced at any time during the project.
  - Be a pessimist: Work under the assumption that the analysis work was incomplete and inaccurate and that the system is full of programming errors.
- The goal of testing is to locate the maximum number of errors in the available time.
  - It is theoretically impossible to guarantee a 100-percent error-detection rate, so you have to settle for this more realistic goal.
- Clearly define the expected results of each test so that test results are easy to analyze.
  - If possible, create electronic versions of expected output files so that the actual outputs can be verified automatically. If not, use hard copy.
- The more removed the test designer is from the project team, the better the test.
  - An outsider is likely to take a more critical approach than an insider, and is less likely to be operating under the same (sometimes mistaken) assumptions as insiders do.

- A complete test plan covers the following:
  - Scenarios based on the basic flow of each system use case.
  - Scenarios based on all the alternate flows of each system use case—that is, all valid but rarely occurring cases.
  - Scenarios based on all the exceptional flows of each system use case.
  - All line-item BRD requirements not included in the preceding (for example, general quality requirements).
  - All features described in the requirements documentation. (The features should be traceable to system use cases.)
  - The domain (valid range) of each input variable of each system use case.[3]
  - All requirements regarding input/output relationships for each system use case.
  - Verification of the specified relative frequency of system use cases.
  - Sequential dependencies among use cases.
- Save test plans, test cases, and test results.
  - By saving tests, you can reuse them in future regression tests.
- Concentrate on the lemons.
  - If your time is limited, concentrate your testing efforts on the areas of the system that have been most problematic in the past.
- Check for unwanted side-effects.
  - Unintended side-effects of a programming change are common sources of errors. When testing a programming change, make sure areas of the system that the change was not supposed to affect are still working correctly.
- Execute tests in a safe testing environment.

Table 10.1 summarizes when to use the testing techniques covered in this chapter.

Structured Walkthroughs

Most people think of testing as a process involving the execution of a program by the computer. This is only one type of testing—referred to, appropriately, as *computer-based testing*. Testing, however, also includes *non-computer-based tests*. How can you test a system without actually executing it? You walk through some aspect of the system manually with a group of participants. The formal method for doing this is the *structured walkthrough*.

TABLE 10.1   Testing Techniques

To Do the Following	Use These Tools
Ensure that all of the code has been covered properly during testing	White-box techniques: statement, decision, condition, multiple condition coverage
Test the requirements for completeness and accuracy	Structured walkthrough
Test functional requirements for end-to-end business process	High-level integration tests based on business use cases
Test the system's response to simple conditions	Condition response tables
Test the system's response to a group of input conditions that might occur in any combination	Decision tables, decision trees
Design test data most likely to uncover bugs	Boundary-value analysis
Test how the system handles high volume	Volume test (a type of system test)
Test how the system handles a high level of activity within a short period of time	Stress test (a type of system test)
Test for user-friendliness	Usability test (a type of system test)
Test speed	Performance test (a type of system test)
Ensure processes that should remain unaffected by the release work as before	Regression test (a type of system test)
Submit the system for final acceptance by the user	User acceptance testing (UAT)

Structured Walkthrough

A *structured walkthrough* is a peer-review process for testing the completeness and accuracy of a project deliverable, such as a portion of the BRD.

Why Are Structured Walkthroughs an Important Aspect of Testing?

Errors are often thought to be exclusively due to bad programming; in fact, they can be introduced at any stage of a project. The beauty of walkthroughs is that, unlike computer-based testing, they can be performed before the software is written.

Early testing means early detection of errors. The sooner errors are found, the easier they are to fix. Also, unlike computer-based tests, walkthroughs tend to find the *cause* of a problem, not just its symptom. For example, a computer-based test may find symptoms, such as scattered situations where credit is advanced to non-worthy applicants; a walkthrough may uncover the cause—an incorrectly documented decision table for evaluating credit applications.

Requirements-Based (Black-Box) Testing

The purpose of *requirements-based testing* is to find variances between the software and the requirements. The business requirements document (BRD) acts as the reference point for these tests. The term *black-box tests* is also used for these types of tests, since the tester does not need to know anything about the internals of the software, such as the code and table structure, to design and run them. This is in contrast to *white-box tests*, which are technical tests that are based on a knowledge of the inner workings of the IT system.

Limitations of Requirements-Based Testing

Since no knowledge of the code is assumed with requirements-based testing, the only way to know definitively the effect that a particular set of inputs will have on the system is to test the system's response to it. This means that for full coverage, you'd have to test every possible set of input values and conditions. In practice, this is an unachievable standard, so instead you use techniques that help you design black-box tests that will uncover the greatest number of bugs in a given amount of time.

Use-Case Scenario Testing

Use-case scenario testing is one approach to requirements-based testing that tests the various scenarios of each use case. Use cases lend themselves well to testing. Because of the narrative style of the use-case documentation, it is already very close to being a testing script. And the way the use cases are organized—into end-to-end business use cases and user-goal system use cases—matches the way the tests are organized. I have often been asked if use cases, then, are *all* you need to design the test. The answer is no. To design tests, you need more detail, such as graphical user interface (GUI) screens, the structural model (which provides validation rules for attributes), and the documentation on business rules (stored in a business rules engine or kept manually in a folder). The system use cases may *refer* to these artifacts, but the artifacts are not part of the use-case documentation itself.

Deriving Use-Case Scenario Tests

Recall that your processing requirements were grouped around system use cases, each with their own group of scenarios. The flows were chosen so that they would cover all important scenarios:

- **Basic flow:** The normal path through the use case
- **Alternate flows:** Rarely occurring flows and other variations from the norm
- **Exception flows:** Unrecoverable errors and any other flows that result in the interaction ending without the user achieving the goal of the use case

Use the flows of the system use case to derive scenarios, then test each scenario. For example, one test scenario might walk through the basic flow. You might be able to design another test scenario that walks through the basic flow and all of the alternate flows. At a bare minimum, you'll want to ensure that the basic flow and each of the alternate and exception flows are covered at least once in the test scenarios. But you may also be interested in designing key tests that use certain combinations of the alternate flows. For example, one alternate flow for a stock-trading site may be "non-standard lot size" and another may be "order can only be partially filled." The software may be able handle each of these alternates one at a time but not when they occur together. To test the system's response to this situation, you'll want to include a test scenario that walks through both alternate flows. If you need to ensure you've covered *all* possible combinations of a set alternate flows, use decision tables, covered later in this chapter.

During test execution, you'll be looking to see whether the sequence of events during the test matches that described in the use case. One way to do this is to use the steps of the system use case as the source for the following test template. Place steps that begin with "The user..." in the "Action/Data" column of the template; place steps that begin with "The system..." in the "Expected Result/Response" column.

Test Template

Test #: _____   Project #: _____

System: _____   Test environment: _____

Test type (e.g., regression/ requirements-based, etc.):

Test objective: _____

System use case: _____   Flow: _____

Priority: _____

Next step in case of failure: _____

Planned start date: _____   Planned end date: _____

Actual start date: _____   Actual end date: _____

Times to repeat: _____

Pre-conditions (must be true before test begins): _____

Test Template (continued)

Req #	Action/Data	Expected Result/Response	Actual Result	Pass/ Fail

Tester ID: _____

Pass/fail: _____   Severity of failure: _____

Solution: _____

Comments: _____

Sign-off: _____

(Req # is short for requirement number and corresponds to the number used to identify the requirement in the BRD. Many organizations number their requirements so that they can be traced forward to test cases and other project artifacts. The numbering may be manual, or automatically generated with the use of a tool such as Rational RequisitePro.)

Decision Tables for Testing

When the input conditions affecting a system use case are interrelated, it is not enough to test for each input condition separately; you must test all *combinations* of input conditions. An input condition is any condition that will have an impact on the system response. Examples from a Web retail site include Item on Sale, Customer Discount, and Fast Delivery Method Selected. You'll find some input conditions documented in the system use case as alternate flows—for example, the alternate flow Non-Standard Lot Size. You might also see them already documented as part of the requirements in a decision table appended to a step of the use case or to the use case as a whole. In this case, you can reuse the decision table for testing purposes.

From a testing perspective, each column in the table identifies a test scenario. Keep in mind, though, that the column only *identifies* the test scenario; it does not fully *specify* it. To properly specify a test, you need to complete the test template for each test scenario you've identified from the columns. Also, as discussed in the upcoming section "Boundary-Value Analysis," you may need to create more than one test scenario per column.

The use of decision tables in this context may be complex, but that does not mean that this approach to testing is "white box." The input conditions and the expected system responses are still derived from the requirements—not from an examination of the code. This classifies the technique as "black box." (Later in this chapter, you'll learn that decision tables can also be used by programmers for white-box testing—but that is another matter.)

Case Study J1:
Deriving Test Cases from Decision Tables

You are designing test cases for the system use case Review Case Report. Fortunately, you earlier created a decision table as part of the requirements documentation, as shown in Figure J1.1. Note how each column in the table identifies the nature of the input data and systems response for each test scenario.

		1	2	3	4	5	6	7	8	9	10	11	12
CONDITION	Code of Good Practice Followed (Y/N)	Y	Y	Y	Y	Y	Y	N	N	N	N	N	N
	Steps and Procedures Followed? (Y/N)	Y	Y	Y	N	N	N	Y	Y	Y	N	N	N
	# PC Members (0–2,3–5,6–99)	0–2	3–5	6–99	0–2	3–5	6–99	0–2	3–5	6–99	0–2	3–5	6–99
ACTION	Mark as Not Payable	X			X			X	X	X	X	X	X
	Mark as Payable		X	X		X	X						
	Pay 1/2 Standard Amount					X	X						
	Pay Standard Amount		X										
	Pay Double Amount			X									

Figure J1.1
Validate case and determine payment amount.

> ## What the Decision Table Does *Not* Say about Testing
>
> The decision table shows only the net result of each test; it does not show the required sequencing of steps. For this reason, you need to complete the test template for each test scenario, indicating the expected sequence of actions. Use the system use-case description to work out the expected workflow for each case.
>
> Also, each column tells you something about the input data for a given test, but does not specify *exactly* which data to test for. For example, for the test corresponding to column 2 in Figure J1.1, the number of Peace Committee members may be three, four, or five. Which of these should you use? What about tests for invalid data? These issues are addressed by boundary-value analysis.

Boundary-Value Analysis

Boundary-value analysis is a technique for targeting test data most likely to reveal bugs. The technique is based on the premise that the system is most error-prone at points of change.

Boundary-value analysis can help you pinpoint test data for any requirements-based (black-box) test. If you are working from a decision table, then boundary-value analysis can help you decide which data to use for the test(s) indicated by each column of the table. The technique covers both positive and negative testing:

- A *positive test* is one that tests the system's response to valid conditions (success scenarios).

- A *negative test* is one that tests the system's response to invalid conditions (errors).

The following is a summary of boundary-value analysis rules:

- If the condition states that the *number* of input (or output) values must lie within a specific range:
  - Create two positive tests, one at either end of the range.
  - Create two negative tests, one just beyond the valid range at the low end and one just beyond the high end.

    For example, for the system use case Update Case that accepts 2–10 parties to a dispute, the positive tests would have the user enter exactly 2 and exactly 10 parties. Negative tests would try for 1 and 11 parties.

- Similarly, if an input or output *value* must lie within a range of values and the whole range is treated the same way:
  - Create two positive tests, one at either end of the range.
  - Create two negative tests, one just beyond the valid range at the low end and one just beyond the high end.

    For example, if the Ward Number attribute of the Peace Committee class has a valid range of 1–100, create two positive tests: 1, 100. Also create two negative tests: 0, 101.

- If an input or output value must lie within a range of values and different valid ranges are treated differently:
  - Create a positive test for each end of each valid range.
  - Create two negative tests, one just below the smallest acceptable value and one just above the highest.

    For example, the decision table for the system use case Review Case Report indicates that system response depends on # Peace Committee Members. The valid ranges are 0–2, 3–5, and 6–99. The positive test values are 0, 2, 3, 5, 6, and 100. The negative tests are −1 and 100.

- If an input or output value must be one of a set of valid options and all options are treated the same way:
  - Create one test for valid data using any value from the set.
  - Create one invalid test using any value not in the set.

    For example, the Reason Code No Gathering attribute of Case must match the code of one of the reason codes in the lookup table. Create one positive test where the code is found in the table and one negative test where it is not.

- If an input or output value must belong to a set of values and each one is treated differently:
  - Create one test for each valid option.
  - Create one invalid test using a value not in the set.

    For example, if the system treats criminal offenses differently from civil offenses, create a positive test for a case whose dispute code refers to a criminal dispute and another test where the code refers to a civil one. Also, create a negative test for where the dispute code is not found in the lookup table.

- If the requirements state that a certain condition must be true:
  - Create one valid test where the condition is satisfied.
  - Create one invalid test where the condition is not satisfied.

    For example, the Testimony attribute of Party to Dispute must be non-null. Create a positive test where testimony is entered and a negative test where it is not.

- To limit the number of tests you have to run, you can combine as many valid tests as possible in a single run. However, you may not combine invalid tests.

- Look out for any boundaries not covered in the preceding rules. For example, for any reports or screens, test one case where exactly one page or screen is filled and one test where the output goes over by one line. Wherever sorting occurs, test cases where everything is presorted; where all values are the same; and where one value is the lowest possible, and one is the highest. For input values, try negative numbers and zero. Try entering no value at all.

Case Study J2: Select Test Data Using Boundary-Value Analysis

You once again refer to the decision table for the system use case's review case report. Earlier, you noted that each column represents one or more test cases. Now you create precise test cases based on what you've learned about boundary-value analysis, as shown in Figure J2.1. (For the purposes of this case study, I've set an upper limit of 99 on the number of Peace Committee members.)

		1	2	3	4	5	6	7	8	9	10	11	12
CONDITION	Code of Good Practice Followed (Y/N)	Y	Y	Y	Y	Y	Y	N	N	N	N	N	N
	Steps and Procedures Followed? (Y/N)	Y	Y	Y	N	N	N	Y	Y	Y	N	N	N
	# PC Members (0–2,3–5,6–99)	0–2	3–5	6–99	0–2	3–5	6–99	0–2	3–5	6–99	0–2	3–5	6–99
ACTION	Mark as Not Payable	X			X			X	X	X	X	X	X
	Mark as Payable		X	X		X	X						
	Pay ½ Standard Amount					X	X						
	Pay Standard Amount		X										
	Pay Double Amount			X									

Figure J2.1
Selecting test data using boundary-value analysis.

Case Study J2: Resulting Documentation

Boundary value analysis leads you to design the test cases in Table J2.1.

TABLE J2.1   Test Cases Resulting from Boundary-Value Analysis*

Test #	Decision Table Col #	Code Followed?	Steps?	# PC Members
1	1	Y	Y	0
2	2	Y	Y	3
3	3	Y	Y	6
4	4	Y	N	2
5	5	Y	N	3
6	6	Y	N	6
7	7	N	Y	2
8	8	N	Y	5
9	9	N	Y	6
10	10	N	N	2
11	11	N	N	3
12	12	N	N	99
13		X	Y	2
14		–	Y	3
15		Y	–	5
16		N	X	2
17				1
18				X
19				100
20		N	Y	–

*Rows 13–20 are negative tests.

White-Box Testing

White-box testing is a testing methodology based on knowledge of the internal workings of the IT system.

Who Does White-Box Testing?

Developers perform these tests, since knowledge of programming code is required. But as a business analyst, you have a supporting role: You may be required to specify the *level* of white-box testing that the software must pass through before it is accepted. And after the tests are run, you might be called on to inspect evidence that the white-box tests have been carried out successfully. This proof sometimes comes in the form of a report produced by an automated testing product, confirming the level of white-box testing to which the software has been exposed. To support white-box testing, you need a basic understanding of what such testing can and cannot achieve and of the meaning of the white-box testing levels.

Limitations of White-Box Testing

To ensure that software is completely error-free, white-box testing would have to include enough tests to thoroughly "exercise" the code. In practice, however, this is impossible. Why? At first glance, it might seem sufficient to execute a set of tests that causes every statement to be executed at least once. Unfortunately, this does not supply sufficient coverage, because some errors show up only when a program's execution follows a specific *path* through the code. To white-box test a program fully, then, you would need to try all possible paths of statement execution. Because the number of tests usually required for full coverage is so high, other approaches are used to winnow the set of tests to a manageable size.

> **Even Small Programs Can Have an Astronomical Number of Pathways**
>
> Consider an operation containing 20 statements that are repeated up to 20 times. The body of the loop includes several nested IF-THEN-ELSE statements. It would take about 10^{14} tests to cover all of the possible sequences in which those statements could be executed.

White-Box Coverage Quality Levels

The following coverage levels are used to specify the degree of thoroughness of white-box testing, listed in order of increasing coverage. Depending on the level of risk, you may specify one of the following coverages:

- **Statement coverage:** Every coding statement is executed at least once. This coverage level is considered to be too low to be acceptable.

- **Decision coverage:** Every decision in the code has taken all possible outcomes at least once during the tests. Decision coverage is the minimum acceptable level of coverage. For example, if the source code contained the decision AGE OVER 20 AND LICENCE IS UNDER SUSPENSION, this expression would have to evaluate to both true and false at least once during the tests.

- **Condition coverage:** Every simple condition takes all possible outcomes at least once. For example, in the preceding example, the decision is actually a complex condition made of two simple conditions: AGE > 20 and LICENSE IS UNDER SUSPENSION. For this level of coverage, the tests must include cases where the condition AGE > 20 takes true and false outcomes and the condition LICENSE IS UNDER SUSPENSION takes true and false outcomes.

- **Multiple condition coverage:** Every combination of outcomes for simple conditions making up a complex condition is tested. For example, for the complex condition AGE > 20 AND LICENSE IS UNDER-SUSPENSION, you'd test the following

  - AGE > 20 is true and LICENSE IS UNDER SUSPENSION is true.

  - AGE > 20 is true and LICENSE IS UNDER SUSPENSION is false (that is, the license is not under suspension).

  - AGE > 20 is false (i.e., AGE <= 20) and LICENSE IS UNDER SUSPENSION is true.

  - AGE > 20 is false and LICENSE IS UNDER SUSPENSION is false.

You might be wondering if decision tables play any part here. There is a role for decision tables—but not the in the context you learned to use them earlier in this chapter. The conditions and actions in the tables discussed earlier were based on the *requirements*. The coverage tests we're currently dealing with, however, involve condition expressions and actions written in the *source code*. (These condition expressions may sometimes have parallel conditions in the requirements—but they often do not.) Decision tables can be used in a programming context to derive multiple condition coverage tests, using source-level conditions and actions. Use of decision tables in this way is beyond your role as BA because of the programming knowledge it requires.

Sequencing of White-Box Tests

When software is written, it is developed in modules, or units. In structured systems, the software unit is the *process*, known by various terms such as *subroutine*, *function*, or *subprogram*. In OO, the basic software unit is the class, which contains code for attributes and operations. In both structured and OO environments, a plan must be put together to sequence the testing of these units and their proper integration within the software. The process of planning and executing these piecemeal tests is called *unit testing*.

Unit Testing and the BA

While the developers usually carry out unit testing, the BA needs to be able to consult with the developers about the planning and scheduling of these tests. Since most systems in large organizations involve a hybrid of structured software (typically for back-end legacy systems) and OO (typically for Web-enabled front-end systems), as a BA, you'll need a basic understanding of unit testing in both environments.

Big Bang Approach to Unit Testing

There are a number of approaches for the sequencing of unit tests. In the *big bang* approach, each unit is first tested individually. Once this is complete, all units are integrated and tested in one "big bang" test.

In a structured system, these units are subroutines or functions. In an OO system, they are classes. In either environment, the developers often need to create "dummy" software to stand in for other units not being tested at that time. One of the disadvantages of the big bang approach is that, since units are first tested in complete isolation from the rest of the program, a large amount of dummy software has to be written. Another disadvantage is that the final big bang test is the first opportunity to test whether the units have been integrated properly in the software. If an integration problem shows up at this time, it will be very hard to diagnose. For this reason, the big bang approach is not advised—but is still used because it is easy to manage.

Incremental Approaches to Unit Testing

A preferred approach is the *incremental* approach, where each unit is added to the system one by one. With each incremental test, the internal workings of a unit *and* its integration with the rest of the system are tested. Since not much is being added with each test, diagnosis is easier.

In a structured environment, there are two types of incremental testing to choose from: *top-down* or *bottom-up*.

Top-Down Testing

In top-down testing, the units are tested starting from the mainline program (the high-level module that coordinates the major functions) and advances toward the low-level units that carry out basic functions. The advantage of this sequence is that it mirrors the order in which software units are usually developed. The disadvantage is that since high-level subroutines are tested before the low-level routines on which they depend, the tester must create stubs—"fake" units that take the place of the real low-level routines during testing.

Bottom-Up Testing

In bottom-up testing, the order is reversed: First the low-level routines are tested, followed by higher-level routines. The advantage of this approach is that it does not require the overhead of creating stubs. It does, however, require the creation of other stand-in software, called *drivers*, but these are usually easier to develop. The big disadvantage is that this sequence may not match the order in which the units are actually coded.

Incremental Testing in an OO Environment

In an OO environment, the units are not organized top to bottom. Rather, objects are seen as being on the same level, collaborating with each other to carry out system use cases. It makes no sense, therefore, to speak of a "top-down" or "bottom-up" approach. Instead, the system use cases direct the sequencing of tests. When software is developed iteratively (as is commonly the case with OO systems), a set of system use cases is developed and released (internally or to the user). During each iteration, only the classes and operations required for the scheduled use cases are developed and tested. With each iteration, more classes and operations are developed and tested until the entire system has been covered.

System Tests

Once the black-box tests have been completed, another battery of tests is executed. These are called *system tests*. With the exception of usability testing (a type of system test), you will not typically perform these tests, but you may be involved in planning them and in verifying that the tests have been conducted, so you should be aware of the tests in this category. The term system tests refers to a grab-bag of tests that go beyond functionality. The purpose of system tests is to test compliance with the non-functional requirements, also known as service-level requirements, or SLRs. The non-functional requirements specify the required level of service—for example, the maximum acceptable response time.

Myers on System Testing

Myers defines system testing as follows: "The purpose of *system testing* is showing that the product is inconsistent with its original objectives."

The idea behind system testing is that even if the code has been adequately tested for coverage (white-box testing) and has been shown to do everything expressed in the user requirements, it may still fail because it doesn't do these things well enough. It may not meet other objectives—such as those related to security, speed, and so on. Myers laid out a set of system tests designed to catch these kinds of failures.[4] These tests are still widely in use today. Following are some of the more popular of these tests.

- **Regression testing:** *Regression testing* validates whether features that were supposed to be unaffected by a new release still work as they should. The test helps avoid the "one step forward, two steps backward" problem: a programming modification designed to fix one problem inadvertently creating new ones. How much regression testing should you do? That depends on the level of risk. Often, organizations create a problem review board to set standards for regression testing and to evaluate on a case-by-case basis the degree of regression testing required.

- **Volume testing:** *Volume testing* verifies whether the system can handle large volumes of data. Why is this necessary? Some systems break down only when volume is high, such as a system that uses disk space to store files temporarily during a sort. When the volume is high, the system crashes because there isn't enough room for these temporary files. Also, some systems may become unbearably slow when volume is high. Often, this is due to the fact that the data tables become so large that searches and lookups take an inordinate amount of time.

- **Stress testing:** *Stress testing* subjects the system to heavy loads within a short period of time. What distinguishes this from volume testing is the time element. For example, an automated teller system is tested to see what happens when all machines are processing transactions at the same time, or a network server is tested to see what happens when a large number of users all log on at the same time.

- **Usability testing:** *Usability testing* looks for flaws in the human-factors engineering of the system. In other words, it attempts to determine whether the system is user-friendly. Isn't it enough that the system does what it's supposed to do? No. Users may reject it due to frustration with the user interface.

Usability Testing Questions

Questions investigated during usability testing include the following:

- Is the user interface appropriate for the educational level of the users?

- Are system messages written in easy-to-understand language?

- Do all error messages give clear, corrective direction? The user must always be given a "way out."

- Are there any inconsistencies in the user interfaces of the system? Look for inconsistencies with respect to screen layout, response to mouse clicks, and so on.

- Does the system provide sufficient redundancy checks on key input? Important data should be entered twice, or in two complementary ways—for example, a social security number *and* a name for financial transactions.

- Are all system options and features actually useful to the user? Unused "extras" make the system harder to learn and clutter the interface.

- Does the system confirm actions when necessary? The system must confirm important actions, such as the receipt of a customer's online order.

- Does the flow dictated by the system support the natural flow of the business?

- **Security testing:** *Security testing* attempts to find holes in the system's security procedures. For example, the tests will attempt to hack through password protection or to introduce a virus to the system.

- **Performance testing:** *Performance testing* locates areas where the system does not meet its efficiency objectives. Performance tests include the measuring and evaluation of the following:

  - **Response time:** The elapsed time it takes the system to respond to a user request.

  - **CPU time:** The amount of processing time required.

  - **Throughput:** The number of transactions processed per second.

- **Storage testing:** *Storage testing* checks for cases where storage objectives are not met. These objectives include requirements for random access memory (RAM) and disk requirements.

- **Configuration testing:** *Configuration testing* checks for failure of the system to perform under all of the combinations of hardware and software configurations allowed for in the objectives. For example, these tests look for problems occurring when a supported processor, operating system revision, printer driver, or printer model is used.

- **Compatibility/conversion testing:** Often, the goal of an IT project is to replace some part of an existing system. The objective of *compatibility testing* is to verify whether the replacement software produces the same result as the original modules (with allowance for new or revised features) and is compatible with the existing system. *Conversion testing* verifies whether the procedures used to convert the old data into new formats work properly.

- **Reliability testing:** *Reliability testing* checks for failure to meet specific reliability objectives. For example, the objectives for one of my early programs—a food-testing program—stated that an automated count of bacteria grown on a grid be correct to a given accuracy. Reliability testing would verify whether this objective was met. Another metric that falls in this category is mean time to failure (MTTF).

▪ **Recovery testing:** *Recovery testing* checks for failure of the recovery procedures to perform as stated in the objectives. For example, an online financial update program keeps a log of all activity. If the master files are corrupted, the objectives state that a recovery procedure will be able to restore files to their state just before the crash by processing the day's transaction log against a backup of the previous day's files. A recovery test would look for failure of this procedure to recover the files.

Beyond the System Tests

The BA should plan for a final set of tests to take place after the system tests are complete. These are UAT, beta testing, parallel testing, and installation testing.

▪ **User acceptance testing (UAT):** Acceptance testing is the final testing of the system before the users sign off on it. This test is often performed by the users themselves, although in some organizations, the BA performs the test while the user looks on. There are two alternative approaches to UAT—a formal and an informal approach.

Formal UAT Versus Informal UAT

In the formal approach, the developers and users sign a document beforehand that lays out the terms of the UAT. The document stipulates that if the users carry out the UAT under the terms described in the agreement and if the tests are successful, the users will accept the system. By having participants sign off on this document before the UAT, the BA sets the stage for a clean end to the project.

Proponents of the informal approach argue that the formal approach is inappropriate. In their view, users should have free reign to experiment with the system to make sure it can let them do their jobs, which might involve unexpected variations of usage. For example, IBM's RUP methodology states:

> "In informal acceptance testing, the test procedures for performing the test are not as rigorously defined as for formal acceptance testing. The functions and business tasks to be explored are identified and documented, but there are no particular test cases to follow. The individual tester determines what to do. This approach to acceptance testing is not as controlled as formal testing and is more subjective than the formal one."

- **Beta testing:** Alpha testing is the testing of the system by the manufacturer. These are the kinds of tests you have been reading about until this point. *Beta testing* occurs after the alpha testing is complete. In beta testing, copies of the system are distributed to a wide group of users, selected to represent the various configurations, volume, stress, and functional needs of the target user population. The developers correct any errors uncovered by beta testing before releasing the production version. Beta testing is often used for systems that will have a wide distribution.

- **Parallel testing:** On some projects, the system undergoes *parallel testing* before final acceptance. With this approach, the new system is put into place and used while the old system is run concurrently. Both systems should provide equivalent outputs (except for any variations resulting from new enhancements and modifications). Parallel testing minimizes risk. If errors arise, the user can quickly revert to the old system until the problem is resolved.

- **Installation testing:** *Installation testing* is performed after the software is installed. Its purpose is to check for errors in the installation process itself. This test checks whether all files that should have been installed are, indeed, present; whether the content of the files is correct; and so on.

Step 2d: Specify Implementation Plan

The BRD must include an implementation plan so that steps required when releasing the system can be planned for in advance. The issues addressed typically include the following:

Training:

- Who is to be trained?
- How will training be done?
- What resources (hardware, software, training rooms, trainers, administration, and so on) will be required?

Conversion:

- Identify existing data that will need to be converted (due to new file formats, new database management software, and so on).
- Plan promotion of programs (from the current version to the new one).
- Plan granting of privileges to the users.
- Schedule jobs (for batch systems).
- Advise operations of which jobs to add to the production run: daily, weekly, monthly, quarterly, semi-annually, or annually.

- Ensure that the job is planned to be executed in the right sequence— that is, after certain jobs are run and before others.

- Advise operations of the reports to be printed and the distribution list for reports and files.

Rollout:

- Advise all affected users of the promotion date for the project.

End-user procedures:

- Write up the procedures for the affected departments.

- Distribute an end-user procedures document to affected departments.

Post-Implementation Follow-Up

Follow up within a reasonable time frame after implementation to ensure that the project is running successfully and to verify that the project is achieving high-level goals. For example, check back six months after installation to see whether market share has indeed increased 6 percent as described in the BRD. Determine whether any further enhancements or changes are needed to ensure the success of the project. Also, the post-implementation follow-up offers a good opportunity to review lessons learned from the project.

Step 2e: Set Baseline for Development

Once the BRD is complete, freeze all analysis documentation. Save this "frozen copy" so that team members will be able to refer back to it later. This copy becomes the "baseline"— or beginning point—for the next step: the actual development of the software.

Chapter Summary

In this chapter, you learned how to design test cases that are most likely to uncover software bugs using the tools and principles of structured testing as applied to OO projects. Also, you learned about the features of an implementation plan and the need for a post-implementation follow-up.

Tools and concepts that you learned about in this chapter include the following:

- *Structured testing* is the process of using standardized techniques to locate flaws (bugs). Flaws detected by structured testing include those introduced during business analysis, design, and programming.

- A *structured walkthrough* is a peer-review process for testing the completeness and accuracy of a project deliverable, such as a portion of the BRD.

- *White-box tests* are technical tests that are based on a knowledge of the inner workings of the IT system.

- The purpose of *requirement-based testing* is to find variances between the software and the requirements. The business requirements document (BRD) acts as the reference point for these tests. The term *black-box tests* is also used for these types of tests, since the tester does not need to know anything about the internals of the software, such as the code and table structure, to design and run them.

- *Use-case scenario testing* is one approach to requirements-based testing that tests the various scenarios of each use case.

- A *decision table* shows only the net result of each test.

- When software is written, it is developed in modules, or units. In both structured and OO environments, a plan must be put together to sequence the testing of these units and their proper integration within the software. The process of planning and executing these piecemeal tests is called *unit testing*.

- *Boundary-value analysis* is a technique for targeting test data most likely to reveal bugs. The technique is based on the premise that the system is most error-prone at points of change.

- Once the black-box tests have been completed, another battery of tests is executed. These are called *system tests*. These are a grab-bag of tests that go beyond functionality. The purpose of system tests is to test compliance with the non-functional requirements, also known as service-level requirements, or SLRs. The non-functional requirements specify the required level of service—for example, the maximum acceptable response time.

- *Regression testing* validates whether features that were supposed to be unaffected by a new release still work as they should.

- *Volume testing* verifies whether the system can handle large volumes of data.

- *Stress testing* subjects the system to heavy loads within a short period of time.

- *Usability testing* looks for flaws in the human-factors engineering of the system.

- *Security testing* attempts to find holes in the system's security procedures.

- *Performance testing* locates areas where the system does not meet its efficiency objectives.

- *Storage testing* checks for cases where storage objectives are not met.

- *Configuration testing* checks for failure of the system to perform under all of the combinations of hardware and software configurations allowed for in the objectives.

- Often, the goal of an IT project is to replace some part of an existing system. The objective of *compatibility testing* is to verify whether the replacement software produces the same result as the original modules (with allowance for new or revised features) and is compatible with the existing system.

- *Reliability testing* checks for failure to meet specific reliability objectives.

- *Recovery testing* checks for failure of the recovery procedures to perform as stated in the objectives.
- The BRD must include an *implementation plan* so that steps required when releasing the system can be planned for in advance.

Endnotes

[1] Recall that an alternate flow is an alternative to the normal path of events for a use case; for example, in the use case Withdraw Funds, the alternate flow is Maximum Daily Limit Exceeded. An exception flow is a path taken when a non-recoverable error occurs, such as Communications Down.

[2] For example, over and above that in the flows described previously.

[3] Boundary-value analysis provides rules for selecting input values within and outside of the domain.

[4] G. Myers, *The Art of Software Testing,* 1978, page 106.

CHAPTER 11

WHAT DEVELOPERS DO WITH YOUR REQUIREMENTS

Chapter Objectives

As the project moves into the Construction phase, the developers (systems analyst, systems architect, database administrator, and so on) start the work of adapting your business model for technical use. On a waterfall project, this is the point at which your active participation stops. On an iterative project, you continue gathering requirements during the Construction phase, completing the requirements needed for the selected use-case scenarios before they are implemented in an iteration. In either case, once design and coding are under way, you need to be available to answer the questions that inevitably arise during the development process. To assist you in communicating with the developers, this chapter looks at some of the issues that occupy them as they turn your business model into a design specification.

Tools and concepts that you'll be introduced to in this chapter include the following:

- OO analysis patterns
- Visibility
- Control classes
- Boundary classes
- Sequence diagrams
- Communication diagrams
- Timing diagrams
- Deployment diagrams
- Layered architecture

- Interfaces
- Implementing OO using procedural languages
- Implementing OO using RDBMS

OO Patterns

Some problems are difficult to design a solution for, yet are common to many systems. The idea of patterns is to provide a "best practices" solution for these common problems. A pattern consists of a problem description, one or more diagrams (class diagrams, sequence diagrams, and communication diagrams) that describe a design solution to the problem and, often, a segment of code that implements the design. It is typically the systems analyst who adapts the business model by incorporating these patterns.

Examples

Following are some examples of OO patterns:

- The business structural model states that an object has many roles and that some operations and attributes apply to all roles. The *strategy* pattern offers a combination of aggregation and inheritance to standardize role handling.
- An object is composed of other objects that may be composed of other objects, and so on. Any composition level may be skipped. If one object at any level needs to be operated on, all the objects below it or above it will require a similar operation (for example, a recall of all components). The *composite* pattern offers a combination of aggregation and inheritance to turn this complicated issue into a simple design solution.

Visibility

Visibility is a property that can be used to describe a class member.

Member

A *member* of a class is an attribute or operation.

Visibility determines whether other classes can refer to a class member, and whether other objects can "see" (and therefore use) this attribute or operation.

What They Say:

Visibility: "The visibility attribute provides the means to constrain the usage of a named element, either in namespaces or in access to the element. It is intended for use in conjunction with import, generalization, and access mechanisms.[1] ...VisibilityKind is an enumeration of the following literal values: public; private; protected; package."[2] (UML)

What They Mean:

Visibility is a property of a model element such as a class member. Visibility may have only specific values. These values—Public, Private, Protected, and Package—describe whether the element can be seen outside of the context in which it is defined.

Example

The CashAccount class has an operation, DepositFunds(), that other classes use. This operation entails adjusting the general ledger, a process described in the internal operation EnterDepositIntoGeneralLedger(). The systems analyst specifies the visibility of DepositFunds() as Public, meaning that operations in other classes can refer to it. The visibility of EnterDepositIntoGeneralLedger(), on the other hand, is specified as Private, meaning that only operations of the CashAccount class can refer to it.

Visibility Options

The options for specifying visibility are as follows:

- **Private:** Code for the class may refer to the member by name. Code in other classes may not. Specializations inherit the member but may not refer to it by name. The symbol for private is a minus sign (–). For example, a specialized CheckingAccount class inherits a private attribute, Balance, from a generalized Account class. Every CheckingAccount object will have a Balance attribute but the attribute will be accessible only by operations defined for the Account class.

- **Protected:** The rules for a protected member are similar to those for a private member, except that specializations may refer to the member by name. The symbol for protected is a pound sign (#). For example, a specialized CheckingAccount class inherits a protected attribute, #AccountNumber, from a generalized Account class. Every CheckingAccount object will have an AccountNumber attribute and be accessible to operations defined in the CheckingAccount class.

- **Public:** Any element may access the member. The symbol for public is a plus sign (+).

- ▪ **Package:** The member is visible to all elements within the nearest enclosing package. Outside the nearest enclosing package, the member is not visible. The symbol for package is a tilde (~).

Control Classes

In this book, we have only dealt with entity classes. Developers add other types of classes to the system, however. One of these is the *control class*. Ivar Jacobson introduced control classes to address one of the shortcomings of OO[3]. He noted that while it is often easier to modify OO systems than the older "structured" systems, some changes are more difficult in OO. In particular, OO makes it harder to change the *sequencing* of the operations required by a system use case. The problem is that, in OO, these operations are scattered among the classes involved in the use case instead of being listed in a single controlling program. To correct the problem, he suggested the addition of a control class to encapsulate, in one software unit, the sequencing logic of a use case. As a rule of thumb, one control class is introduced for each system use case.

Boundary Classes

Systems should be insulated as much as possible from changes in other systems. Otherwise, a change in one would create an unacceptable ripple effect on others. The OO approach is to define a boundary class for each external system. This creates a bottleneck to the other system: The only way that the system under design is allowed to communicate with another is by sending a message to the boundary object. The advantage of this approach is that any changes or bugs affecting communication with the external system will be localized in the boundary class—and, therefore, easy to fix or modify[4]. As a rule of thumb, one boundary class is allocated for each external system and one for each interaction between a human actor and a system use case, as depicted on the system use case diagrams.

Sequence Diagrams

A *sequence diagram* describes the sequence of operations during one scenario of a system use case and determines which object carries out each operation.[5] The UML categorizes it as an *interaction diagram*—a diagram that highlights how objects interact with each other.

Some business analysts use sequence diagrams as an alternative to activity diagrams with partitions (swimlanes). Instead of drawing one complex activity diagram to cover all scenarios, the BA draws one simple sequence diagram for each scenario. Each diagram is simple, since it describes only one scenario. The disadvantage of sequence diagrams for this purpose is that they require the BA to work out not only which object *performs* each action but also which object *requests* the action. This is often difficult to determine in a business context. In addition, BAs tend to have more difficulty using this diagram than its counterpart, the activity diagram with partitions. For these reasons, sequence diagrams are not advised for BA use. On the other hand, sequence diagrams are an excellent way to design the distribution of operations among classes for programming purposes.

Example: A Sequence Diagram

Figure 11.1 shows how a systems analyst might attempt to design the object interactions required for the steps within the Disburse Payments system use case required to create a payment to a Peace Committee member. An excerpt from the use case follows:

System use case: Disburse Payments

2. Flow of Events

   Basic Flow:

   ...

   2.2 The user selects a case.

   2.3 The system displays the amount payable for the case.

   2.4 The system displays each Peace Committee member assigned to the case.

   2.5 The system displays the Peace Committee member account owned by each of the displayed Peace Committee members.

   ...

   2.7 The user approves the disbursement.

   2.8 The system creates payments for the case.

   2.9 The system marks the case as Paid.

Using modeling tools (such as those in the Rational suite of products) the operations identified during the drawing of the sequence diagram can be automatically added to the classes involved, making the design process easier.

The diagram in Figure 11.1 indicates the following:

- The convener selects a case on the Disbursement GUI (graphical user interface) screen.

- The Disbursement GUI sends the message QueryCase() to the Disbursement Control object, requesting it to query payment-related details about the case.

- The Disbursement Control object services this request by passing a number of messages to the Case object. These include GetPayableAmount(), GetPcMember(), and GetPcAccount(). These are requests to retrieve payment and Peace Committee member information relevant to the case. (To keep the diagram simple, only one Peace Committee member account is shown, though more are involved.)

- The convener approves the disbursement for the case.
- The GUI responds to the approval by sending the message CreatePayments() to the Disbursement Control object.
- The Disbursement Control object responds by sending a Create() message to each required Payment object. (The diagram only shows one of these.) Though not shown on this draft of the diagram, payment details such as the destination and amount of the payment are passed at this time as arguments.
- The Payment object sends a Withdraw() message to the cash account and a Deposit() message to the Peace Committee member account.
- The Disbursement Control object finishes the process by sending the message SetPaidStatus() to the Case object to indicate that payments have been made.

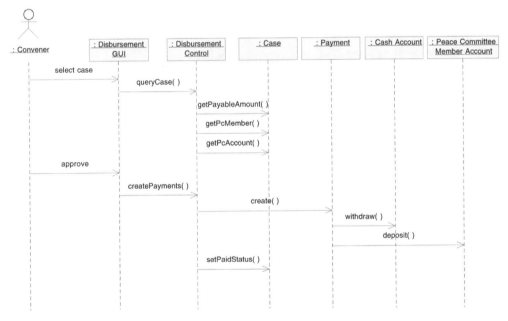

Figure 11.1
Designing object interactions with a sequence diagram.

Later, the systems analyst could add more steps to the diagram to indicate how payments are also made to the fund accounts.

Communication Diagrams

Like the sequence diagram, the communication diagram is categorized in the UML as an interaction diagram. Both diagrams can show the sequencing of operations for a scenario and indicate which object does which operation. However, each highlights a different aspect of the collaboration: The communication diagram highlights *structure*—the ways in which objects are linked to each other—while the sequence diagram highlights *timing*—the order in which messages are sent between objects.

In a communication diagram, objects are connected by solid lines (links). The messages are indicated as labeled arrows above the links. Each message is numbered to indicate sequencing. The communication diagram in Figure 11.2 illustrates the scenario shown in the previous sequence diagram shown in Figure 11.1.

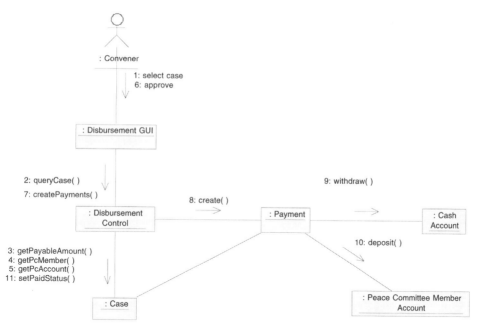

Figure 11.2
Designing object interactions with a communication diagram.

Other Diagrams

The UML contains other diagrams you might come across occasionally. Following is a brief introduction to two of these—the timing diagram and the deployment diagram.

Timing Diagrams

The timing diagram is a new UML 2 feature. It can be used to show the length of time that an object stays in each state. For example, suppose that rules dictated that a Peace Gathering had to spend 30 minutes in a fact-finding state, 60 minutes in deliberation, and 15 minutes in closing. A timing diagram might show all of this, as shown in Figure 11.3.

Timing Diagram

"Timing Diagrams are used to show interactions when a primary purpose of the diagram is to reason about time. Timing diagrams focus on conditions changing within and among Lifelines along a linear time axis. Timing diagrams describe behavior of both individual classifiers and interactions of classifiers, focusing attention on time of occurrence of events causing changes in the modeled conditions of the Lifelines."[6] (UML)

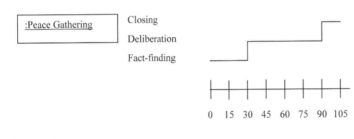

Figure 11.3
A timing diagram.

Deployment Diagrams

Deployment diagrams indicate how the software is to be installed across systems—for example, what will be installed on the server and what will be installed on the admin PCs.

Layered Architecture

Layered architecture is an approach to splitting up software into packages. The term refers to breaking up a software application into distinct layers or tiers[7]. These levels are arranged above one another, each serving distinct and separate tasks. Software in one tier may only access software in another tier, according to strict rules. In an OO system, systems analysts create class packages for each tier and populate these with classes that implement the architecture. For example, they might add a class to handle the saving and retrieving of objects from the database.

There are a number of approaches to layered architecture:

- Monolithic (One-tier)
- Two-tier
- Three-tier
- *N*-tier

Monolithic, Two-Tier, Three-Tier, and *N*-Tier Architecture

Any software application can be seen as consisting of three broad areas:

- **Data logic:** The software to manage the data
- **Business (processing) logic:** The software that enacts the business rules
- **Presentation (interface) logic:** The software that manages the presentation of the output (such as screens)

In *monolithic architecture*, these three areas are all bundled together in a single application. Monolithic architecture is often employed on mainframe systems.

The common approach for new systems is to separate the application into various layers, or tiers. In *two-tier architecture*, there are two layers: a server (a central computer system) and a client (one system at each desk). In the "thin client, fat server" variation on this theme, the presentation logic and minimal business logic reside on the client system; the rest is on the server. In "fat client, thin server," the presentation logic and much of the business logic reside on the client.

In *three-tier architecture*, there are three layers, or subsystems: a client system, loaded with presentation logic; an application server[8] with business logic; and a data server with data logic.

Finally, in *N-tier architecture* any number (*N*) of levels is arranged, each serving distinct and separate tasks.

Interfaces

Developers may also add to the classes introduced by the BA by designing interfaces. An *interface*[9] acts like a generalized class except that it has no attributes and no process logic; only operation names and standard rules for invoking them are defined. Each class that obeys the interface must conform to the interface's rule regarding the operations. A class that obeys the interface is said to be a *type* of the interface.

> **Interface**
>
> "A named set of operations that characterize the behavior of an element." (UML 2)

There are a number of ways to indicate an interface in the UML. The simplest way is to use the simple box notation, with the stereotype <<Interface>>. The types are connected to the interface with an arrow that looks like the generalization relationship, except that it is dashed, as shown in Figure 11.4[10]. The figure shows three different systems for checking a person's credit: Verify, CCCheck, and CCRater. Each must have methods for performing the operations defined in the interface Bank-to-Bank Common Interface—but the methods may differ from system to system.

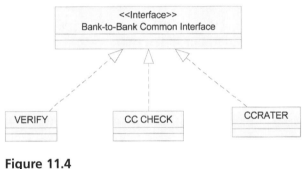

Figure 11.4
An interface.

Mix-Ins

A *mix-in* is a generalized class used to add functionality to any class that inherits from it, such as the mix-in Saveable to Disk. Mix-ins are added to the model to avoid the problems usually associated with multiple inheritance.

Implementing OO Using an OO Language

Once the systems analyst has added to and adapted the classes defined by the BA, the next step is to create code that conforms to the model. When the target programming language is OO-compliant (such as the .NET languages and C++), specifications for the classes and their relationships, attributes, and operations can all be converted to code in a straightforward manner. In fact, tools such as Rational Rose can do this automatically. Some tools rely on the class diagrams for code generation. Others rely on the state-machine diagrams.

Implementing OO Using Procedural Languages

The developers may use object-oriented design approaches despite the fact that the target programming language is written in a non-OO, procedural language such as COBOL.[11] In fact, I worked in such an environment many years ago. The organization decided on this path because it wanted to take advantage of OO's reusability without having to convert to a new language. Non-OO languages can be used so that they emulate OO languages. The key is to use the available units—subroutines—and make them act like classes. In most cases, however, OO design is usually used only when the implementing language is object-oriented.

Implementing a Database from a Structural OO Model Using an RDBMS

You've learned that the class diagrams provide guidance in the design of the database. OO database management systems that support OO ideas such as inheritance do exist, but currently, they are rarely used. Most organizations use another technology called relational database management systems (RDBMS). Examples of RDBMS technology are DB2, SQL, and Access.

RDBMS does not directly support OO features such as inheritance and class operations. Nevertheless, with a little effort, you can implement the class diagrams of OO using RDBMS; in fact this is commonly done. To do this, each entity class is implemented as a table (file) in the RDBMS database. The attributes are implemented as fields. Extra attributes (called *foreign keys*) are added, when necessary, in order to link records to each other.

While RDBMS databases do not directly support inheritance and aggregation, they can be adapted to behave as though they do. For example, each generalized and specialized class is implemented as a table. Each specialized object appears twice: once as a record in the generalized file and once in the specialized file. The records share the same unique identifier (primary key).

Chapter Summary

In this chapter, you were introduced to advanced OO topics. Tools and concepts in this chapter included the following:

- *OO patterns* describe best practices for modeling commonly occurring situations.
- *Visibility* defines the degree to which a model element may be accessed by other elements.
- *Control classes* manage the sequencing of steps over the course of a use case.

- *Boundary classes* handle communication between the system and external systems.

- *Sequence diagrams* depict workflow for a particular scenario and are used primarily in design.

- *Communication diagrams* depict the passing of messages between objects in a way that highlights structure.

- *Timing diagrams* can depict how long an object stays in each state.

- *Deployment diagrams* indicate how software is to be installed.

- *Layered architecture* is an approach to splitting up software into distinct tiers.

- An *interface* defines the operations that classes that conform to it must be able to support.

- OO models may be implemented as code using *procedural languages* and as RDBMS tables even though those target development environments were not originally designed to support OO.

Endnotes

[1] *UML Superstructure Specification*, v2.2, OMG, 2009, page 99.

[2] *UML Superstructure Specification*, v2.2, OMG, 2009, page 139.

[3] However, the control stereotype (used to identify this type of class) is not a predefined, standard UML stereotype.

[4] Please note that *boundary* is not a predefined, standard UML stereotype.

[5] This is a feature it shares with activity diagrams with partitions.

[6] *UML Superstructure Specification*, v2.2, OMG, 2009, page 521.

[7] The terms *layer* and *tier* are often used synonymously. The term *tier* emphasizes the "one-above-the-other" arrangement of the levels.

[8] Also called *middle tier*.

[9] This is not to be confused with classes that define user interfaces.

[10] Other notations are the lollipop and ball-and-socket notations.

[11] OO COBOL exists but is not widely used.

THE B.O.O.M. PROCESS

Adapt the following process to your project-management methodology. For example, on iterative projects, step 2 peaks during the Discovery phase, but continues afterward because not all requirements are gathered before design and coding begin. As well, on such projects, an entire cycle of analysis, design, coding, and testing occurs during each iteration of a phase. Moreover, on agile projects, the requirements are not baselined because they may be changed at any time as long as they are not being implemented. (For a complete discussion of the impact of the lifecycle approach on BA activities, see the section "Adapting the Noble Path" in Chapter 2, "Overview of BA Activities Throughout the Life Cycle" in *The Business Analyst's Handbook*, by this author.)

Please note that, in the following steps, artifacts created or revised by each activity are shown in brackets.

1: Initiation

The purpose of the Initiation phase is to make the business case for the project and create UI prototypes and architectural proofs of concept. (Prototypes at this stage are likely to be disposable. Any proofs of concept are largely paper-based.)

1a) Model business use cases

    i)   Identify business use cases (business use-case diagram)

    ii) Scope business use cases (activity diagram)

1b) Model system use cases

    i)   Identify actors (role map)

    ii) Identify system use-case packages (system use-case diagram)

    iii) Identify system use cases (system use-case diagram)

1c) Begin structural model (class diagrams for key business classes)

1d) Set baseline for Discovery (BRD/Initiation)

2: Discovery

The purpose of this phase is to conduct investigations leading to an understanding of the solution's desired behavior. Requirements analysis peaks during this phase but never disappears entirely. During this phase, the BA elicits detailed requirements from stakeholders, analyzes them, and documents them for verification by stakeholders and for use by the developers. Architectural proofs of concept are also constructed during the Discovery phase.

2a) Behavioral analysis

    i) Describe system use cases (use-case description)

    ii) Describe state behavior (state-machine diagram)

        1. Identify states of critical objects

        2. Identify state transitions

        3. Identify state activities

        4. Identify superstates

        5. Identify concurrent states

2b) Structural analysis (class and object diagrams): Perform in parallel with 2a

   i)   Identify entity classes

   ii)   Model generalizations

   iii)   Model transient roles

   iv)   Model whole/part relationships

   v)   Analyze associations

   vi)   Analyze multiplicity

   vii)   Link system use cases to the structural model

   viii) Add attributes

   ix)   Add lookup tables

   x)   Distribute operations

   xi)   Revise class structure

2c) Specify testing (test plan/decision tables)

   i)   Specify white-box testing quality level

   ii)   Specify black-box test cases

   iii)   Specify system tests

2d) Specify implementation plan (implementation plan)

2e) Set baseline for Construction (BRD/Discovery)

BUSINESS REQUIREMENTS DOCUMENT (BRD) TEMPLATE

Following is a template for a business requirements document (BRD). The document includes many best practices in use today. Don't be limited by the template, however; adapt it to your needs, adding or subtracting sections as required.

Once your organization has settled on a template, adjust it regularly based on lessons learned from previous projects. After each project, ask, "What type of requirements documentation did we miss on this project?" "Where did we go into more detail than we needed to?" Based on the responses to these questions, your organization may decide to add, contract, or remove entire sections of the BRD.

The best way to use the template is to allow for some flexibility: Allow individual projects to deviate from the template, but define how and when deviations may occur, and require any project that uses an altered template to justify the deviation. The BRD template that follows gives each technique covered in this book a "home" in the final requirements documentation.

Keep in mind, as well, that the BRD may not actually reside in one place, but may be assembled from separate components, with different assemblies geared for different audiences.

Business Requirements Document (BRD)

Project No.: _____

Production Priority: ____

Target Date: _____

Approved by:

_____   _____

Name of user, department   Date

_____   _____

Name of user, department   Date

Prepared by:

_____   _____

Name of user, department   Date

Filename: _____

Version No.: _____

Table of Contents

- Version Control
  - Revision History
  - RACI Chart
- Executive Summary
  - Overview
  - Background
  - Objectives
  - Requirements
  - Proposed Strategy
  - Next Steps
- Scope
  - Included in Scope
  - Excluded from Scope
  - Constraints
  - Impact of Proposed Changes
- Risk Analysis
  - Technological Risks
  - Skills Risks
  - Political Risks
  - Business Risks
  - Requirements Risks
  - Other Risks
- Business Case
- Timetable
- Business Use Cases
  - Business Use-Case Diagrams
  - Business Use-Case Descriptions
- Actors
  - Workers
  - Business Actors
  - Other Systems
  - Role Map

- User Requirements
  - System Use-Case Diagrams
  - System Use-Case Descriptions
- State-Machine Diagrams
- Nonfunctional Requirements
  - Performance Requirements
    - Stress Requirements
    - Response-Time Requirements
    - Throughput Requirements
  - Usability Requirements
  - Security Requirements
  - Volume and Storage Requirements
  - Configuration Requirements
  - Compatibility Requirements
  - Reliability Requirements
  - Backup/Recovery Requirements
  - Training Requirements
- Business Rules
- State Requirements
  - Testing State
  - Disabled State
- Structural Model
  - Class Diagrams: Entity Classes
  - Entity-Class Documentation
- Test Plan
- Implementation Plan
  - Training
  - Conversion
  - Scheduling of Jobs
  - Rollout
- End-User Procedures
- Post-Implementation Follow-Up
- Other Issues
- Sign-Off

Version Control

Completing the following table makes it easy to come back later and track what changes were made to the requirements at each point in the project, who made them, and why they were made. This is a way of implementing change control on the BRD.

Revision History

Version #	Date	Authorization	Responsibility (Author)	Description

RACI Chart for This Document

The RACI chart identifies the persons who need to be contacted whenever changes are made to this document. RACI stands for responsible, accountable, consulted, and informed. These are the main codes that appear in a RACI chart, used here to describe the roles played by team members and stakeholders in the production of the BRD. They are adapted from charts used to assign roles and responsibilities during a project.

The following describes the full list of codes used in the table:

Codes Used in RACI Chart

*	Authorize	Has ultimate signing authority for any changes to the document.
R	Responsible	Responsible for creating this document.
A	Accountable	Accountable for accuracy of this document (for example, the project manager).
S	Supports	Provides supporting services in the production of this document.
C	Consulted	Provides input (such as an interviewee).
I	Informed	Must be informed of any changes.

RACI Chart

Name	Position	*	R	A	S	C	I

Executive Summary

The "Executive Summary" section should be a précis of the entire document. It should summarize, in a page or two, the context for the document (why it was written), the main issues raised within, and the main conclusions of the document. The purpose of the summary is to provide just enough detail for a high-level stakeholder (who may not have time to read the whole thing) and to help any other potential reader ascertain whether it is worth reading the rest of the document.

This is a one-page summary of the document, divided into the following subsections.

Overview

This subsection of Executive Summary is a one-paragraph introduction that explains the nature of the project.

Background

This subsection of Executive Summary provides details leading up to the project that explain why the project is being considered. Discuss the following where appropriate: marketplace drivers, business drivers, and technology drivers.

Objectives

This subsection of Executive Summary details the business objectives addressed by the project.

Requirements

This subsection of Executive Summary is a brief summary of the requirements addressed in this document.

Proposed Strategy

This subsection of Executive Summary recommends a strategy for proceeding based on alternatives.

Next Steps

This subsection of Executive Summary describes specific actions to be taken next. Complete the following for each action.

- **Action**: Describe the specific action to be taken.
- **Responsibility**: State who is responsible for taking this action.
- **Expected Date**: State when the action is expected to be taken.

Scope

The "Scope" section defines what is to be included and excluded from the project, what has been predetermined about the project (constraints), the business processes affected by the project, and the impact of the project on stakeholders.

Included in Scope

This subsection of Scope is a brief description of business areas covered by the project.

Excluded from Scope

This subsection of Scope briefly describes business areas *not* covered by the project.

Constraints

This subsection of Scope documents predefined requirements and conditions.

Impact of Proposed Changes

This subsection of Scope describes the impact of proposed changes in the business area. Use the following table to document the impact.

Business Use Case	New?	Desired Functionality	Current Functionality (If a Change)	Stakeholders/ Systems	Priority

Risk Analysis

In this section of the BRD, you describe risks. A *risk* is something that could affect the success or failure of a project. Analyze risks regularly as the project progresses. While you may not be able to avoid every risk, you can limit each risk's impact on the project by preparing for it beforehand.

For each risk, you'll note the likelihood of its occurrence, the cost to the project if it does occur, and the strategy for handling the risk. Strategies include the following

- **Avoid:** Do something to eliminate the risk.
- **Mitigate:** Do something to reduce damage if risk materializes.
- **Transfer:** Pass the risk up or out to another entity.
- **Accept:** Do nothing about the risk. Accept the consequences.

Technological Risks

This subsection of "Risk Analysis" specifies new technology issues that could affect the project.

Skills Risks

This subsection of "Risk Analysis" specifies the risk of not getting staff with the required expertise for the project.

Political Risks

This subsection of "Risk Analysis" identifies political forces that could derail or affect the project.

Business Risks

This subsection of "Risk Analysis" describes the business implications if the project is canceled.

Requirements Risks

This subsection of "Risk Analysis" describes the risk that you have not correctly described the requirements. List areas whose requirements were most likely to have been incorrectly captured.

Other Risks

In this subsection of "Risk Analysis," document any other risks not covered in the prior subsections.

Business Case

Describe the business rationale for this project. This section may contain estimates on cost/benefit, return on investment (ROI), payback (length of time for the project to pay for itself), market-share benefits, and so on. Quantify each cost or benefit so that business objectives may be measured after implementation. Revise estimates periodically as the project progresses.

Timetable

In this section of the BRD, provide a timetable for the project.

Business Use Cases

Complete this section if the project involves changes to the workflow of end-to-end business processes. Document each end-to-end business process affected by the project as a business use case. If necessary, describe existing workflow for the business use case as well as the new, proposed workflow.

Business Use-Case Diagrams

Business use-case diagrams describe stakeholder involvement in each business use case.

Business Use-Case Descriptions

Describe each business use case with text and/or an activity diagram. If you are documenting with text, use an informal style or the use-case template described in the upcoming "User Requirements" section.

Actors

In this section, describe the actors (people, organizations, or other entities) that participate in the execution of business processes, that interact with the business and/or interact with the IT system.

Workers

List and describe stakeholders who act within the business in carryi[ng]
business use cases.

Department/ Position	General Impact on Project

Business Actors

List and describe external parties, such as customers and partners, who interact
with the business.

Actor	General Impact on Project

Other Systems

List computer systems potentially affected by this project. Include any system that
will be linked to the proposed system.

System	General Impact on Project

Role Map

The role map describes the roles played by actors (users and external systems)
that interact with the IT system.

ients for automated processes from a user

ns

ribe which users use which feature and the

tions

short descriptions of the use cases are pro-
...... Discovery phase, the following template is filled out for each medium- to high-risk use case. Low-risk use cases may be described informally. This template may also be used to document the business use cases included earlier in the BRD.

Use-Case Description Template

1. Use Case: The use-case name as it appears on system use-case diagrams

   Perspective: Business use case/system use case

   Type: Base use case/included/extending/generalized/specialized

   1.1 Brief Description: Describe the use case in approximately one paragraph.

   1.2 Business Goals and Benefits: Briefly describe the business rationale for the use case.

   1.3 Actors

       1.3.1 Primary Actors: Identify the users or systems that initiate the use case.

       1.3.2 Secondary Actors: List the users or systems that receive messages from the use case. Include users who receive reports or online messages.

       1.3.3 Off-Stage Stakeholders: Identify non-participating stakeholders who have interests in this use case.

   1.4 Rules of Precedence

       1.4.1 Triggers: Describe the event or condition that "kick-starts" the use case (for example, "User calls Call Center; inventory low"). If the trigger is time-driven, describe the temporal condition, such as "end-of-month."

       1.4.2 Pre-Conditions: List conditions that must be true before the use case begins. (If a condition *forces* the use case to occur whenever it becomes true, do not list it here; list it as a trigger.)

1.5 Post-Conditions

    1.5.1 Post-Conditions on Success: Describe the status of the system after the use case ends successfully. Any condition listed here is guaranteed to be true on successful completion.

    1.5.2 Post-Conditions on Failure: Describe the status of the system after the use case ends in failure. Any condition listed here is guaranteed to be true when the use case fails as described in the exception flows.

1.6 Extension Points: Name and describe points at which extension use cases may extend this use case.

    1.6.1 Example of Extension Point Declaration: "Preferred Customer: 2.5–2.9."

1.7 Priority

1.8 Status: Your status report might resemble the following:

    Use-case brief complete: 2009/06/01.

    Basic flow + risky alternatives complete: 2009/06/15

    All flows complete: 2009/07/15

    Coded: 2009/07/20

    Tested: 2009/08/10

    Internally released: 2009/09/15

    Deployed: 2009/09/30

1.9 Expected Implementation Date

1.10 Actual Implementation Date

1.11 Context Diagram: Include a system use-case diagram showing this use case, all its relationships (includes, extends, and generalizes) with other use cases, and its associations with actors.

2. Flow of Events

Basic Flow

2.1 (Insert basic flow steps.)

Alternate Flows

2.X.a (Insert the Alternate Flow Name): The alternate flow name should describe the condition that triggers the alternate flow. "2.X" is the step number within the basic flow where the interruption occurs. Describe the steps in paragraph or point form.

Exception Flows

2.Xa (Insert the Exception Flow Name): The exception flow name should describe the condition that triggers the exception flow. An exception flow is one that causes the use case to end in failure and for which "post-conditions on failure" apply. "2.X" is the step number within basic flow where the interruption occurs. Describe the steps in paragraph or point form.

3. Special Requirements: List any special requirements or constraints that apply specifically to this use case.

   3.1 Non-Functional Requirements: List requirements not visible to the user during the use case—security, performance, reliability, and so on.

   3.2 Constraints: List technological, architectural, and other constraints on the use case.

4. Activity Diagram: If it is helpful, include an activity diagram showing workflow for this use case or for select parts of the use case.

5. User Interface: Initially, include description/storyboard/prototype only to help the reader visualize the interface, not to constrain the design. Later, provide links to screen-design artifacts.

6. Class Diagram: Include a class diagram depicting business classes, relationships, and multiplicities of all objects participating in this use case.

7. Assumptions: List any assumptions you made when writing the use case. Verify all assumptions with stakeholders before sign-off.

8. Information Items: Include a link or reference to documentation describing rules for data items that relate to this use case. Documentation of this sort is often found in a data dictionary. The purpose of this section and the following sections is to keep the details out of the use case proper so that you do not need to amend it every time you change a rule.

9. Prompts and Messages: Any prompts and messages that appear in the use case proper should be identified by name only, as in "Invalid Card Message." The "Prompts and Messages" section should contain the actual text of the messages or direct the reader to the documentation that contains text.

10. Business Rules: The "Business Rules" section of the use-case documentation should provide links or references to the specific business rules that are active during the use case. An example of a business rule for an airline package is "Airplane weight must never exceed the maximum allowed for its aircraft type." Organizations often keep such rules in an automated business rules engine or manually in a binder.

11. External Interfaces: List interfaces to external systems.

12. Related Artifacts: The purpose of this section is to provide a point of reference for other details that relate to this use case, but would distract from the overall flow. Include references to artifacts such as decision tables, complex algorithms, and so on.

State-Machine Diagrams

Insert state-machine diagrams describing the events that trigger changes of state of significant business objects.

Nonfunctional Requirements

Describe across-the-board requirements not covered in the use-case documentation. Details follow.

Performance Requirements

Describe requirements relating to the system's speed.

Stress Requirements

This subsection of performance requirements describes the degree of simultaneous activity that the system must be able to support. For example, "The system must be able to support 2,000 users accessing financial records simultaneously."

Response-Time Requirements

This subsection of performance requirements describes the maximum allowable wait time from the moment the user submits a request until the system comes back with a response.

Throughput Requirements

This subsection of performance requirements describes the number of transactions per unit of time that the system must be able to process.

Usability Requirements

Describe quantitatively the level of usability required. For example, "A novice operator, given two hours of training, must be able to complete the following functions without assistance...." Also, refer to any usability standards and guidelines that must be adhered to.

Security Requirements

Describe security requirements relating to virus protection, firewalls, the functions and data accessible by each user group, and so on.

Volume and Storage Requirements

Describe the maximum volume (that is, the number of accounts) that the system must be able to support, as well as random access memory (RAM) and disk restrictions.

Configuration Requirements

Describe the hardware and operating systems that must be supported.

Compatibility Requirements

Describe compatibility requirements with respect to the existing system and external systems with which the system under design must interact.

Reliability Requirements

Describe the level of fault-tolerance required by the system.

Backup/Recovery Requirements

Describe the backup and recovery facilities required.

Training Requirements

Describe the level of training required and clearly state which organizations will be required to develop and deliver training programs.

Business Rules

List business rules that must be complied with by the solution. For example, a flight-reservation system might have a rule that the baggage weight on an aircraft must never exceed a given maximum. If an external rules engine is being used, this section should refer the reader to the location of these rules.

State Requirements

Describe how the system's behavior changes when in different states. Describe the features that will be available and those that will be disabled in each state.

Testing State

Describe what the user may and may not do while the system is in the test state.

Disabled State

Describe what is to happen as the system goes down (that is, how it "dies gracefully"). Clearly define what the user will and will not be able to do.

Structural Model

The structural model describes business concepts and categories of business objects that are tracked by the business and that must be tracked by the solution. The model also includes business rules pertaining to those objects, such as the rule that an account may be tied to more than one customer.

Class Diagrams: Entity Classes

Insert class diagrams representing classes of business objects and relationships among the classes. This section centralizes rules that govern business objects, such as the numerical relationships among objects, the operations associated with each object, and so on.

Entity Class Documentation

Insert documentation to support each of the classes that appear in the class diagrams. Not every class needs to be fully documented. First do a risk analysis to determine where full documentation would most benefit the project. Complete the following for each class you document.

- **Class Name**: Name the class, as it appears in the structural model.
- **Alias:** List any other names by which the class is known within the business domain.
- **Description:** Provide a brief description of the class.
- **Example:** Provide an example of an object of this class.
- **Attributes:** These may be documented in a table as follows:

Attribute	Derived?	Derivation	Type	Format	Length	Range	Dependency

When your requirements are complete up to this point and approved by the appropriate people, submit them to developers. You can then work on the test plan, implementation plan, and end-user procedures.

Test Plan[1]

To standardize the testing, you should develop a test-plan document for analysts to follow when constructing the project's test plans. Although every project is different, the following may be used as a guideline. Each project should consider the following stages during testing:

1. **Submit the requirements to the technical team.** The technical team completes development. Concurrently, the BA builds numbered test scenarios for requirements-based testing. Consider using decision tables to identify scenarios and boundary-value analysis to select test data. The technical team conducts white-box testing to verify whether programs, fields, and calculations function as specified. The BA or technical team specifies the required quality level for white-box testing, such as multiple-condition coverage.

2. **Perform requirements-based testing.** The BA or dedicated quality-assurance (QA) staff administers or supervises tests to prove or disprove compliance with requirements. Ensure that all formulae are calculated properly. Describe principles and techniques to be used in black-box testing, such as structured testing guidelines and boundary-value analysis.

3. **Conduct system testing.** Ensure that the integrity of the system and data remain intact. For example:

   - **Regression test:** Retest all features (using a regression test bed).
   - **Stress test:** Test multiple users at the same time.
   - **Integration tests:** Make sure that the changes do not negatively affect the overall workflow across IT and manual systems.
   - **Volume test:** Test the system with high volume.

4. **Perform user-acceptance testing.** Involve the end-users at this stage. Choose key users to review the changes in the test environment. Use the testing software as a final check.

Implementation Plan

In this section of the BRD, describe plans for deploying the solution into production.

Training

In this subsection of "Implementation Plan," describe training plans. For example:

- Specify who is responsible for training.
- Specify who is to be trained.
- Specify how training will be done.

Conversion

In this subsection of "Implementation Plan," describe plans for converting and upgrading the existing infrastructure, data, and software. For example:

- Specify existing data that must be converted.
- Specify how software will be promoted to new release.
- Specify plans for granting privileges to the users.

Scheduling of Jobs

In this subsection of "Implementation Plan," specify plans for adding batch jobs to the production run. The plans should include instruction regarding the following issues:

- Advising IT operations of which jobs to add to the production run. Specify the frequency of the run: daily, weekly, monthly, quarterly, semi-annually, or annually.
- Ensuring that the job is placed in the correct sequence.
- Advising IT operations of the reports to be printed and the distribution list for reports and files.

Rollout

Advise all affected users when the project is promoted.

End-User Procedures

Write up the procedures for the affected departments. Distribute this document to members of those departments in addition to providing any hands-on training.

Post-Implementation Follow-Up

Follow up within a reasonable time frame after implementation to ensure that the project is running successfully. Determine whether any further enhancements or changes are needed to ensure success of the project.

Other Issues

In this section of the BRD, add any other issues that were not addressed in prior sections.

Sign-Off

Use this section of the BRD for sign-offs on the requirements. Sign-offs should include the sponsor and representatives of the solution provider.

Endnote

[1]These requirements are often described in a separate test plan. If they are not addressed elsewhere, describe them here in the BRD.

BUSINESS REQUIREMENTS DOCUMENT EXAMPLE: CPP CASE STUDY

Business Requirements Document (BRD)

Project No.: _____

Production Priority: ____

Target Date: _____

Approved by:

_____   _____

Name of user, department   Date

_____   _____

Name of user, department   Date

Prepared by:

_____   _____

Name of user, department   Date

Filename: _____

Version No.: _____

Table of Contents

- Version Control
    - Revision History
    - RACI Chart for This Document
- Executive Summary
    - Overview
    - Background
    - Objectives
    - Requirements
    - Proposed Strategy
    - Next Steps
- Scope
    - Included in Scope
    - Excluded from Scope
    - Constraints
    - Impact of Proposed Changes
- Risk Analysis
    - Technological Risks
    - Skills Risks
    - Political Risks
    - Business Risks
    - Requirements Risks
    - Other Risks
- Business Case
- Timetable
- Business Use Cases
    - Business Use-Case Diagrams
    - Business Use-Case Descriptions
        - Business Use Case: Manage Case (Dispute)
        - Business Use Case: Administer Payments

- Actors
  - Workers
  - Business Actors
  - Other Systems
  - Role Map
- User Requirements
  - System Use-Case Diagrams
  - System Use-Case Descriptions
    - Package: Manage Administration
    - Package: Administer Payments
- State-Machine Diagrams
  - State Machine Diagram: Case
- Nonfunctional Requirements
  - Performance Requirements
    - Stress Requirements
    - Response-Time Requirements
    - Throughput Requirements
  - Usability Requirements
  - Security Requirements
  - Volume and Storage Requirements
  - Configuration Requirements
  - Compatibility Requirements
  - Reliability Requirements
  - Backup/Recovery Requirements
  - Training Requirements
- Business Rules
- State Requirements
  - Testing State
  - Disabled State

- Structural Model
  - Main Entity-Class Diagram
  - Package: People and Organizations
  - Package: Products and Services
  - Package: Events/Transactions
  - Package: Lookup Tables
  - Account Ownership
  - Entity-Class Documentation
- Test Plan
- Implementation Plan
  - Training
  - Conversion
  - Scheduling of Jobs
  - Rollout
- End-User Procedures
- Post-Implementation Follow-Up
- Other Issues
- Sign-off

Version Control

Revision History

Version #	Date	Authorization	Responsibility (Author)	Description
0.1	06/05		Mbuyi Pensacola	Initial Draft
1.0	07/05	J. Carter	Mbuyi Pensacola	Final Version/ Initiation
2.0	08/05	J. Carter	Mbuyi Pensacola	Final Version/ Discovery

RACI Chart for This Document

*	Authorize	This individual has ultimate signing authority for any changes to the document.
R	Responsible	This individual is responsible for creating this document.
A	Accountable	This individual is accountable for the accuracy of this document (e.g., project manager).
S	Supports	This individual provides supporting services in the production of this document.
C	Consulted	This individual provides input (interviewee, etc.).
I	Informed	This individual must be informed of any changes.

Name	Position	*	R	A	S	C	I
C. Ringshee	Director, CPP	X					
J. Carter	Manager, Operations			X			
Mbuyi Pensacola			X				

Executive Summary

Overview

This project is for a software system to govern the tracking and reporting of cases by the Community Peace Program (CPP).

Background

The project is being developed for the Community Peace Program (CPP), a South African non-profit organization that provides infrastructure for community-based justice systems based on the model of restorative justice. The main objective of the CPP is to provide an effective alternative to the court system. Its advantages are improved cost-effectiveness and a decreased recurrence rate, since problems are treated at their source. All parties to a dispute must consent to having the case diverted to the CPP. The advantage to the perpetrator is the avoidance of incarceration and other severe punishment; for the complainant, the advantages lie in the possibility for a true resolution to the problem and a decreased likelihood that the problem will recur. The advantages to the justice system are as follows:

- A reduction in case volume due to the offloading of cases to the CPP and a decrease in recurrence rates.
- A decrease in the cost of processing a case.

The system is being deployed in the townships of South Africa under the auspices of the CPP and with the support of the Justice Department. Similar approaches are being used throughout the world—for example, the Forum, in use by Canada's Royal Canadian Mounted Police (RCMP).

The CPP operates by working with local communities to set up Peace Committees. Most of these are currently in townships on the Cape Town peninsula. Each Peace Committee is composed of "peacemakers"—members of the community who are trained in conflict-resolution procedures based on principles of restorative justice. The complainants and accused must all agree to adhere to the procedure or the case is passed on to the state justice system.

Due to increasing demand for its services in conflict resolution, the CPP is undergoing a rapid expansion. Current manual practices will not be able to keep up with the expected rise in case volume.

Objectives

The most urgent need is for timely statistics regarding cases handled by the CPP. Because of the anticipated increase in caseload, these statistics will be difficult to derive using the current manual systems. Timely statistics will be essential in justifying the project to its funders. Also, the tracking of funds disbursement and monitoring of cases will become increasingly difficult as the program expands.

Requirements

The project will leave current manual systems in place for the initial recording of case information up to and including the conduct of a Peace Gathering and the completion of subsequent monitoring. Workflow after that point will be within the scope of the project—i.e., recording of case data, validation of CPP procedures, disbursement of payments, and the generation of statistical reports.

Proposed Strategy

An iterative SDLC will be employed as follows: The business analyst(s) will analyze all use cases at the start for the project (the Discovery phase); the design and coding will proceed iteratively. In the first iteration, general administration and case tracking will be developed. In the second iteration, payments will be disbursed and reports generated.

Next Steps

- **Action:** Select software developer
- **Responsibility:** J. Carter
- **Expected Date:** One month after acceptance of this document

Scope

Included in Scope

The system will provide statistical reports for use by funders. Also, it will provide limited tracking of individual cases to the degree required for statistics and, wherever possible, in a manner that will facilitate expansion of the system to include complete case monitoring. The project includes manual and automated processes. The system will encompass those activities that occur after a case has been resolved.

These are primarily the recording of case data, the disbursement of payments, and the generation of reports. CPP members will be the only direct users of this system.

Excluded from Scope

The system becomes aware of a case only when it has been resolved. All activities prior to this point are not included in this project—i.e., it excludes the tracking of cases from the time of reporting, convening of Peace Gathering, and monitoring of cases. The activities will continue to be performed manually, although the manual forms will be changed to comply with new system requirements.

Constraints

1. Eighty-percent match (minimum) between CPP's needs and COTS (commercial-off-the-shelf) product(s).
2. One integrated solution is preferred. No more than two COTS products should be needed.
3. M. Williams will be main liaison for the project.
4. Final approval for a system is estimated to take six weeks to two months.

Impact of Proposed Changes

Business Use Case	New?	Desired Functionality	Current Functionality (If a Change)	Stakeholders/ Systems	Priority
Manage administration	Yes	General administrative functions, e.g., creation/updating of Peace Committees, members, etc.	Manual systems only in place	CPP general administration	High
Manage case	Yes	Manage a case: identify new cases, update case information, etc.	Manual systems only in place	Peace Committee, facilitator, monitor, convener	High

Business Use Case	New?	Desired Functionality	Current Functionality (If a Change)	Stakeholders/ Systems	Priority
Administer payments	Yes	Make payments to individuals who assisted in a case and to various funds	Manual systems only in place	Convener, Peace Committee member, AP system	Medium
Generate reports	Yes	Report on cases by region and by period; compile stats on caseload, # cases per type of conflict, etc.	Manual systems only in place	Any worker (members of the CPP), government body (any governmental organization receiving reports), funder	High

Risk Analysis

Strategies for dealing with risk include the following:

- **Avoid:** Do something to eliminate the risk.
- **Mitigate:** Do something to reduce damage if risk materializes.
- **Transfer:** Pass the risk up or out to another entity.
- **Accept:** Do nothing about the risk. Accept the consequences.

Technological Risks

- **Risk:** Difficulty linking database management system (DBMS) to programming language. Programmers have had experience using proposed DBMS but not with accessing it from proposed programming language.
- **Likelihood:** Medium.
- **Cost:** Project delays.
- **Strategy:** Mitigate. Build early proof-of-concept in order to iron out problems early.

Skills Risks

TBD.

Political Risks

- **Risk:** Source of funding for the organization discontinued. Funding for this organization is provided by a foreign government and is granted only on an annual basis after yearly inspections of the organization and based on the government's policy toward foreign aid.
- **Likelihood:** Low.
- **Cost:** Shutting down of the organization.
- **Strategy:**
  - **Avoid:** Avoid through regular project reports to funders and lobbying of government ministers.
  - **Mitigate:** Search out "plan B" funders.

Business Risks

- **Risk:** IT project cancelled.
- **Likelihood:** Medium.
- **Cost:** Increase in administration costs to handle growing volume. Inability to produce timely progress reports may lead to loss of funder.
- **Strategy:** Mitigate. Plan early release of highest-priority system use cases.

Requirements Risks

- **Risk:** Payment disbursement rules improperly documented. Rules regarding payments made due to a case are volatile and complex and therefore may not be accurately described to programmers.
- **Likelihood:** High.
- **Cost:** Faulty payments, software modifications.
- **Strategy:** Plan structured walkthroughs with stakeholders. Review again before coding begins.

Other Risks

TBD.

Business Case

- **Initial investment:** Two person-years @ US$50,000/yr = $100,000. Hardware: Use existing PCs at office location.
- **Annual cost:** One new half-time position, IT maintenance staff = US$25,000/yr.
- **Annual benefits:** Reduce administration staff by two due to automatic generation of reports to funders and increased efficiency of case tracking = US$60,000/yr.
- **Return on investment (ROI):** ([Annual benefit] – [Annual cost])/ [Initial investment] = (60,000 – 25,000)/100,000 = 35%.
- **Payback period:** [Initial investment]/([Annual benefit] – [Annual cost]) = 100,000/(60,000–25,000) = 2.9 or approximately 3 years.

These numbers are expected to improve over the years as the project expands, since the efficiencies of the IT system relative to a manual system are more pronounced the greater the volume of the cases.

Timetable

- **Discovery:** Complete 08/2009
- **Construction:** TBD
- **Final V&V:** TBD
- **Closeout:** TBD

Business Use Cases

Business Use-Case Diagrams

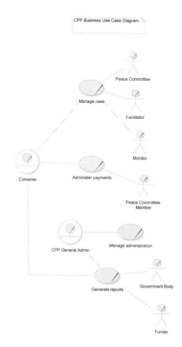

Business Use-Case Descriptions

Business Use Case: Manage Case (Dispute)

(Semi-formal style)

Pre-condition: A Peace Committee has been established in the township.

Post-conditions on success: A case report has been prepared.

Flow:

1. The Peace Committee in the area initiates a Peace Gathering.
2. The Peace Committee prepares an individual interview report for each party to the dispute.
3. Once all reports have been taken, the facilitator summarizes the reports to the Peace Gathering.
4. The facilitator verifies the facts in the reports with those present.

5. The facilitator solicits suggestions from the gathering.

6. The facilitator solicits a consensus for a plan of action.

7. If the gathering has decided to refer the case to the police, the facilitator escorts the parties to the police station, after which the convener prepares a case report as per step 10.

8. If, on the other hand, a consensus has been reached, the facilitator appoints a monitor.

9. The monitor performs ongoing monitoring of the case to ensure its terms are being met.

10. When the deadline for monitoring has been reached, the ongoing monitoring immediately ends. At this time, if the conditions of the case have been met, the convener prepares a case report. If the conditions have not been met, then the process begins again (return to step 1).

   10.1 The conditions described in step 10 do not apply to cases referred to police. That is, once the parties have been escorted to the police, a case report is always prepared.

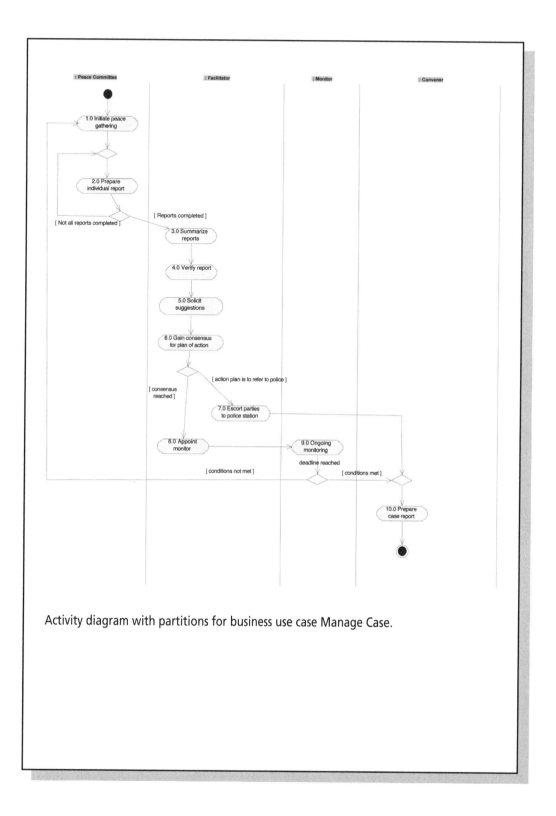

Activity diagram with partitions for business use case Manage Case.

Business Use Case: Administer Payments

(Semi-formal style)

Pre-condition: A case report has been submitted.

Post-conditions on success: Payments have been made to funds and to accounts of Peace Committee members involved in the case.

Flow:

1. The convener reviews the case report to determine whether rules and procedures have been followed.

2. If rules and procedures have been followed:

    a) The convener marks the case as payable.

    b) The convener then disburses payments to the various funds and to the accounts of Peace Committee members who worked on the case.

    c) The existing accounts payable system actually applies the payments. (Constraint: The AP system must continue to be used for this purpose when the project is implemented.)

3. If the rules and procedures have not been followed, the convener marks the case as non-payable.

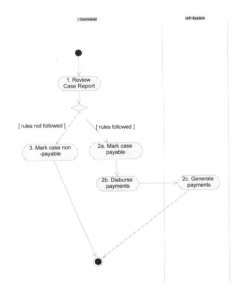

Activity diagram with partitions for business use case Administer Payments.

Actors

Workers

Department/Position	General Impact on Project
Convener	(Member of the CPP.) Will use IT to update cases and administer payments.
CPP General Admin	(Member of the CPP.) Will use IT to perform administrative functions such as updating Peace Committees and members in the system.

Business Actors

Actor	General Impact on Project
Facilitator	A member of the community trained to facilitate Peace Gatherings. Current manual processes will remain with slight changes to forms as required for reporting purposes.
Monitor	A member of the community assigned to monitor parties' compliance with plan of action agreed to during Peace Gathering. Current manual process will remain in place.
Peace Committee	An organization set up within a community and consisting of local members of the community, trained by the CPP to assist in dispute resolution. Current manual process will remain in place. Will need to report to head office about any changes to the organization, membership, etc.
Peace Committee member	A member of a Peace Committee. A local, trained by the CPP to assist in dispute resolution. Will receive notification of payment for services by the IT system.
Government body	Represents any government organization that receives reports from the new system.
Funder	Source of CPP funding. Will receive analytical reports from IT system.

Other Systems

System	General Impact of Project on External System
AP System	Existing system for tracking accounts payable. This system must remain in place.

Role Map

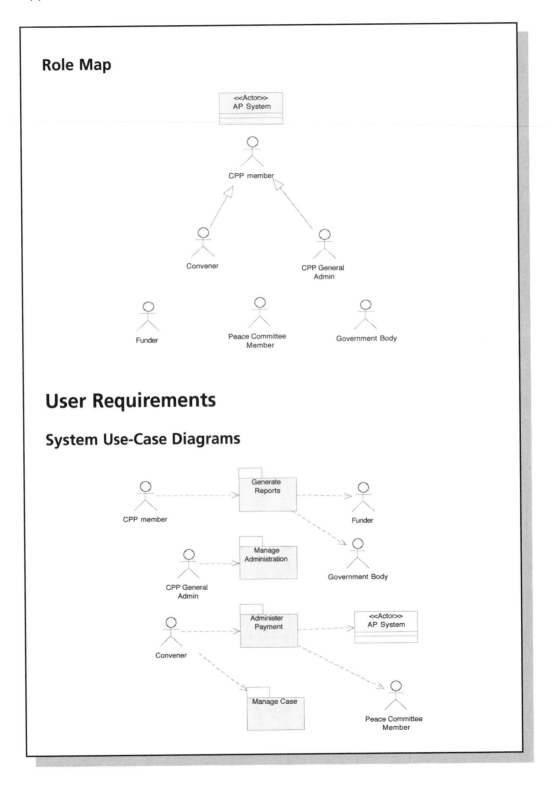

User Requirements

System Use-Case Diagrams

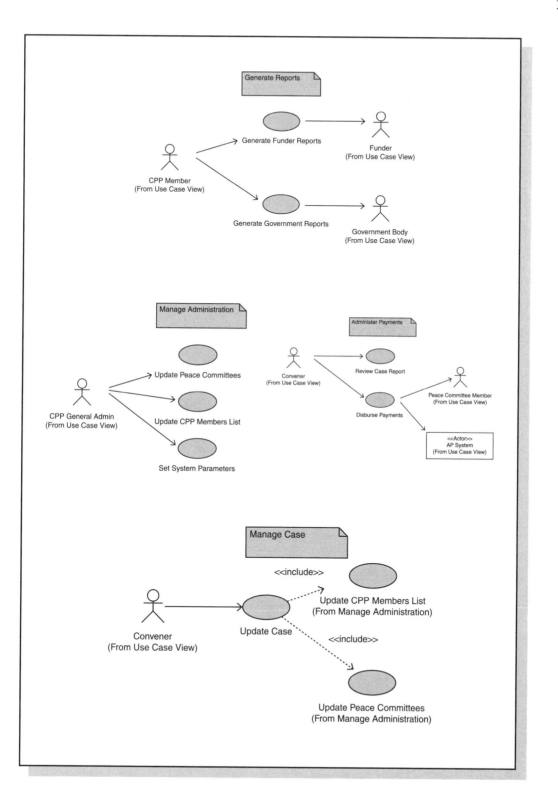

System Use-Case Descriptions

Package: *Manage Administration*

Following is an example of a brief description used for a low-risk use case.

- **System use case:** Update Peace Committees
- **Description:** Add/change/delete Peace Committees; update Peace Committee membership.

Package: *Administer Payments*

Following is an example of a formal use-case description:

System Use Case: *Review Case Report*

1. Use Case: Review Case Report

   Perspective: System use case

   Type: Base use case

   1.1 Brief Description: Review a case report in order to determine whether it is payable based on adherence to rules and procedures. Mark case as payable/non-payable.

   1.2 Business Goals and Benefits: IT tracking of payments will allow for generation of up-to-date reports to funders upon request, required for continuance of funding for the organization.

   1.3 Actors

       1.3.1 Primary Actors: Convener

       1.3.2 Secondary Actors: N/A

       1.3.3 Off-Stage Stakeholders: Funders

   1.4 Rules of Precedence

       1.4.1 Triggers: Convener calls up Review option.

       1.4.2 Pre-conditions: Case has transitioned from Monitored state and monitoring conditions have been met, or case has transitioned from Referred to Police state. Case must not have already been reviewed.

   1.5 Post-conditions

       1.5.1 Post-conditions on Success: Case is marked as Reviewed and prevented from being reviewed again.

       1.5.2 Post-conditions on Failure

   1.6 Extension Points

   1.7 Priority: High

1.8   Status

Use-case brief complete: 2009/06/01

Basic flow + risky alternatives complete: 2009/06/15

All flows complete: 2009/07/15

1.9   Expected Implementation Date: TBD

1.10   Actual Implementation Date: TBD

1.11   Context Diagram

Convener   Review Case Report

2. Flow of Events

Basic Flow:

2.1   The system displays a list of resolved cases that have not been reviewed.

2.2   The user selects a case.

2.3   The system validates that the case is payable. (12.1)

2.4   The system determines the payment amount. (12.1)

2.5   The system marks the case as payable.

2.6   The system records the payment amount.

2.7   The system checks the cash fund records to ensure adequate funds exist.

    2.7.1   No funds shall be removed from cash fund or disbursed at this time.

2.8   The system records the fact that the case has been reviewed.

Alternate Flows:

2.3a   Non-payable case:

    2.3a.1   The system marks the case as non-payable.

    2.3a.2   The user confirms the non-payable status of the case.

    2.3a.3   Continue at step 2.8.

2.3a.2a User overrides non-payable status:

    2.3a.2a.1 The user indicates that the case is to be payable and enters a reason for the override and a payment amount.

    2.3a.2a.2 Continue at step 2.5.

2.7a   Cash funds low but sufficient:

    2.7a.1   The system marks the case as payable.

    2.7a.2   The system displays the low funds warning. (9.1)

Exception Flows:

2.7b   Insufficient cash funds:

2.7b.1   The system informs the user that funds are not available.

2.7b.2   The use case ends in failure.

3. Special Requirements

3.1   Nonfunctional requirements

3.1.1   Security: Case details must only be accessible by CPP members.

3.2   Constraints

4. Activity Diagram: N/A

5. User Interface: TBD

6. Class Diagram

7. Assumptions

8. Information Items

9. Prompts and Messages

9.1   Low Funds Warning: See external design specifications/messages

10. Business Rules:

Rule 103: Cash fund low trigger point

11. External Interfaces

12. Related Artifacts

12.1   Decision Table A: Validate case and determine payment amount.

		1	2	3	4	5	6	7	8	9	10	11	12
CONDITION	Code of Good Practice Followed (Y/N)	Y	Y	Y	Y	Y	Y	N	N	N	N	N	N
	Steps and Procedures Followed (Y/N)	Y	Y	Y	N	N	N	Y	Y	Y	N	N	N
	# PC Members (<3,3–5,6+)	<3	3–5	6+	<3	3–5	6+	<3	3–5	6+	<3	3–5	6+
ACTION	Mark as Not Payable	X			X			X	X	X	X	X	X
	Mark as Payable		X	X		X	X						
	Pay ½ Standard Amount					X	X						
	Pay Standard Amount		X										
	Pay Double Amount			X									

System Use Case: Disburse Payments

1. Use case: Disburse Payments

   Perspective: System use case

   Type: Base use case

   1.1 Brief Description: Create record of payments made for the case to Peace Committee members and fund accounts.

   1.2 Business Goals and Benefits: IT tracking of payments will allow for generation of up-to-date reports to funders upon request, required for continuance of funding for the organization.

   1.3 Actors

       1.3.1 Primary Actors:
   Convener

       1.3.2 Secondary Actors:
   Peace Committee Member, AP System

       1.3.3 Off-Stage Stakeholders:
   Funders

   1.4 Rules of Precedence

       1.4.1 Triggers: The user calls up the Disburse Payments option.

       1.4.2 Pre-conditions: The case is in the Payable state and a payment amount for the case has been determined.

   1.5 Post-conditions

       1.5.1 Post-conditions on Success

           1.5.1.1 Payments are made into the accounts of all Peace Committee members involved in the case and into the fund accounts.

           1.5.1.2 The case is in the Paid state.

   1.6 Extension Points

   1.7 Priority: High

   1.8 Status

   Basic flow + risky alternatives complete: 2009/06/20

   All flows complete: 2009/07/27

   1.9 Expected Implementation Date: TBD

   1.10 Actual Implementation Date: TBD

1.11 Context Diagram

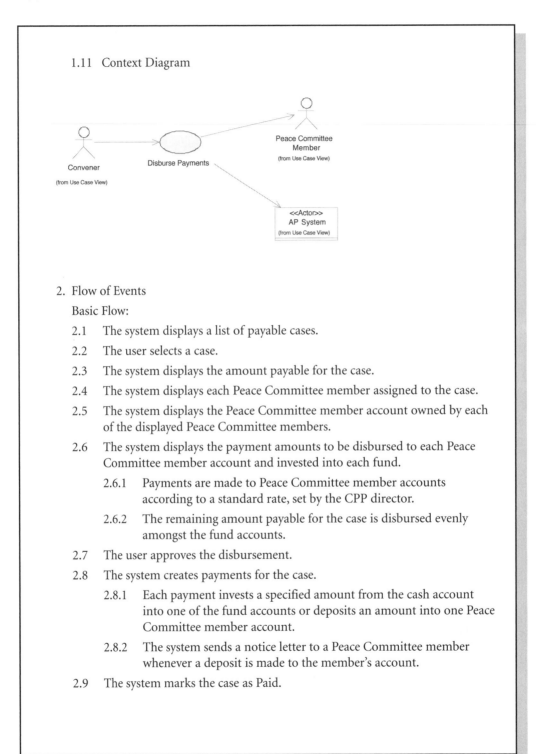

2. Flow of Events

Basic Flow:

2.1 The system displays a list of payable cases.

2.2 The user selects a case.

2.3 The system displays the amount payable for the case.

2.4 The system displays each Peace Committee member assigned to the case.

2.5 The system displays the Peace Committee member account owned by each of the displayed Peace Committee members.

2.6 The system displays the payment amounts to be disbursed to each Peace Committee member account and invested into each fund.

2.6.1 Payments are made to Peace Committee member accounts according to a standard rate, set by the CPP director.

2.6.2 The remaining amount payable for the case is disbursed evenly amongst the fund accounts.

2.7 The user approves the disbursement.

2.8 The system creates payments for the case.

2.8.1 Each payment invests a specified amount from the cash account into one of the fund accounts or deposits an amount into one Peace Committee member account.

2.8.2 The system sends a notice letter to a Peace Committee member whenever a deposit is made to the member's account.

2.9 The system marks the case as Paid.

Alternate Flows:

2.7a   User does not approve disbursement amounts:

    2.7a.1   The user overrides the disbursement amounts.

    2.7a.2   The system confirms that the total payable for the case has not changed.

2.7a.2a Total payable has changed:

    2.7a.2a.1   The system displays a message indicating the amount of the discrepancy.

    2.7a.2a.2   Continue at step 2.7a.1

2.8a   Payment causes a withdrawal from cash that pushes balance below a specified trigger point:

    2.8a.1   The system sends a notice to admin requesting new cash funds.

6. Class Diagram

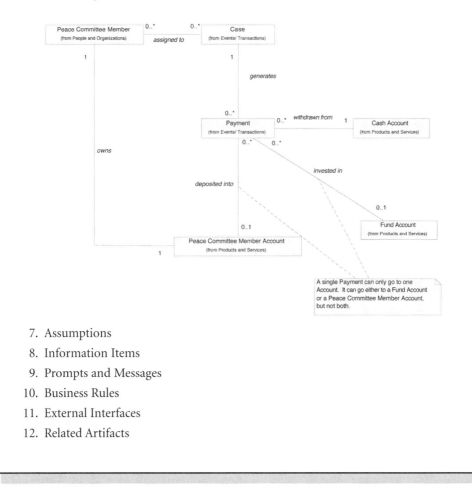

7. Assumptions

8. Information Items

9. Prompts and Messages

10. Business Rules

11. External Interfaces

12. Related Artifacts

State-Machine Diagrams

State-Machine Diagram: Case

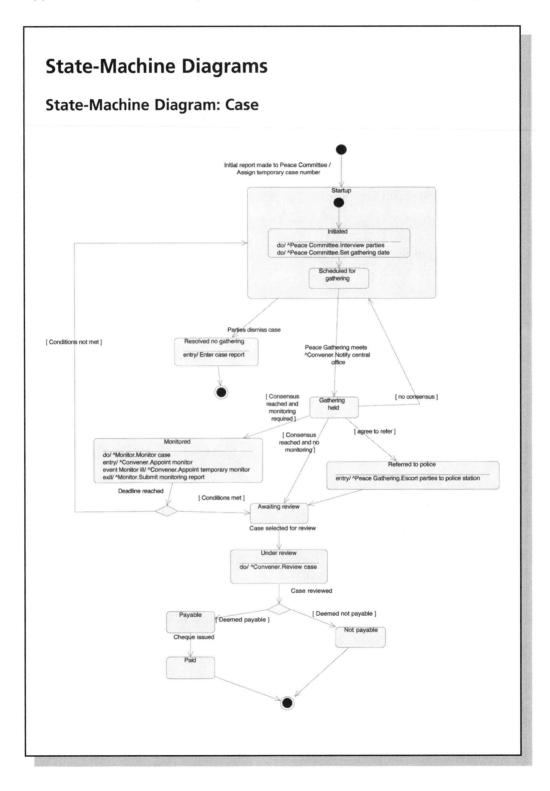

Nonfunctional Requirements

Performance Requirements

Stress Requirements

The system must be able to support 10 users accessing case records simultaneously.

Response-Time Requirements

Three seconds.

Throughput Requirements

TBD.

Usability Requirements

System must conform to usability guidelines V2.1.

Security Requirements

Case details must only be accessible to CPP officials.

Volume and Storage Requirements

First iteration of the system must support a volume of 60 Peace Committees and a total case load of 25,000 cases/year.

Configuration Requirements

PC-compatible. Microsoft XP Professional.

Compatibility Requirements

System must interface with existing AP system.

Reliability Requirements

Total daily downtime must not exceed 1 hour during normal business hours (9:00 a.m.–5:00 p.m.).

Backup/Recovery Requirements

Daily backup of data files onto DVD. Weekly backup of entire system.

Training Requirements

Software development company to be responsible for end-user training.

Business Rules

See business rules engine. *BR09-35*.

State Requirements

Testing State

TBD.

Disabled State

TBD.

Structural Model

Main Entity-Class Diagram

Package: People and Organizations

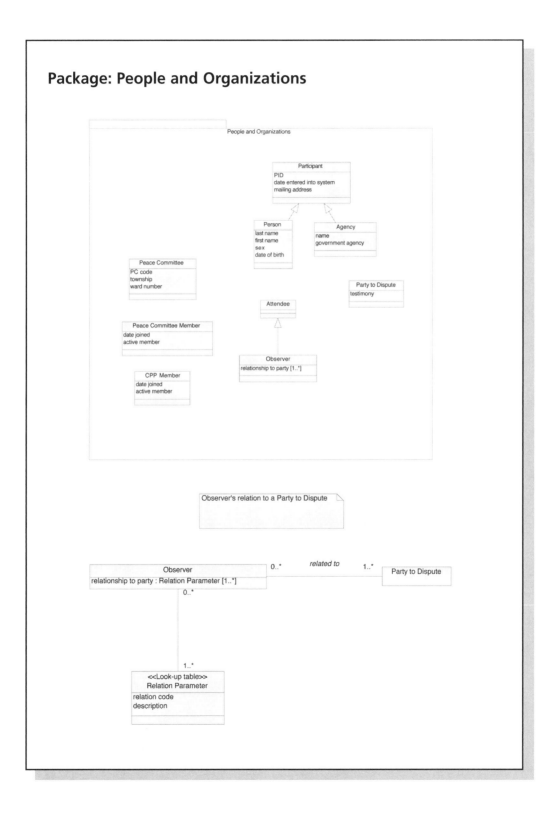

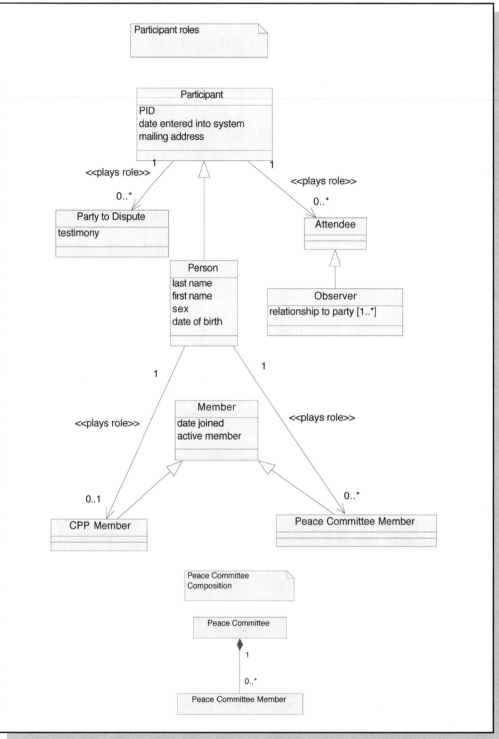

Package: Products and Services

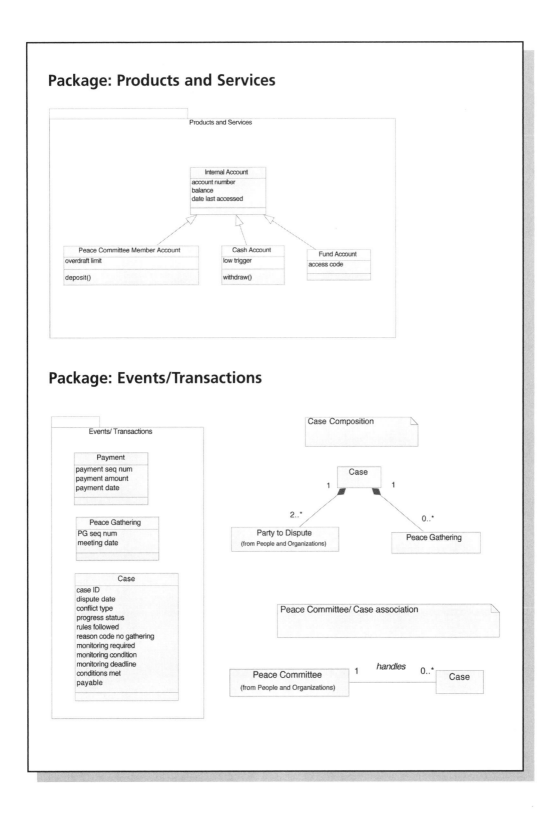

Package: Events/Transactions

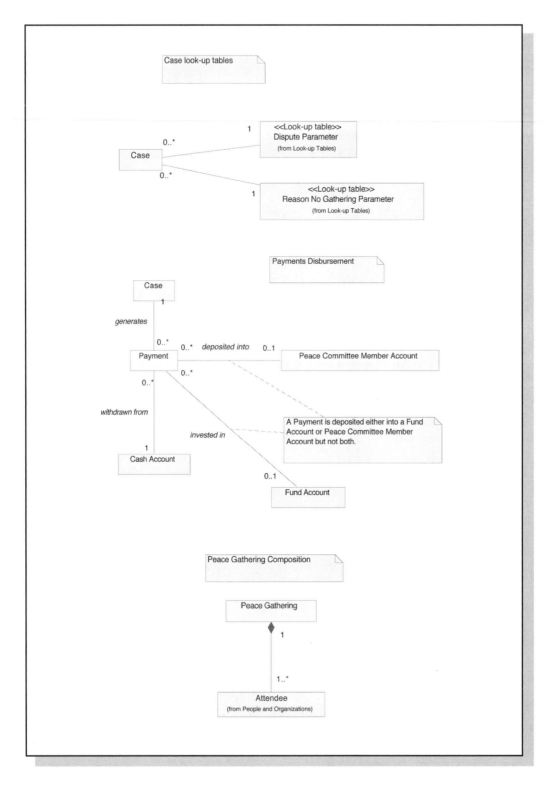

Package: Lookup Tables

Look-up tables

<<Look-up table>> Reason No Gathering Parameter
reason code no gathering description

<<Look-up table>> Dispute Parameter
dispute type description criminal offense

<<Look-up table>> Relation Parameter
relation code description

Account Ownership

Peace Committee Member Accounts

Peace Committee Member —— *owns* —— Peace Committee Member Account
1   1

Entity-Class Documentation

Payment
payment seq num case ID withdrawal account num deposit account num payment amount payment date

Example of entity-class documentation: Payment.

- **Class name:** *Payment*
- **Alias:** *Payout*
- **Description:** One of many possible payments made per case. Each payment is deposited into a single account, such as a Peace Committee member account.
- **Example:** Payment #111000 for Case #134567 to the Microenterprise Fund.
- **Attributes:** See Table C.1.

TABLE C.1

Attribute	Derived?	Derivation	Type	Format	Length	Range	Dependency
payment seq num			Char	999999	6	000001– 999999	
case ID							
withdrawal account num							
deposit account num							Must not be same as withdrawal account num
payment amount			Num	999,999.99		0– 999,999.99	
payment date			Date	yy/mm/dd		On or before system date	

Test Plan

1. Submit the requirements to the technical team.

2. The technical team completes development. Concurrently, the BA builds numbered test scenarios for requirements-based testing. Use decision tables to identify scenarios and boundary-value analysis to select test data. The technical team conducts white-box testing to verify whether programs, fields, and calculations function as specified. The BA or technical team specifies the required quality level for white-box testing, such as multiple-condition coverage.

3. Perform requirements-based testing. The BA or dedicated quality-assurance (QA) staff administers or supervises tests to prove or disprove compliance with requirements. Ensure that all formulae are calculated properly. Describe principles and techniques to be used in black-box testing, such as structured testing guidelines and boundary value analysis.

4. Conduct system testing. Ensure that the integrity of the system and data remain intact. Conduct the following tests:

   - **Regression test:** Retest all features (using a regression test bed).

   - **Stress test:** Test multiple users at the same time.

   - **Integration tests:** Make sure that the changes do not negatively affect the overall workflow across IT and manual systems.

   - **Volume test:** Test the system with high volume.

5. Perform user acceptance testing. Involve the end-users at this stage. Choose key users to review the changes in the test environment. Use the testing software as a final check.

Implementation Plan

Training

- IT firm is responsible for training.
- **Training audience:** Conveners, general administrators, director.
- **Forum:** Four one-day sessions on-site.

Conversion

- Convert existing manual case records to electronic records.
  - Scheduled completion date: 07/15/2012
- Grant privileges to the users.
  - Scheduled date: 07/20/2012

Scheduling of Jobs

- Government reports to be run on demand and at end of month.
- Funder reports to be run on demand and at end of year.

Rollout

Advise all affected users when the project is promoted.

End-User Procedures

TBD.

Post-Implementation Follow-Up

TBD.

Other Issues

Sign-Off

DECISION TABLE TEMPLATE

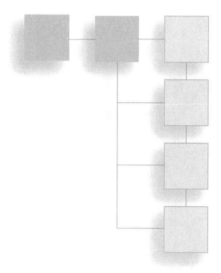

		1	2	3	4	5	6	7	8	9	10	11	12
CONDITION													
ACTION													

TEST SCRIPT TEMPLATE

Test Template

Test #: _____   Project #: _____

System: _____   Test environment: _____

Test type (e.g., regression/ requirements-based, etc.):

Test objective: _____

System use case: _____   Flow: _____

Priority: _____

Next step in case of failure: _____

Planned start date: _____   Planned end date: _____

Actual start date: _____   Actual end date: _____

Times to repeat: _____

Pre-conditions (must be true before test begins): ____

Req #	Action/Data	Expected Result/Response	Actual Result	Pass/ Fail

Tester ID: _____

Pass/fail: _____   Severity of failure: _____

Solution: _____

Comments: _____

Sign-off: _____

(Req # is short for requirement number and corresponds to the number used to identify the requirement in the BRD. Many organizations number their requirements so that they can be traced forward to test cases and other project artifacts. The numbering may be manual, or automatically generated with the use of a tool such as Rational RequisitePro.)

Appendix F

Glossary of Symbols

Business Use-Case Diagram

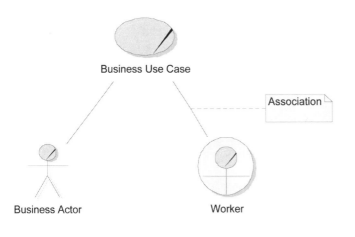

347

System Use-Case Diagram

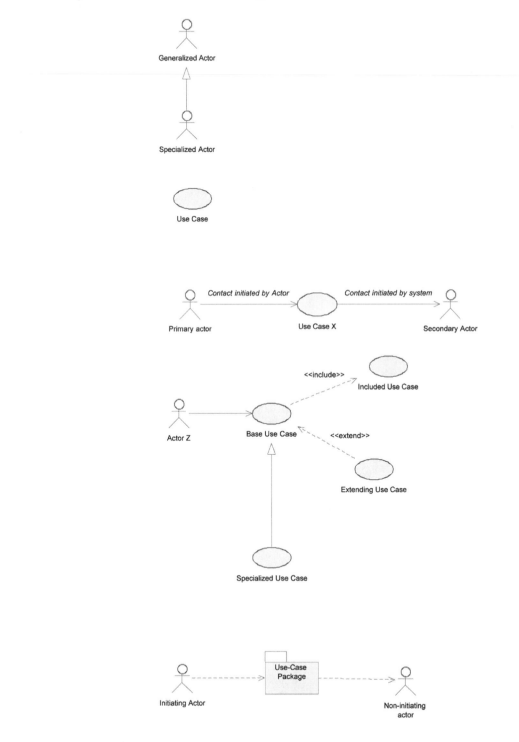

Package Diagram

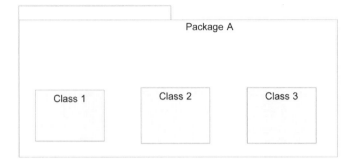

Class Diagram

Allowable multiplicities[1]:

1   One and only one

0..1   Zero or one

0..*   Zero or more

1..*   One or more

n   *n* and only *n* (for example, 5)

n..m   *n* through *m* (for example, 5..10)

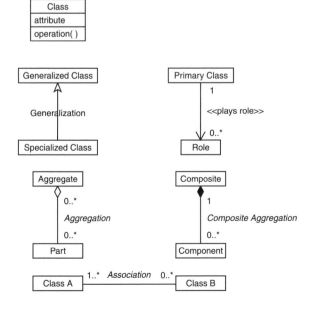

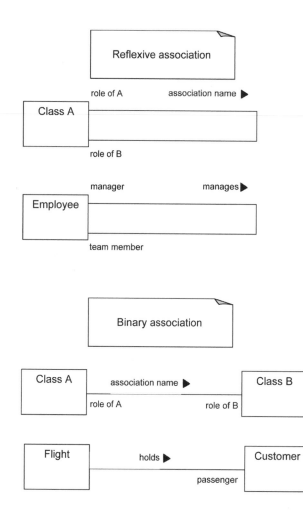

Object Diagram

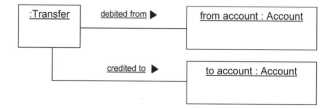

Composite Structure Diagram

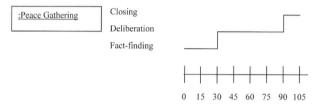

Timing Diagram

:Peace Gathering	Closing
	Deliberation
	Fact-finding

0   15   30   45   60   75   90   105

Activity Diagram

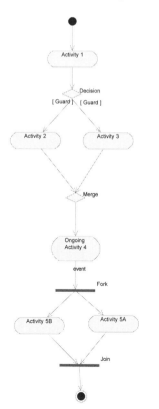

State-Machine Diagram

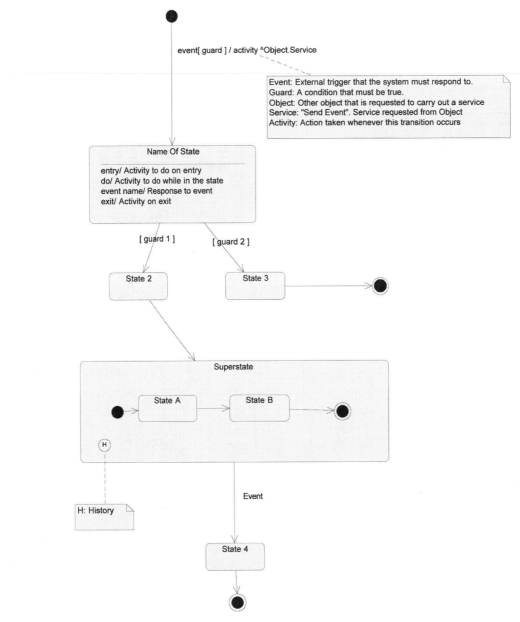

event[guard] / activity ^Object.Service

Event: External trigger that the system must respond to.
Guard: A condition that must be true.
Object: Other object that is requested to carry out a service
Service: "Send Event". Service requested from Object
Activity: Action taken whenever this transition occurs

Name Of State

entry/ Activity to do on entry
do/ Activity to do while in the state
event name/ Response to event
exit/ Activity on exit

[guard 1]   [guard 2]

State 2   State 3

Superstate

State A   State B

H

H: History

Event

State 4

Endnote

[1]Discontinuous multiplicities such as 5, 8 were dropped from the standard in UML 2.

APPENDIX G

GLOSSARY OF TERMS AND FURTHER READING

A

activity: (UML term) A task or process.

activity diagram: (UML term) A diagram that describes the sequencing of business activities. An *activity diagram* with *partitions* (swimlanes) also describes which object is responsible for each activity.

actor: (UML term) A type of user or an external system that interacts with a *use case*. For example, the Customer actor initiates the use case Deposit Funds.

aggregation: (UML term) The relationship that exists between a whole and its parts. For example, the relationship between Line-Of-Products and Product is an aggregation.

association: (UML term) A relationship defined at the class level that describes a link that the business maintains between objects belonging to classes at either end of the association. Objects may be linked because information about one is tied to data about the other, for example, information about an invoice object is *associated* with data about a Customer object. Other reasons for an association between objects include the following: One object collaborates with another to complete a task (for example, an ATM object collaborates with an Account object during cash withdrawal); one object acts on the other object (for example, a manager *manages* an employee).

attribute: (UML term) An attribute is defined at the class level to identify a property that the system tracks for all the objects of that class. Similar to the term "field." (*Field* is used within the context of database design.) For example, an attribute of Car is Year of Manufacture.

B

behavioral model: (UML term) The part of the model that describes dynamic behavior—what the system does and how it does it. Diagrams included as part of the behavioral model include *use-case diagram*, *activity diagram*, *state-machine diagram*.

black-box test: (structured testing term) A test that can be designed without knowledge of the inner workings of the system. (See *requirements-based testing*.)

business model: An abstract representation of a business system.

C

class: (UML term) A category that a group of objects may belong to. Objects in the same class share the same *attributes* and *operations*.

class diagram: (UML term) Describes how classes are related to other classes.

composite aggregation: (UML term) Describes the association between a whole and its parts in cases where the whole completely owns the part and where destruction of the whole causes destruction of the part. For example, an *invoice* is composed of line items; when the Invoice object is destroyed, so are the Line Item objects.

E

encapsulation: (OO term) A principle that states that the description of a class encompasses both its operations (actions) and attributes (data) and that no object may refer directly to another's attributes or rely on a knowledge of how its operations are carried out. Encapsulation requires that objects only interact by passing messages—that is, by asking other objects to perform operations.

entity class: (UML term) A subject that the business tracks. For example, Customer, Invoice.

ERD: (data-modeling term) *ERD* stands for entity relationship diagram. An ERD describes the relationships between subjects tracked by the business—for example, the relationship between customers and their accounts. ERDs were developed prior to OO. The UML *class diagram* encompasses everything that can be depicted in an ERD.

extend: (UML term) A use case can be described as *extending* a base use case if it adds to or alters the behavior of the base at specified extension points and under a specified condition. For example, the use case Apply for Preferred Mortgage extends the base use case Apply for Mortgage.

F–G

fork: (UML term) A bar on an activity diagram that indicates a point after which parallel activities are executed. Parallel activities may begin in any order after the fork.

generalized class: (UML term) A class that describes features common to a group of classes. For example, Account is a generalized class that describes features that the specialized classes Checking Account, Power Account, and Savings Account all have in common. (Also called *generalization class, superclass, parent class, base class*.) Specialized classes inherit the attributes, operations, and relationships of the generalized class.

guard: (UML term) A condition that must be true before something may occur. For example, a deposit transaction may only be processed if the guard Funds Available in Account is True. Guards may appear on *activity diagrams* and *state-machine diagrams*.

I

include: (UML term) When a number of use cases share some common requirements, the commonalities may be factored out into an included use case. Each of the original use cases is said to *include* this new use case. For example, each of the two use cases Withdraw Cash and Pay Bills includes the use case Check Available Funds.

inheritance: (UML term) A relationship that models partial similarities between elements. In the context of classes, inheritance is used when a number of classes share some but not all features. The shared features are described in a generalized class. Each variation is described as a specialized class. A specialized class inherits all the operations, attributes, and relationships of the generalized class. For example, Checking Account inherits the attributes, etc., of Account.

instance: (UML term) An object is an *instance* (specific case) of a class. For example, the customer Jane Dell Ray is an object—an instance of the class Customer.

J–M

join: (UML term) A bar on an activity diagram marking the end of parallel activities. All parallel activities flowing into it must end before flow can proceed beyond the join.

merge: (UML term) A diamond on an activity diagram marking the point where divergent paths off of a previous decision converge back to a common flow.

method: The procedure used to carry out an operation.

multiplicity: (UML term) Defines the number of objects that may be associated with each other. In structured analysis, the equivalent term is *cardinality*. For example, a mortgage is signed by at least one and at most three parties.

O

object: (UML term) A thing that is a part of the system. In business analysis, something is considered an object if it is responsible for carrying out business activities or if the business needs to track information about it. An object is an *instance* (specific case) of a class. For example, the customer Jane Dell Ray is an object—an instance of the class Customer.

object-oriented: (UML term) An approach to analysis, design, and coding based upon a view of a system as a composition of basic units, called *objects*, each of which represents information and operations related to one aspect of the system. A system described as *object-oriented* must also support other concepts such as *classes* and *inheritance*.

OMG: Object Management Group. Sets OO standards.

OO: See *object-oriented*.

operation: (UML term) A function that an object may carry out or that is carried out on the object. For example, Apply Price Increase is an operation of Product. Alternative terms: *service*, *message*.

P

package: (UML term) A container used to organize model elements into groups. Packages may be nested within other packages. Alternative term: *subsystem*.

package diagram: (UML term) A diagram that depicts how model elements are organized into packages and the dependencies among them, including package imports and package extensions.

polymorphism: (UML term) May take many forms. The term is applied to objects and operations. With respect to operations, it means that the same operation may be carried out in different ways (that is, using different methods) by different classes. For example, Checking Account and Savings Account each have their own polymorphic version of the operation Determine Service Charge.

R–S

requirements-based testing: (structured testing term) Testing techniques that determine the degree to which a system complies with the requirements set out in the business requirements document (BRD). The test cases are designed based on knowledge of the requirements, but not on the inner workings of the system. Equivalent term: *black-box testing*.

sequence diagram: (UML term) A diagram that depicts how operations are sequenced and which objects carry them out.

specialized class: (UML term) If a group of classes shares some but not all features, then the commonalities are described in a generalized class and the peculiarities of the subtypes are described in specialized classes. A specialized class acquires all the relationships, attributes, and operations of the generalized class. A specialized class should be used only for full-time subtypes. (Part-time subtypes are described as *transient roles*.) For example, a Checking Account is a specialization of Account. Alternative terms: *subclass, child class, derived class*.

state-machine diagram: (UML term) A diagram that depicts the different states of an object and the rules that govern how it passes from state to state. For example, a state-machine diagram for Insurance Claim describes how the claim's state passes from Initiated to Adjusted to Paid.

structural model: (UML term) The portion of a business model that describes static, structural aspects of a system—in particular, business classes and their relationships.

structured analysis: Structured analysis is a set of techniques for analyzing a system by organizing processes hierarchically—from general to specific. Predates OO analysis.

subclass: (OO term) See *specialized class.*

superclass: (OO term) See *generalized class.*

T–U

transient role: (B.O.O.M. term) A role that may change during an object's lifetime. (If the role is not likely to change, describe it instead as a specialized class.) For example, PTA Board Member is a transient role played by a parent in a school.

UML: Unified Modeling Language. A standard notation owned by the Object Management Group (OMG), a not-for-profit computer industry–specifications consortium. The UML is used for the specification, visualization, and modeling of the structure and behavior of business and software systems.

use case: (UML term) An interaction between an actor and a system that achieves an observable and (usually) useful result for the actor.

use-case diagram: (UML term) A diagram that depicts the main services that the system performs and the actors that interact with the system during each use case.

Further Reading

Booch, Grady. *The Unified Modeling Language User Guide.* Addison-Wesley Professional: 2005.

Cockburn, Alistair. *Writing Effective Use Cases.* Pearson Education Canada: 2000.

Eriksson, Hans-Erik, and Magnus Penker. *Business Modeling with UML: Business Patterns and Business Objects.* Wiley: 1999.

Eriksson, Hans-Erik, Magnus Penker, Brian Lyons, and David Fado. *UML 2 Toolkit.* Wiley: 2003.

Fowler, Martin, and Kendall Scott. *UML Distilled: A Brief Guide to the Standard Object Modeling Language, 2nd Edition.* Addison-Wesley Professional: 2003.

Gamma, Erich, Richard Helm, and Ralph Johnson. *Design Patterns: Elements of Reusable Object-Oriented Software.* Pearson Education Canada: 1994.

Hoffer, Jeffrey A. *Modern Systems Analysis and Design.* Pearson Education Canada: 2004.

Jacobson, Ivar. *The Unified Software Development Process.* Pearson Education Canada: 1999.

Larman, Craig. *Applying UML and Patterns: An Introduction to Object-Oriented Analysis and Design and Iterative Development.* Prentice Hall PTR: 2004.

Leffingwell, Dean, and Don Widrig. *Managing Software Requirements: A Unified Approach.* Pearson Education Canada (Addison-Wesley): 1999.

Marshal, Chris. *Enterprise Modeling with UML: Designing Successful Software through Business Analysis*. Pearson Education Canada: 1999.

Podeswa, Howard. *The Business Analyst's Handbook*. Cengage: 2008.

Robertson, Suzanne, and James Robertson. *Mastering the Requirements Process*. Pearson Education Canada: 1999.

Rumbaugh, James, Ivar Jacobson, and Grady Booch. *The Unified Modeling Language Reference Manual, 2nd Edition*. Addison-Wesley Professional: 2004.

Schneider, Geri, and Jason P. Winters. *Applying Use Cases: A Practical Guide*. Addison Wesley Longman: 2001.

Wiegers, Karl. *Software Requirements*. Microsoft Press: 2003.

Related Sites

Please be advised that Web site URLs are always subject to change.

www.nobleinc.ca

Home page for Noble Inc., a business analysis training and consulting organization, offering a business analysis program designed by the author.

www.ideaswork.org

Home page for Ideaswork, the organization behind the South African restorative justice project that is the basis of the CPP case study.

www.omg.org

Home page for the OMG—the organization that sets standards for OO.

www.theiiba.org

Home page for the International Institute of Business Analysis.

www.uwsg.iu.edu/usail/network/nfs/network_layers.html

ISO/OSI Network Model, Trustees of Indiana University.

www.15seconds.com/issue/011023.htm

The article is called "Application Architecture: An *N*-Tier Approach—Part 1" by Robert Chartier, INT Media Group, Inc.

www-128.ibm.com/developerworks/rational/rationaledge

For business use-case modeling, see "Effective Business Modeling with UML: Describing Business Use Cases and Realizations" by Pan-Wei Ng of the Rational Edge at www.therationaledge.com/content/nov_02/t_businessModelingUML_pn.jsp.

INDEX

A

abstract generalized actors, 83

Access, 281

Accounts package in Community Peace Plan
(CPP) case study, 339

activity. *See also* state activities
defined, 353
element in activity diagram, 65–66
in state transition, 147

activity diagrams, 3, 5–6
business use cases, documenting, 47
defined, 353
elements of, 65–67
in Initiation phase, 34
nested activities, 67–68
object flows in, 68–71
stakeholders, presentation to, 41
symbols, glossary of, 351
for system use cases, 115
without partitions, 65–68
workflow, depicting, 63–64

activity diagrams with partitions, 6, 64, 71–72
for Community Peace Program (CPP)
case study, 73–77
example of, 72

actors. *See also* generalized actors; role maps;
specialized actors; system use-case
diagrams; system use-case packages
BRD template section for, 296–297
in business use-case diagrams, 47–48

in Community Peace Program (CPP)
case study, 59–60, 323–324
defined, 353
FAQs about, 81
generalization relationship between, 82–84
in Initiation phase, 34
overlapping roles, modeling actors with,
82–84
with partially overlapping roles, 82–83
stereotypes and, 81–82
system use-case diagram, identifying in,
80–82
totally overlapping roles, actors with, 83–84

adaptability of lifecycle, 39

advanced use-case features, 125–137
in Community Peace Program (CPP) case
study, 136–137

aggregation. *See also* composite aggregation
challenge questions about, 190
in Community Peace Program (CPP) case
study, 190–192
composite structure diagrams, 188–191
defined, 353
indicating, 187–188
information sources for finding, 187
interview questions for determining, 189–190
in OO (object orientation), 25–26
rules about, 187
and whole/part relationships, 186

alias for class, 170

alpha testing, 267

alternate-alternate flow, documenting, 114

alternate flows
  alternate-alternate flow, documenting, 114
  Community Peace Program (CPP) case study
    for, 113
  defined, 111
  documenting, 111–114
  typical alternate flows, 111
  use-case scenario testing for, 253

"Application Architecture: An *N*-Tier
  Approach—Part 1" (Chartier), 358

*Applying UML and Patterns: An Introduction
  to Object-Oriented Analysis and Design and
  Iterative Development* (Larman), 357

Applying Use Cases: A Practical Guide
  (Schneider & Winters), 358

The Art of Software Testing (Myers), 248

artifacts
  attributes, information sources for finding, 222
  generalized use cases and, 133
  and use-case description templates, 115–125

associations. *See also* multiplicity
  analysis of, 25
  business reality, reflection of, 195–196
  in business use-case diagrams, 47–48
  in Community Peace Program (CPP) case
    study, 199–201
  defined, 6, 353
  discovering, 193, 198–199
  examples of, 192
  indicating, 192–193, 194
  naming conventions for, 193–194
  notes explaining issues and, 199
  object diagrams, modeling object links with,
    197–198
  in OO (object orientation), 24–25
  part-time subtypes and, 175
  redundant association rule of thumb,
    196–199
  rules about, 193–194

asynchronous interruptions, 129

attributes
  adding attributes, 221–230
  Community Peace Program (CPP) case study,
    adding attributes in, 226–230
  defined, 6, 353
  defining, 37–38
  derived attributes, 223
  for entity classes, 167
  importance of derived attributes, 223
  indicating, 221, 223–225
  information sources for finding, 222
  meta-attributes, 225–226
  multiplicity of, 225
  in OO (object orientation), 19
  rules for assigning, 222–223
  in structural models, 214–215
  verification rules about, 221

B

backup requirements
  in BRD template, 302
  in Community Peace Program (CPP) case
    study, 334

base class, 23

baseline
  for analysis, 101–102
  for development, 268
  in Initiation phase, 35

basic flow
  Community Peace Program (CPP) case study,
    110–111
  documenting, 109–111
  extend feature and, 132
  generalized use cases and, 135–136
  and include feature, 129
  use-case scenario testing for, 253

behavioral analysis
  in Discovery phase, 36
  structural analysis and, 165–166

behavioral models, 3–4
  B.O.O.M, developing in, 38
  defined, 354

beta testing, 267

big bang tests, 262

binary associations, 193

black-box testing, 252–254
  defined, 354

Blueprint's Requirements Center, 3

Booch, Grady, 18, 357–358

B.O.O.M. *See also* **specific phases**
   behavioral model, developing, 38
   customizing for specific project, 38–41
   and SDLCs (systems development lifecycles), 33–34
   stakeholders, presentations to, 41
   structural model, developing, 38
bottom-up testing, 263
boundary classes, 274
boundary-value analysis, 256–259
   in Community Peace Program (CPP) case study, 258–259
brainstorming interviews, 44
BRD. *See* **business requirements document (BRD)**
budgets and B.O.O.M, 40
bugs, 247. *See also* **testing**
Business Analysis Body of Knowledge Version 2.0 (BABOK 2), **2, 6–13**
business analysis planning/modeling, 7–8
The Business Analyst's Handbook (Podeswa), **283, 358**
business case
   in BRD template, 296
   in Community Peace Program (CPP) case study, 58, 319
Business Modeling with UML: Business Patterns and Business Objects (Eriksson & Penker), **357**
business models, 3
   defined, 354
Business Object Oriented Modeling. *See* **B.O.O.M**
business process diagrams (BPDs) for workflow, 64
business requirements document (BRD).
   See also **implementation plans**
   baseline for development, setting, 268
   in Community Peace Program (CPP) case study, 49–62, 307–342
   in Discovery phase, 104–105
   in Initiation phase, 35
   and requirements-based testing, 252
   template for, 287–306
   test plan document for, 304
business rules, 124–125
   attributes, finding, 222
   in BRD template, 303
   in Community Peace Program (CPP) case study, 334

business use-case descriptions, 319–322
   in BRD template, 296
business use-case diagrams, 47–48
   in BRD template, 296
   case study on, 49–62
   in Community Peace Program (CPP) case study, 62, 319
   symbols, glossary of, 347
business use cases, 29–30. *See also* **activity diagrams**
   in BRD template, 296
   business use-case diagrams, 47–48
   in Community Peace Program (CPP) case study, 59, 319–322
   documenting, 47
   in Initiation phase, 34, 46–48
   system use-case packages for, 86

C

candidate classes, 167
   alias for, 170
   follow-up questions on, 170–171
case workers, 48
cases, 101. *See also* **system use cases**
Chartier, Robert, 358
choice pseudostate, 149
class diagrams, 6, 164
   defined, 354
   in Discovery phase, 35–36
   stakeholders, presentation to, 41
   symbols, glossary of, 349–350
class name, 170
classes. *See also* **candidate classes; entity classes**
   association of, 24
   boundary classes, 274
   control classes, 274
   defined, 6, 354
   generalization and, 22–24
   interview questions for finding, 169–170
   lookup tables and, 231–232
   mix-ins, 280
   in OO (object orientation), 21–22
   revising class structure, 241–243
   rules about, 166
   in UML (Unified Modeling Language), 21
   visibility of members, 272–274

Closeout phase, 37
    of SDLC, 34
COBOL, 281
Cockburn, Alistair, 109, 112, 357
cognitive psychology and OO, 18–19
communication diagrams, 277
Community Peace Program (CPP) case study
    activity diagrams with partitions for, 73–77
    advanced use-case features in, 136–137
    alternate flow in, 113
    associations in, 199–201
    attributes, adding, 226–230
    basic flow example, 110–111
    boundary-value analysis, selecting test data using, 258–259
    business requirements document (BRD) for, 49–62, 307–342
    business use-case diagrams for, 62
    composite states in, 157–158
    decision tables in, 119–121, 255–256
    decision tree, 123
    distribute operations in, 238–241
    entity classes in, 172–174
    generalizations in, 179–180
    linking system use case to structural model, 216–220
    lookup tables in, 233–235, 339
    multiplicity in, 205–208
    revising class structure, 241–243
    role map for, 84–85
    state activities in, 154–155
    state transitions in, 150–152
    states in, 145–146
    system use-case diagrams in, 95–100
    system use-case packages in, 89–90
    test cases from decision tables, deriving, 255–256
    transient roles in, 184–185
    whole/part relationships in, 190–192
compatibility requirements
    in Community Peace Program (CPP) case study, 333
    testing for compatibility, 265
completion transitions, 147

composite aggregation, 26–27
    challenge questions about, 190
    in Community Peace Program (CPP) case study, 190–192
    composite structure diagrams, 188–191
    defined, 354
    indicating, 187–188
    information sources for finding, 187
    interview questions for determining, 189–190
    multiplicity and, 203
    rules about, 187
    and whole/part relationships, 186
composite patterns, 272
composite states, 156–158
    in Community Peace Program (CPP) case study, 157–158
composite structure diagrams, 188–191
    symbols, glossary of, 351
computer-based testing, 250
Computing Technology Industry Association (CompTIA), 2
concrete generalized actors, 83
concurrent states, 159–160
condition/response tables, 124
conditions
    extend feature and, 130
    white-box testing, coverage of, 261
configuration requirements
    in BRD template, 302
    in Community Peace Program (CPP) case study, 333
    testing, 265
constraints on scope in Community Peace Program (CPP) case study, 315
Construction phase, 37
    interviews during, 43–44
    of SDLC, 33
control flow in activity diagram, 65–66, 68
convergence point for alternate flow, 112
conversion plan, 267–268
    in BRD template, 305
    in Community Peace Program (CPP) case study, 342
    testing, 265
customer-relations management (CRM), 3

D

data flow diagrams (DFDs), 5

database, implementing, 281

DB2, 281

decision coverage in white-box testing, 261

decision element in activity diagram, 65–66

decision tables, 116–121

    in Community Peace Program (CPP) case study, 119–121

    example of, 117–118

    stakeholders, presentation to, 41

    step-by-step procedure for using, 118–119

    template for, 343

    for testing, 254–256

    underlying concept for, 117

    usefulness of, 117

decision trees, 122–123

    in Community Peace Program (CPP) case study, 123

    stakeholders, presentation to, 41

dependency in system use-case package, 87

deployment diagrams, 278

derived attributes, 223

derived class, 23

Design Patterns: Elements of Reusable Object-Oriented Software (Gamma, Helm & Johnson), 357

developers and B.O.O.M, 40

diagrams. *See also* specific types

    importance of, 3

disabled state requirements in BRD template, 303

Discovery phase, 35–37, 104–105

    interviews during, 43–44

    lifecycle considerations, 104

    purpose of, 284–285

    of SDLC, 33

    use-case description template, 105–108

distribute operations, 237–241

    in Community Peace Program (CPP) case study, 238–241

divergence point for alternate flow, 112

Do/activity, 153

dynamic models. *See* behavioral models

E

"Effective Business Modeling with UML: Describing Business Use Cases and Realizations" (Ng), 358

elicitation, 8

encapsulation, 20

    defined, 354

end-to-end business processes, 43–78

end-users

    BRD template, procedures in, 306

    and Community Peace Program (CPP) case study, 342

    implementation plan addressing, 268

enterprise analysis, 10

Enterprise Modeling with UML: Designing Successful Software through Business Analysis (Marshal), 358

entity, defined, 6

entity classes, 166–174. *See also* candidate classes

    attributes specified for, 167

    BRD template, documentation in, 303–304

    in Community Peace Program (CPP) case study, 172–174, 339–340

    defined, 354

    examples of, 167

    FAQs about, 167

    lists of, 167

    naming conventions, 167–168

    package diagram for, 169

    packages, grouping classes into, 168

    supporting documentation, 171

entity relationship diagrams (ERDs), 6

    defined, 354

Entry/activity, 153

Envisioning phase (Microsoft Solutions Framework), 45

Eriksson, Hans-Erik, 357

event

    in activity diagram, 65–66, 68

    in state transition, 147

Eventname/activity, 153

Events/Transactions package, Community Peace Program (CPP) case study, 337–338

exception flows
    documenting, 114
    and include feature, 129
    use-case scenario testing for, 253
executive summary
    in BRD template, 292–293
    in Community Peace Program (CPP) case
        study, 54, 313–314
Exit/activity, 153
extend feature, 129–132
    defined, 354
    drawing an extension, 131
    examples of extending use cases, 130
    rules for, 132
    use-case documentation, extend relationship
        affecting, 132
extension point, 130
external agents/external entities, 80

F

Fado, David, 357
FAQs
    on actors, 81
    on entity classes, 167
    on structural analysis, 165–166
final node in activity diagram, 66
final states, 144
Final Verification and Validation (V&V) phase,
    37
    interviews during, 43
    of SDLC, 34
finite state, 145
flexibility in BRD template, 287
follow-up plan
    in BRD template, 306
    in Community Peace Program (CPP) case
        study, 342
forks
    in activity diagrams, 66–67
    defined, 354
formality of lifecycle, 39
Fowler, Martin, 95, 357
full-time subtypes, 175
further reading, 357–358

G

Gamma, Erich, 357
generalizations, 175–180
    actors, generalization relationship between,
        82–84
    advanced challenge questions, 178
    challenge questions on, 178
    in Community Peace Program (CPP) case
        study, 179–180
    example, 176
    indicating in UML, 177
    information sources for, 176
    interview questions for finding, 177–178
    in OO (object orientation), 22–24
    overuse of, 177
    reasons for modeling, 176
    rules on, 176
    subtypes, 175
generalized actors, 83–84
    system use-case package and, 88
generalized classes, 23
    defined, 355
generalized use cases, 133–136
    drawing, 134–135
    examples of, 134
    rules for, 135
    use-case documentation, effect on, 135–136
generic products, extend feature and, 129
glossaries
    symbols, glossary of, 347–352
    terms, glossary of, 353–357
guard condition
    in activity diagram, 65–66
    defined, 355
    in state transition, 148–149
GUI (graphic user interface) and attributes, 221

H–I

Helm, Richard, 357
Hoffer, Jeffrey A., 357

IBM Rational Software Modeler (RSM), 3
ideaswork.org, 358
IF-THEN-ELSE statements, 260